Where the Caribou Still Roam

In the Barren Lands of Arctic Canada

Guy Mueller

© Guy Mueller. 2020.

All rights reserved. No part of this publication may be reproduced, distributed, or transmitted in any form or by any means, including photocopying, recording, or other electronic or mechanical methods, without the prior written permission of the publisher, except in the case of brief quotations embodied in critical reviews and certain other noncommercial uses permitted by copyright law.

ISBN: 978-0-9986042-3-7
Second Edition

Book Design: Patti Frazee
Cover Design: Guy Mueller

Little Sticks Publishing
Madison, WI USA

Contents

About this Book v
Acknowledgments vii

Prologue 1

Maps 3

Part I   Into the Barren Lands

Chapter 1   The Decisions 17
Chapter 2   The Questions 27
Chapter 3   The Prairie Highways.................................. 43
Chapter 4   The Boreal Forest....................................... 55
Chapter 5   The Flight Over the Tree Line................... 71

Part II   Down the Big River

Chapter 6   The Land of the Little Sticks..................... 83
Chapter 7   The Singing Hills and the Quiet Stream..... 95
Chapter 8   The Black Flies 109
Chapter 9   The Birds Above, the Peat Below.............. 115
Chapter 10   The Mists of Time 123
Chapter 11   The Last of the Little Sticks..................... 129
Chapter 12   The Tuktu... 137

Photos 147

Part III   With the People

Chapter 13   The Whalers 175
Chapter 14   The Road to Arviat 193

Chapter 15 The Northern Store and the Bay 201

Chapter 16 The Walk around Town... 209

Chapter 17 The Trip Home... 237

Epilogue 247

Afterword... 251

Selected Bibliography 269

End Notes 281

About this Book

    This book has three main parts, as well as a prologue, an epilogue, and an afterword. For the motivated reader, the prologue and epilogue are recommended; they should not be skipped. The afterword updates some of the content in the main text and also covers additional topics relevant to the themes of the book. The afterword also tells the story of the writing of this book and explains the reasons for the lapse of time between the completion of the manuscript's first rough draft and the final publication of the book, the short explanation being that editing never ends. At some point it simply has to be euthanized.

    I have endeavored, in this book, to report conversations in a straightforward manner. In many instances, I compressed exchanges among people in time and place to convey their dialogue more informatively. A few of my memory gaps required infilling with reconstructive content, not to distort but to present a coherent continuum. Rest assured, even where I took such creative license, I have remained faithful to the character of the places and people involved.

    I hope you enjoy *Where the Caribou Still Roam* and joining me on my travels in the forests and Barren Lands of northern Canada.

—Guy Mueller, 2017

ACKNOWLEDGMENTS

I treasure my friendships with Tom and Ruth Moore and Mel Baughman. There is no better crew with whom to hike, paddle, and camp. Their company and kindness have enriched me. Mel's daily journal of the canoe trip was invaluable in filling the gaps in my memory about the sequence and content of many events. Tom and Mel also generously shared their photographs for this publication.

As long as I can remember things, I will remember the hospitality of Joe Savikataaq, Sr., his son, Jamie, and their family. In addition to yanking us out of turbulent seas, Joe and Jamie patiently tolerated my questions and introduced us to Peter and his fellow whalers. As they promised, Peter was a great storyteller.

Several people read the first drafts of this book and offered suggestions that dramatically improved the structure, clarity, and focus. These include my cousin, Annie Kuhn, an authentic English major, who is a writer and poet. I also wish to thank Mel Baughman's wife, Sue Spalding, who, during her sadly abbreviated life, was an exceptionally well-read, kind, and constructive coach. Sandra Becker also encouraged me and offered instruction at a critical time, as did Paulette Bates Alden, April Michelle Davis, and Patti Frazee, all of whom who reviewed my work and provided valuable editorial suggestions. Bob Nagel painstakingly proofread one of the drafts and offered additional recommendations as did Craig Weflen. In the same vein, I wish to thank all of the teachers of the world who inspire their students, from my daughter, Melissa, to my tenth-grade English teacher, in 1965, Mrs. Jane Katz.

My eldest daughter, Emily, an archaeologist, provided guidance in my research and writing as did her husband, Ethan Epstein, who is also an archaeologist. Over the years, they have both shared their knowledge about the pre-history and early human occupation of North America with me. We have had many conversations about these topics during which I have enjoyed my role as their student and proud father and father-in-law.

Mostly, I wish to thank my wife, Marsha, who tended to family matters while I trekked off to the Barren Lands and then sequestered myself to read, think, and finally write this book. The spouses of writers, at least those who remain faithful, must have angelic qualities, and Marsha is indeed one of these miraculous people. Despite the loss of time together, she stood by me with encouragement and help. Writing is never done, but circumstances eventually conspire to force a closure to the effort. Now that the job is finished, there will be more time for family and friends.

—*Guy Mueller, 2019*

For my wife, our children, and our grandchildren.

Where the Caribou Still Roam

In the Barren Lands of Arctic Canada

Guy Mueller

Prologue
Spring 2004

This was the fifty-fifth time in my life that the vernal sun had freed the ground from winter's imprisonment. The crystalline had once again had become the friable. The earth yearned, and Midwestern mud oozed from her pores.

In this flux of living things and the lengthening of days, two certainties emerged. First, I would resign from the job that I had held for 25 years. Next, I was going to canoe down the Thlewiaza River on its run to the sea through the Canadian tundra, a region known as the Barren Lands. My friends and I expected to reach the mouth of the Thlewiaza on the northwestern shores of Hudson Bay, near the Inuit hamlet of Arviat, by the end of July. After that, I didn't know what I was going to do with the rest of my life.

As I would learn, the tundra, lying just below the polar ice cap, captivates all who enter. Both desolate and beautiful, it extends, across the top of the continent like a boundless rumpled blanket woven with mottled textures of mosses, lichens, sedges, and traces of ground-hugging woody plants. In the lower latitudes, in the Land of the Little Sticks, a scattering of stunted trees follows the folds of hills and protected valleys. The thin layer of peaty soil supporting this meager vegetation rests on the Precambrian Canadian Shield, bedrock from the beginning of time.

Much of the tundra is generally, but deceptively flat, a deceptiveness that derives from the Barrens' glacial heritage. The continental sheets of ice that once bore down and smoothed the Barrenlands during their advance also sculpted them in retreat, leaving a relief of abrupt hills and winding ridges. Anyone who has attempted to walk across the Barrenlands knows the staggering attributes of this topographical diversity.

The tundra, it turns out, is also a sponge-like land, dappled with countless marshes and overlaid with a maze of lakes and rivers whose waters reflect every mood of the tundra's vast skies. Despite the pervasiveness of water, the Barren Lands, ecologically speaking, are as dry as the Sahara. Precipitation is scanty and variable, often no more than the equivalent of ten inches of rain per year. Most of it falls in the summer, and even then, not always as rain. The curiosity of plentiful surface water is explained by the short, cool summers that curtail evaporation and is also explained by the permafrost. This perennially frozen underlying layer of land, which is as hard as concrete and just as impervious, impedes seepage and curtails drainage. While the water stands about before it can escape to a river or evaporate into the sky, the wind in this treeless land never stands still. It is the Barrenlander's constant companion.

What follows is my story about the Barren Lands. More than a travelogue, this story is an eclectic weave of personal memoir, environmental and cultural commentary, and even some spiritual inquiry. In part, it is also a coming of age story, not about adolescent rites of passage, but a story about coming to terms with middle age, much of which I tell from the perspective of the aft end of a red canoe while paddling down the Thlewiaza River in Nunavut Canada. Perhaps no matter whether we are in the spring or summer, or even the autumn of our lives, we are always coming of age.

While chronicling aspects of my personal journey, I share my concerns about the struggle of our planet and humankind to coexist. Remarkably, some of the most pronounced frontlines of this struggle have collided in the Boreal Forest and the Barren Lands of the Far North. I pay tribute to the continent's last free-flowing rivers, lament the ruin of others, and invite the reader to join me in learning about the peoples of the Far North, including the Inuit, a people formerly known as the Eskimos.

These northern hunters, whose Siberian ancestors crossed the Bering Strait thousands of years ago, have persevered into the modern era amid changes of nearly unfathomable magnitude. Few have experienced the phenomenon of culture shock more recently or more profoundly than the Canadian Inuit. In sum, this is a story about my home continent of North America, but it is also a story about the searches for individual *and* cultural identity, and these searches, never ending, link us in shared humanity.

Finally, this is a story about questions. In one of the last wild places on earth, how and why did the formerly nomadic people there, the Inuit, in a place where the caribou still roam, come to live in permanent urbanized settlements along the coastlines, many as wards of the Canadian government? As we submit to the juggernaut of industrialism and as the distinctions among cultures fade, are any of us better off? Do we face a brighter dawn? I answer the first question while leaving the others for my readers to ponder.

List of Maps on the Following Pages, 5-13

Overall Trip Route and Central Northern Canada, page 5
Topographic Route Maps (8), pages 6-13

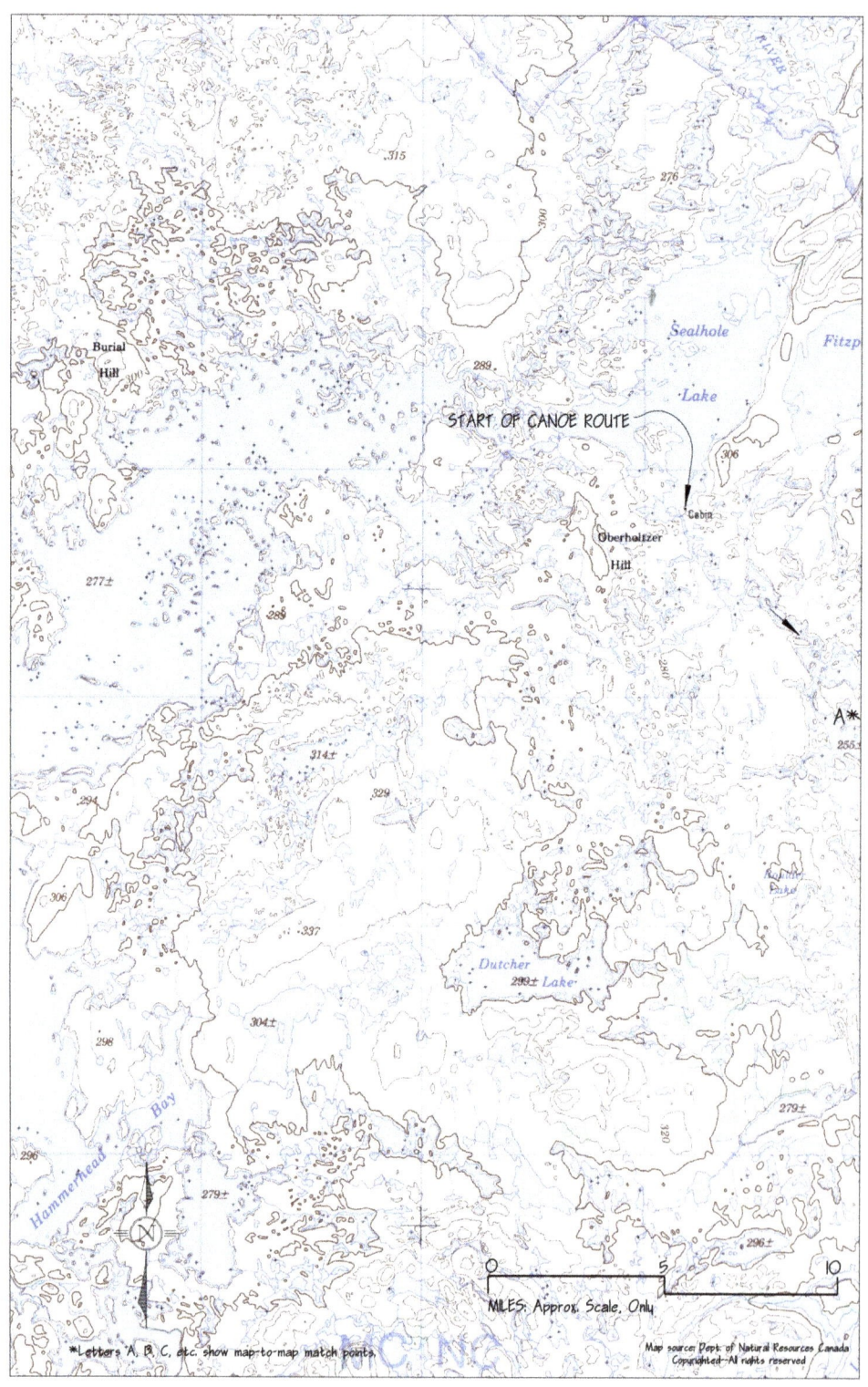

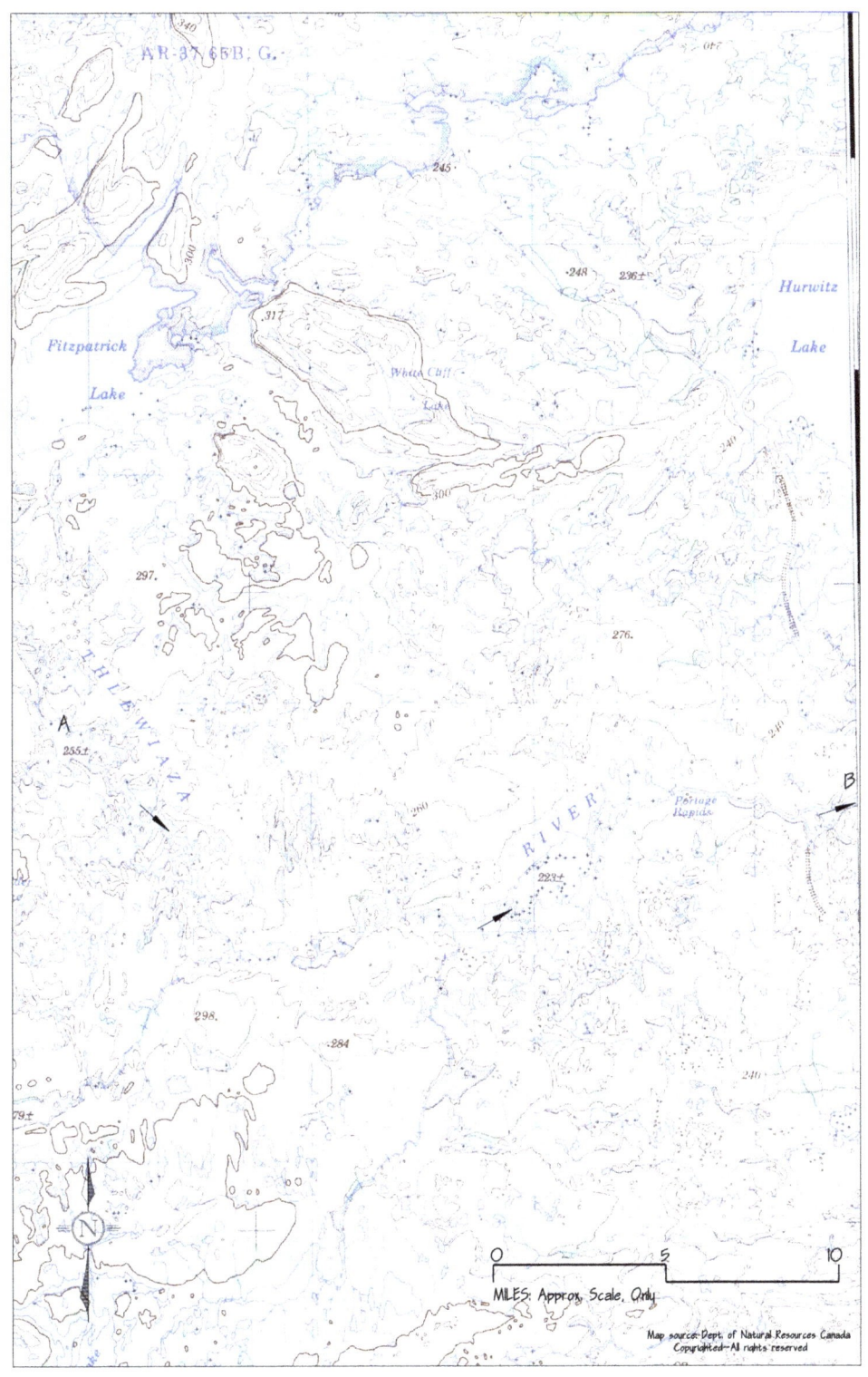

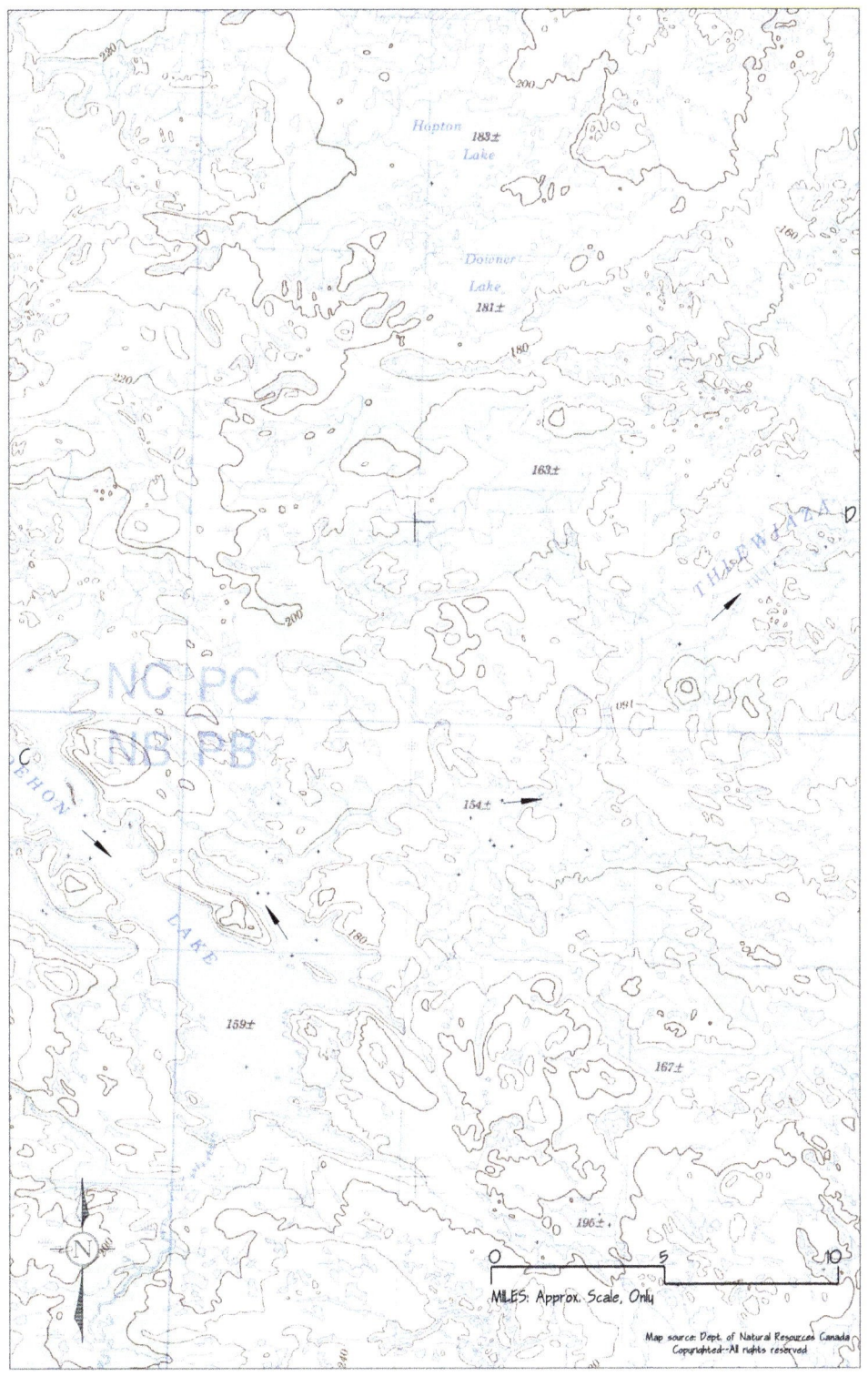

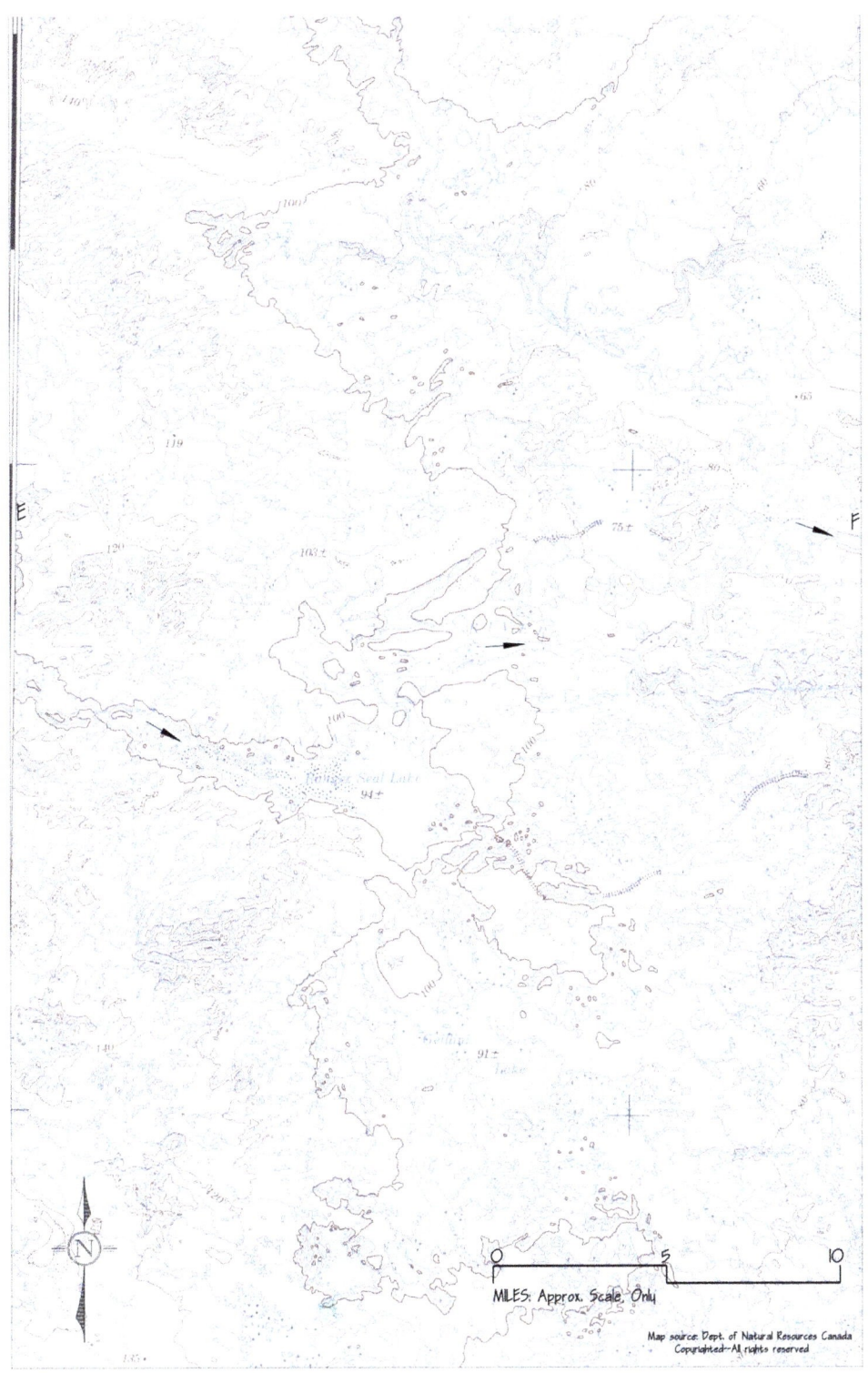

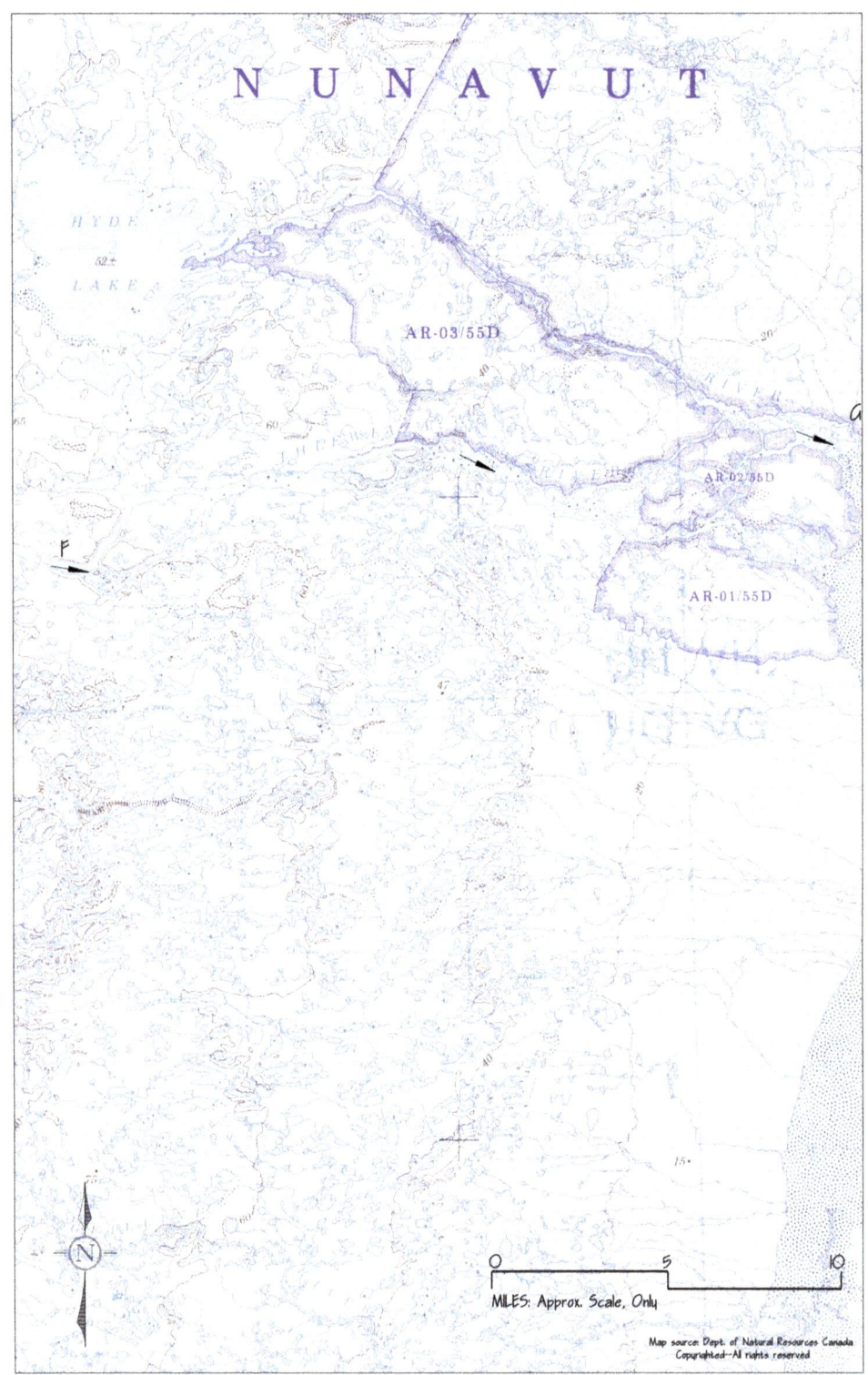

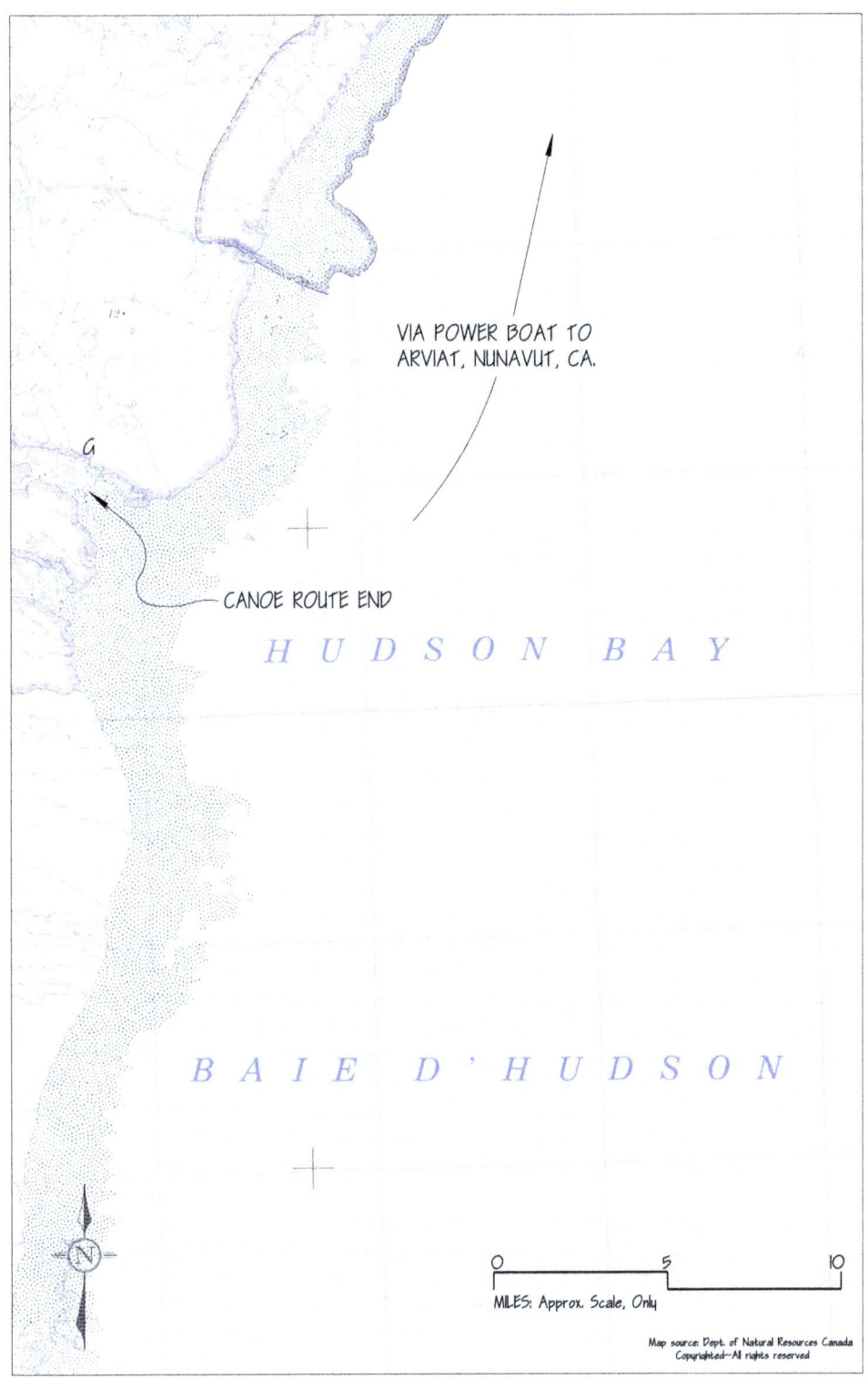

Part I
Into the Barren Lands

Chapter 1
The Decisions

Dad had good business sense. "Son," he said, "starting a business is easy. It's like having babies. But running one, that's like raising kids." As it turned out, running the business was only one part of the challenge. Getting out of it, with something to show for his efforts and cushion his retirement, proved to be the other. After you've poured your life into a family enterprise, practical and emotional reasons preclude putting a "closed" sign on the front door and simply walking away. Dad and his business partner, Howard, who was also Dad's older and only brother, looked at me. Together, they saw the embodiment of their business transition plan—their means for executing a successful exit. And so, at the relatively youthful age of twenty-nine, I was drafted into the family firm.

Prior to reaching the watershed of this induction, I had steered my young career in the direction of public service rather than private business. Perhaps I should have held to that course or chosen any of the others my youth afforded, but I followed my twenty-nine-year-old instincts. In one moment, I struggled with the burden of choice, an opportunity behind every door in a seemingly endless hallway of possibilities. In the next, I opened a single door and the others started locking behind me. I could almost hear the latches clicking.

For the next twenty-five years, the family business consumed me. During the first ten of those years, Dad and I bought out Uncle Howard. Then I took the helm and bought out my father. The business was like a prizefight with an endless number of rounds. I won some, but all were pounding and some were bruising. They swallowed up sixty-hour workweeks, golf-less Saturdays, and more than a few unholy Sabbaths. Fortunately, I didn't golf, still don't, and what I lacked in efficiency and cleverness, I made up for in doggedness.

At the time, my father and mother lived comfortably in Iowa where they remained for most of the rest of their lives. Together, these two octogenarians had shared over sixty years of marriage and traveled every continent, except Antarctica. Occasionally they roughed it by staying in hotels without room service. When I told them about tenting in the wilds and packing out everything packed-in including, in some places, used toilet paper, they forced polite smiles. Their body language was sufficient to communicate the question that they politely declined to verbalize. Had they chosen ask aloud, "Where, dear God, did we go wrong?" might have been the gist of it. When it came to roughing it, it was clear that one of the fruits of their marriage, their son, had fallen a bit beyond the canopy of the family tree.

Meanwhile, back at the business, I was mindful of my father's advice, to keep an eye on the exit, but the spirit of the contest was in my blood. Eventually, the final bell rang. Had a panel of hypothetical judges and referees issued a verdict, my business career probably would have produced a split decision. I made a few good moves, but I also tended to lead with my chin and got my head snapped back more than once. In the end, I avoided getting knocked out and made the family's industrial distribution business a little less small, but I was no titan of industry.

My decision to sell the business that bore the family name for three generations wasn't easy, but the circumstances, aligned like a rare planetary eclipse, made it compelling. My children did not see the company as their calling. Although I still considered myself squarely in the middle of middle age, the time had come to reap what my grandfather had sown and what my father, uncle, and I had devoted our lives to cultivating.

On my last day on the job, I cleaned out the laminate-topped desk in my utilitarian office and then handed the keys to an optimistic manager full of answers and young enough to be my child. My co-workers had the obligatory potluck lunch and presented me with a card full of signatures and clever farewells. We shook hands, and I said good-bye. Some had spent more wakeful time with me during the last twenty-five years than my wife.

I swung open the glass door in the front lobby. Quickly and eerily, I was outside. The building's leaky roof, a nagging, sieve-like membrane of tar and gravel, was no longer my concern. Just the same, I paused to place my hand on the sun-warmed bricks that once were mine.

In the few strides that it took to reach the parking lot, I mused about my recent status as a lame duck boss. Clearly, my jokes were no longer triggering the hearty laughs they once did. No matter, I smiled; this lame duck was waddling away. It was the eve of May Day, the unofficial day for celebrating the contributions of the workers of the world, and I had just quit working, unsure whether I would ever sit in an office again.

During the next couple of weeks, I caught up with tasks around the house, and then I nearly electrocuted myself while attempting to assume the role of backyard arborist. Certain, in my lofty squirrel-like position, that I could lop off that one last silver maple branch and keep it clear of the power lines, I instantaneously learned that the un-insulated wire at the top of the power pole, also known as the "primary," is the bad boy of high voltage. I also learned that while dry dead wood might be an insulator, sap-flowing green wood conducts electricity rather well, actually, shockingly so—at the speed of light. It definitely gave me a buzz and not the kind you get from two martinis, more like the kind that produces a rapidity of flashbacks before the screen goes black.

With the aroma of burnt wood wafting about, I shinnied down the tree, ran to the house, and called the power company. Minutes later, an Xcel Energy supervisor showed up and began to pummel me with reprimands while deservedly making me feel like a naughty child. Then he directed one of his crew to retrieve my pruning saw, still wedged in the treetop branch about thirty feet off the ground. The rescued saw blade bore the black and blue marks of severe heat treatment. As the power company man said, I was lucky to be alive. A week later, another crew came back to top the errant silver maple, leaving trunk- and ground-level cleanup for the mentally challenged homeowner. The whole episode gave new meaning to the phrase, "You work hard; then you die." Almost, anyway.

A few more days passed, and then the latches on some of the doors that had closed so long ago began to loosen. Cracks of light shone through, but they led to no clear direction. I was free of the vocational burdens of toil and task only to find them replaced by a perplexing array of choices—an overload of ill-defined options. I could while away the rest of my middle and golden years as a gentleman of modest distinction, trying to be a kinder friend and family man. I could team up with a former competitor or start a new business, even though my mental T-shirt said, "been there, done that." I could also soil my family's reputation and devote myself to public service, maybe even dirty my hands in politics. Some of these options weren't mutually exclusive, but I tended to avoid the "R" word (retirement).

Half-jokingly and somewhat truthfully, I told people that I was on perpetual furlough, unpaid sabbatical, between jobs, becoming a full-time backyard gardener, or among the "idle" middle class. I was trapped in a fifty-five-year-old body but had been reincarnated with the angst of a college freshman, the kind who is vexed with the "what's your major" question, not in school, but in the university of life.

When I was in business, a three-day weekend was worrisome, and a week's vacation an indulgence. Now, I faced an indefinite furlough of disquieting flexibility. My friend, Mel, had given me a standing invitation to join him on one of his Arctic canoe trips. Previously, three or four weeks would have been out of the question. Routinely, Mel asked. Routinely, I declined. Now, things were different. A few weeks would be feasible, a sort of vacation from the vacation.

Mel, an Eagle Scout in youth, never lost his fervor for preparedness, and nothing beat preparation in Mel's mind better than *advance* preparation. This time, Mel asked not weeks in advance, but months. He asked in early January about canoeing in July, and he knew that I would be "unemployed" then. The inviolate family summer reunion hadn't even been thought of in those bleak winter days, let alone scheduled. My calendar was an open field waiting to be tilled. Truthfully, I felt ambivalent, but I had no honest way to evade Mel's entreaty. If I consented, I would be joining Mel on a canoe trip down the Thlewiaza River in Nunavut, a newly formed territory carved out of the northern and eastern portions of Canada's Northwest Territory. Our final destination would be a coastal village, known as Arviat, on the shores of Hudson Bay.

My unease stemmed from the trip's length as well as my wariness about defying Ben Franklin's advice, the advice about fish and visitors stinking after three days. If I went on this trip, Tom Moore and his wife, Ruth, Mel, and I would be continuous visitors in each other's campsite homes for almost a month. Why put good friendships at risk with too much togetherness, especially given my lack of Arctic experience?

This reluctance, like a shallow puddle, however, soon began to evaporate. The four of us had previously paddled down rivers in the forested regions of Canada without acrimonious effects. Ben Franklin's advice notwithstanding, the more I thought about a three-week trip in the Arctic, the more I warmed to the prospect. Soon, I was informing associates that I wouldn't be available for much of the summer.

When they asked what I meant by being "unavailable," I said that it wasn't much, just a little expedition to the Arctic. Courteously, some responded with affirming oohs and aahs. Others implied by raised eyebrows that I might be crazy. The replies that struck deepest, however, were the questions: "What about your wife? Are you going to leave her alone?"

"You mean Marsha, my wife and the mother of my two daughters?" It was an awkward response. At the same time that I was leaving the family business, Marsha was winding down her own career. She was grappling with her life's roles, sandwiched between being the mother of our adult children and caring for elderly parents. To Marsha, my temporary Arctic exile seemed like a separate vacation for me at a time when she, too, needed a break.

Marsha's enthusiasm for my escape, an excursion that would carve out the heart of the summer, lagged behind that of the escapee. Actually, this assessment might win a place in the Guinness World Records for one of history's greatest understatements. Marsha's aversion finally surfaced one evening around the kitchen table. We were bussing supper dishes when she spoke her mind.

"Why are you doing this? Why are you going away for three weeks to swat bugs and risk your life just so you can catch a few fish? You know, no one will be able to reach you! What happens if something happens? You need to call your parents and explain to them that they won't be able to reach you."

"But I already said yes. I can't back out now. If something happens, it will have to wait or take care of itself. You can send in a helicopter or put the Mounties on our trail. Anyway, why don't you come with us?"

This was a rhetorical question and, after it came out of my mouth, one that struck both of us as insensitive. It ignored Marsha's diminishing interest in carrying packs over portage trails. It also ignored the heartache that anchored her in the Midwest. In a few months, we would reluctantly move her parents to the nursing home of their retirement community in suburban Chicago. Marsha would not forego the tenderness of heart to be near them if needed. She would not allow herself to be beyond the reach of a telephone or the seven-hour drive to northern Illinois, which she made on a monthly basis. Northern Canada was out of the question, but I persisted.

"It's not just a fishing trip. We'll be going to Nunavut, Canada's newest and most northern territory, a part of the world I've never seen before."

"Why go there when you can see the same things in *National Geographic*?"

"Touché." I said this, because Marsha's laments about my reluctance to travel had often evoked the same annoying refrain from me. We could adequately and more efficiently experience exotic destinations, I would say, by leafing through the pages of the yellow-rimmed magazine that arrived in our mailbox each month. We didn't actually have to *go* to these places.

"Look," I said, "it's not just about the scenery or the fishing. It's about the wilderness and the handful of people who live there, the Inuit, you know, the Eskimos." We would be visiting an Inuit village near the end of the earth. The land there never fully thawed and, for much of the year, exposed flesh froze in minutes.

"Sounds delightful." Then after a pause, she asked a question that I knew wouldn't have a satisfying answer. "What about the bears?"

"Well, you're right. There are bears in the tundra." I confessed that we might encounter a grizzly and, if we were lucky, some polar bears, too.

Anxiety and annoyance exuded from my beloved. I sat down, sighed, opened my arms, and then levitated my hands, palms up, a few inches above the walnut tabletop. Marsha stood with arms crossed and leaned back against the white counter, her aquamarine eyes as sparkling as they were thirty-five years ago, her once auburn hair now flecked with honest gray.

"Don't worry. Camping with Mel is a plus. Besides, I can outrun Mel, and that's the important factor if a bear is lunging for our behinds."

"Ha, ha." Marsha's derisive laughter proved that old jokes sometimes don't work, even when they're heard for the first time.

"Seriously, Mel's packing a 12-gauge shotgun with firecracker shells and also lead slugs—if we need them. We'll be packing another kind of heat, too, pepper spray, to be exact. With that arsenal, a bear would be crazy to charge us."

"Oh, that's comforting. Besides, don't you think that bears are generally crazy? You know, crazy with hunger?"

Marsha's apprehension about polar bear hunger cycles was correct. We would be on the shores of Hudson Bay during the seasonal interval when this inland sea, free of its ice, would be rolling with open waters. Deprived of their favorite haunts, the ice floes, and separated from their favorite nourishment, the ringed seal, Hudson Bay's polar bears would roam the coastlines in search of a more meager assortment of food. For *ursus maritimus*, when it's summertime, the livin' ain't so easy. It's the season of hunger, and they would be desperate for anything edible.

"Look," I said, "if all else fails, we'll have our fish filet knives. We can do the Davy Crocket thing." I probably should have humored her in some way or said nothing. The hole I was digging for myself got deeper when I started to sing, at a barely audible level, the song that school kids from the 1950s knew by heart, the one about Davy Crocket being born on a mountain top, raised in the woods, and killing a "b'ar" when he was only three.

My feeble humor about Mel's role as a sacrificial decoy and the annoying singsong about killing b'ars fell flat in a variety of ways. Silence stilled the room. Our aging white refrigerator clicked on. We listened to it drone.

Marsha broke the silence by reminding me that her family never had guns and that her grandfather never allowed them on the farm in Iowa. "Why do you need guns? You're a middle-aged man who has never owned, much less used a gun. This is crazy!"

"Mel is an expert shooter, a veteran hunter. He sleeps with his gun (which would later prove true). Mel will handle the shotgun, not me. *Don't worry*," I continued. "Polar bears are supposed to be sociable and good-natured." Wisely, I omitted their distinction as the world's largest land-based carnivore and the only predator in North America known to not only kill humans but also to stalk them.

"Grizzlies, on the other hand, are heavyweights, too, close to polar bears in size, but they have a reputation of being … well … unpredictable."

"And do you expect anything 'unpredictable' from them?" Marsha asked, incredulously.

"There might be some Barren Ground grizzlies in the scrubby hills during the first half of our trip, through the Land of the Little Sticks." Then I stopped. My persuasive tactics had crumbled under the weight of too much information.

"We'll probably not even see a single bear," was my last, hollow effort. Then each of us left the kitchen and found other things to do.

Many people, of course, Marsha notwithstanding, ranked among the admiring defenders of polar bears. It was easy to see how they could become smitten with their remarkable attributes and affable good looks. These surprisingly agile, roly-poly creatures could accelerate from a dead stop to twenty-five miles per hour to ambush a caribou. Webbed front feet could propel them at speeds faster than Olympians could paddle a loaded canoe and they could do so over distances of forty to sixty miles between ice floes. From a swimming start, they could also jump clear out of the water; the gunnels of our canoes being easy hurdles for them.[1] Despite their carnivorous instincts, which included a taste for human flesh, the bears' defenders claimed that altercations with people were uncommon. Typically, if they occurred, they took root in the fertile grounds of stupidity and food, especially in combination.

In Churchill, Manitoba, the polar bear capital of the world, roughly 150 miles south of our paddling destination, modern history had recorded only two known deaths. In one case, a group of teenagers tracked down a polar bear after a fresh snow. Previously, someone had riddled the poor creature with .22 caliber bullets. Curling up under a tree, the bear tried to sleep away its misery. A few hours later, one of the adolescent assailants made the fatal mistake of stumbling into the bear's hideout.[2]

In another case, a man scavenged some fresh meat from a hotel that had just burned down. Feeling awkward about his theft, he put the cuts under his jacket and, in the manner of walking bait, waddled home. His final step fell short of his front door.[3]

Despite Marsha's misgivings and the risk of polar bear hostilities, the more I thought about it, the more I embraced this expedition. It wasn't the absence of scheduling conflicts or my disregard of Ben Franklin's advice that enticed me. Real desire was building within me. Truthfully, I relished the chance to see a polar bear, a member of that select group of about 25,000 that still lived outside the bars of a zoo. More seriously I wanted to learn more about the Inuit, their history, and their adaptations to the industrialized world.

My deeper desire, however, derived from the prospect of *wilderness*, a prospect inspired by Mel's slideshows of previous trips. Our destination wasn't going to be a highway-fragmented park or designated "nature preserve." No, we would *not* be purchasing permits at a gated pass or subordinating ourselves to a litany of regulations about where and when to camp. This was a boundless, roadless region of continental proportions, a region that encompassed three time zones and a land area as large as Western Europe. With no cities to speak of and only a couple of dozen hamlets dotting the coastlines, it was one of the least crowded places on earth. The entire population of 30,000, eighty-five percent of whom were aboriginal Inuit, could have fit themselves into the Metrodome football stadium in Minneapolis and still left half the seats empty.

It was later that I learned about the truer character of this wilderness. The Arctic was not an unaltered, pristine place. It was a fragile union of human cultures and delicate ecosystems, neither of which had escaped the tentacles of the industrialized world. Not the lesser of these were global climate change and a toxic cocktail of industrial emissions that paid no heed to national boundaries.

In one respect, I did *not* misinterpret Mel's slideshows. These threats to the arctic biome were deceptively invisible or at least not yet readily apparent. Much of the Far North's original visual character had remained intact, including the Kivalliq (Keewatin) region of Nunavut's Barren Lands where we would travel. Yes, there were blemishes: a couple of derelict mines, some prospecting sites, and a few isolated weather stations. Farther north, abandoned DEW Line (Defense Early Warning) outposts and military bases from the cold war era had left a scattering of toxic dumps. Nunavut's coastal settlements also occasionally dealt with contaminated water supplies; and, owing to global warming, willow thickets and dwarf birch had crept farther north.

Despite these scattered alterations, by general appearances, the Barren Lands were much the same as they were prior to the arrival of the first Europeans. For now, this region of low Arctic tundra lay in wait, substantially pristine, although imperfectly so, and ominously as vulnerable as any place on Earth. This enormous swath of undulating tawny green, in the general shape of an upside-down right triangle, stretched from the Mackenzie River delta near the Alaska border to the Melville Peninsula—the most northeastern point of Canada's mainland. The north-south leg of the triangle followed the western shore of Hudson Bay and the tree line, diagonally from southeast to northwest, formed the thousand-mile-long hypotenuse

With a frigid demeanor and neither timber to fell nor arable land to put under the plow, the Barren Lands had avoided the onslaught of European settlement. For the most part, it had escaped the kinds of changes that had so profoundly altered the rest of North America.

In comparison, I sometimes wondered how it might have been to stride through the oak savannah of southern Minnesota in circa 1700–1800, prior to the explosion of Europeans across the continent and their invasion of the Midwest. Maybe I was hopelessly romantic, but I wondered what it would be like to see and hear the thunderous hooves of thousands of bison charging across the wind-stroked prairies of my home state. I wondered what it would be like to grab the mane of a spirited horse and, in the manner of a Dakota hunting party, engage hot pursuit through seas of waving grass, prior to the fences, prior to the tilling and the tiling of the fields and the draining of the wetlands, prior to the agricultural subsidies that had induced farmers to lay open the prairie from fence row to fence row, prior to the sprawl of pavement that had concreted and asphalted the thirteen counties of the Minneapolis–St. Paul metropolitan area, and prior to the flood of street lights and billboards that had washed away the shine of the stars. I supposed that I had to endure such progress, but I wondered how it would be to set foot into a region nearly as God gave it to us. And that wonder drew me to the Far North, to a place where the caribou still roamed.

The planet was not the only thing that was teetering on the threshold of change. My sore knee, thinning shoulder cartilage, and repeated junk mail solicitations from the American Association of Retired People and various providers of prepaid cremation services reminded me that I, too, was neither invincible nor infinite. I wanted to call the CEOs of these companies, especially the cremators, and lay into them with the line that finally brought down an infamous 1950's commie-baiting Senator: "Have you no sense of decency, sir?" But the fact was that I could no longer deny it. I had become a member of that subset of the human species whose chronological stature manifested itself in the swelling up and sagging of the body in inconvenient and unattractive places. Despite what the smiley-faced refrigerator magnet proclaimed, today wasn't necessarily the first day of the rest of my life. It occurred to me that it might be my last.

At twenty, I was a *man*, and the sand in the hourglass of life looked like the Sahara Desert. Thirty-five years later, I was a man, but only a man, and I was counting the individual grains. Moreover, if truth were told, the few grains remaining were passing so quickly that I could barely keep count. As I saw those remaining grains drain away, procrastination became a game of chicken that I no longer wished to play.

So, in the summer of my life before the spring of the year that I quit work, I picked up the phone, sat down at the kitchen table, and called Mel. I would not say no anymore.

Chapter 2
The Questions

Our tundra-bound flotilla of two red canoes would be paddled by a crew of four: Mel and I in one canoe, and Tom and Ruth Moore in the other. The Moores, younger than Mel and me by a couple of years, had previously joined us on several canoe trips in the forested regions of southern Canada. These below-the-tree-line trips had successfully tested our compatibility. Mostly, I knew that both Mel and the Moores were fond of good "experiences" but adamantly opposed to "adventures." Adventures, they said, did not always have happy endings. In Tom's mind, it was a simple formula: unexpected events plus improvisation equaled adventure followed be misery. Thus, there would be no canoe trip with Mel and the Moores without a rigorous regimen of planning. All events that could possibly be foreseen would be foreseen and all foreseen events would be tightly managed.

Our planning sessions took place at Mel's gray-stuccoed house, a proper Art Deco specimen, located near the University of Minnesota's St. Paul campus. Flat-roofed and boxy, Mel's house sat on a snug corner lot that bookended the brick-faced Georgians and faux-timbered Tudors, eclectically lining the rest of the street. Swaying shade from tall-masted oaks drew us to the front door, which, upon opening, led to a curious chorus of assorted ticking and clicking clocks, narrow-slatted oak floors, and the occasional respite of pale blue interior walls. The latter bore the burden of lifelong accumulations of memorabilia and sundry artistic objects.

Sue, Mel's wife, who served as chief curator of clocks and collections, cheerfully facilitated our meetings but did not directly participate. She preferred shorter trips of the day or weekend variety, not arctic expeditions. Like Marsha, she had elected to remain "down south" for the summer.

Mel's dining room was our "war room." Here, around a circular table of antique oak, the four of us ate dinner, laughed at the world, and then got down to the business of discussing trip details and coordinating schedules. There were maps to be poured over, equipment lists to be reviewed, menus to be planned, and food rations to be bagged.

Mel and I had been canoeing and fishing together for nearly twenty years, and during these years I had benefited from and had occasionally been rescued by his preparedness. Attentive and cautious, this former West Point Cadet was the consummate planner for contingencies. Things didn't work out between Mel and the Army, but that turned out to be the Army's loss and the University of Minnesota's gain, where Mel became a professor of forestry and an associate dean. I sometimes wondered, however, which was his real vocation, professor or outdoorsman. Without equivocation, Sue said it was the latter. The professorship, she said, was only an avocation.

Having taken the Boy Scout motto to heart and into adulthood, Mel was a truly prepared person. He had dutifully engraved his driver's license number onto every piece of personal property, from fish landing net to pocketknife. This he did to facilitate their recovery if lost or stolen. The Department of Motor Vehicle's eventual decision to change and to thereby obsolete all existing drivers' license numbers was thus lamentingly received as a tragic consequence of public policy.

With my inclination toward risk and random fun, Mel was my complement. In the chilling downdrafts of advancing thunderstorms, Mel took cover while I stood on the water's edge and casted with a graphite fishing rod, a perfect grounding device for lightning bolts. I figured that my odds of getting zapped were slim, but Mel would remind me that my behavior was not always prudent. His knots were square and taut, mine sometimes more like granny reunions or macramé assemblages.

Mel's remarkable punctuality also accentuated my deplorable lameness in that regard. If I invited Mel to my house and suggested that he arrive between 6:30 and 6:45 p.m., he would arrive at precisely the mid-point, thirty seconds past 6:37. A semi-trailer truck carrying flammable liquids could jackknife across all lanes of traffic and explode into a wall of flames, but Mel would still show up on my doorstep. On time. The National Institute of Standards and Technology would do well to check the oscillations of the nation's master clocks against Mel's arrivals.

Relatively short, Mel fit neatly into a canoe, but he had the shoulders of a linebacker and a paddle stroke to match. In his one deviation from prudent conduct, which regularly occurred at the lips of rapids, Mel had the alarming habit of standing up in the canoe—often on his tiptoes! Craning his neck, he would scout the rapids and then devise maneuvers to descend them. Despite this tiptoe teetering, I couldn't complain. We had some bumps and scrapes, but to Mel's credit, we had never pretzeled our canoe and, aside from a single harmless dunk, which was only a slight blemish on our record, we had never lost it in a true Maytag experience.

Watching Mel tiptoe in the canoe, however, was like watching a tightrope walker without a safety net. I was not in the circus audience looking up at him either; I was with him, just him and me in the skinny canoe. Perched at the fluidic precipice, the tippy canoe would teeter. My paddle grip would tighten and my breath would deepen. Then Mel would sit down, I would exhale, and we would shoot the rapids.

Tom was the husband of our canoe-tripping couple. When he was not skiing down a mountain or making furniture in his home woodshop, he managed the office and kept the books for a food distributor in Minneapolis. He was an unabashed gearhead with more accoutrements for his canoe—clips, carabineers, pouches, kneeling pads, compass holder, waterproof map case—than doodads in a jumbo Swiss Army knife, and he had a couple of those, too. Tom and Ruth also paddled with ergonomically bent, black graphite paddles that didn't weigh much more than a feather and required a credit application prior to purchase. Mel and I, with clunky wood paddles, coveted them.

Tom liked to thumb his nose at our cosmic insignificance. His hair-trigger wit, always cocked, was as sharp as the shock of dark hair that matched the color of his eyes and lopped over his tanned forehead. His purposeful malapropisms and flip-flop puns about pouring me some "watt hotter" or "chalk hot late" made me smile even while I shook my head in feigned regret. Quickly incisive, Tom claimed to be apolitical, which alone may have proved the power of his intellect. Rather than discuss the great issues of the day, which seemed to resolve themselves independently of our expressed opinions, Tom proclaimed greater interest in the correlations between the smells of farts and the ingestion of different kinds of cheeses.

He and his wife, Ruth, were veteran wilderness trekkers whose talents and energies around the campsite were unceasing. When we camped with the Moores, we knew that we had to move fast to help or they would finish the chores before we had a chance to start. Ruth never missed a beat in attending to the details and tidying the campsite, including her observation of smudges on my reading glasses before I could sense any impairment of my own vision. This attentiveness undoubtedly served her well vocationally.

Her day job was to run the payroll for an industrial supply company, which I knew to be an essential but underappreciated job of exacting detail. Even when the payroll department performs flawlessly, most workers, I reflected, tended to see their paychecks as insults. Few, if any employees, it seemed to me, ever felt fully liberated from the perception that they were overworked and underpaid. I knew of no instance in any company when someone sent a little note or called up the payroll department to say, "Gee, I wanted to thank you guys. Everything on my paycheck—deductions, vacation balance, net take home pay, et cetera—is just peachy. You're doing a wonderful job. These flowers are for *you*."

Cautiously inclined to follow established order, Ruth was a remarkable knot of contradictions. What was this seemingly risk-averse wisp of a woman doing gallivanting to the Arctic where she would follow an unmarked trail, plunge down unrated rapids, and be hundreds of miles away from any outpost of civilization, doctors and hospitals included?

Each member contributed to the shared equipment. My veteran canoeing partners honored me by consenting to use my water filter and my tiny Himalayan Primus stove that folded into a bag the size of a grapefruit. In addition to my stove and filter, the group gear included canoes, sponges, bailers, ropes, parachute cord, packs, tents, wind screens, fuel bottles, matches, lighters, kettles, cooking utensils, soap, tents, back-up water filter, collapsible bucket, wire, replacement bolts and nuts for canoe thwarts, sewing kit, boot goop, seam sealer, miscellaneous tools, first-aid kit, fish hook remover, bear repellant, shotgun with slugs and firecracker shells, and emergency flares. Oh yes, I almost forgot to mention—that universal problem solver—duct tape.

Our first-aid kit included clever items, such as a toothache patch and filling repair kit as well as a lightweight SAM splint. It also included a reassuring how-to book entitled *Wilderness Medicine.* The SAM people touted their waterproof splint, which conveniently rolled into fist-sized coil, for use on everything, from fibulas to phalanges. Of course, if one of us were to snap a femur and shish kabob it through a hamstring muscle, the entire contents of this first-aid kit, SAM splint included, would be no more effective than a Band-Aid.

Given the plethora of possible hazards, the greatest utility of our first-aid kit was its placebo effect. Got a fracture, severed artery, cardiac infarction? No problem! We've got all of the medical accouterments and the how-to book right inside this little pouch.

Our most important first-aid item resided not in the first-aid kit but in a black Pelican case. Made of lightweight Space Age plastic and favored by Navy SEAL teams, Pelican cases are crushproof, dustproof, and watertight to a depth of thirty feet. Our chubby little Pelican case held our real lifeline, a rented satellite phone. We would use it only when all else failed.

"Mel," I asked, "What happens if we have to use the satellite phone to call for help?"

"The Royal Canadian Mounted Police will search by helicopter or floatplane. When they find us, we'll have to hand over our credit cards, wedding rings, wristwatches, billfolds, and pocket change as earnest money before they take us out."

At our final meeting at Mel's house, Tom presented something that looked like a fabric cannon ball and a clutch of aluminum poles.

"What's that?" asked Mel.

"This, my friends," announced Tom, "is a portable gazebo stuffed in a pressure pack. When you pop it open, you have a twelve-foot square fabric shed with a nylon roof and mosquito netting for walls. You prop it up with these poles and lines. What do you think? It only weighs ten pounds, maybe fifteen with the poles."

"I don't know," I said. "I like traveling light. One less item, one less headache. An extra fifteen pounds could sink a canoe in a storm or strain someone's back." I started to sound like an uncharacteristically serious person.

"Don't worry," Tom pleaded. "We'll carry it in our canoe."

"No," said Mel, "we'll all pitch in and share the load."

With the debate cut off and seeing that my lean strategy would not prevail, I cast an affirmative vote and made it unanimous. Besides, being eristic was unbecoming as the expedition's rookie member. In addition to our two sleeping tents, one for the Moores and one for Mel and me, we would take Tom's screened-in shelter.

On the trip, we would use it as our combined screened-in living and dining room and affectionately refer to it as the Tundra Tarp. On our third day on the river, with our campsite engulfed in clouds of mosquitoes and assorted flies, I started saying a daily prayer of thanksgiving for having lost this debate.

By mid-April, the details fell into place. Tom emerged as the mastermind of the trip's logistics. These included an intricate ten-point plan, as all good plans should be—just like Moses' commandments.

1. Rent a satellite phone, learn how to operate it, and pack it with the rest of the gear.

2. Leave Minneapolis late in the afternoon, drive eleven hundred miles overnight to Lynn Lake, Manitoba.

3. Advance a respectable sum of money to the heretofore unknown Lynn Lake Esso station operator, whom we hoped would shuttle our van back to the local fire station at Thompson, Manitoba, instead of, say, taking it for a joy ride and dumping it in a swamp.

4. Fly our canoe party, gear, and canoes via Trans West Twin Otter floatplane from Lynn Lake 290 miles north to Seal Hole Lake, while praying for decent weather and enough ice out of the lake to land the plane on open water.

5. Paddle approximately two hundred miles down the Thlewiaza River to its mouth at Hudson Bay.

6. Using the satellite phone, call Joe Savikataaq Sr. the only person in Arviat, Nunavut, reputed to have a boat big enough to transport our canoes and us on the high seas of Hudson Bay. Joe would ferry us in his boat sixty miles north to Arviat where we would have to find a place to stay overnight.

7. Fly via Calm Air passenger service from Arviat to Thompson, Manitoba, with an interim stop in Churchill, Manitoba.

8. Arrange to have our canoes flown from Arviat via a cargo flight to Thompson, where upon a third party, another Barren Lands-bound group of friends, would pick up our canoes and drive them back to the Twin Cities.

9. Take a taxi from the Thompson airport to a community building where the man from the Esso station was supposed to have parked the van. The success of this step depended on the assumption that there was at least one taxi in Thompson.

10. Drive the van and trailer from Thompson back to the Twin Cities.

Although this ten-point plan was masterfully designed, I sensed the presence of Murphy's Law lurking in the shadows. The odds that our trip might entail not just good experiences but some actual adventures seemed strong.

My share of the preparatory work involved getting Nunavut fishing licenses and finding accommodations in Arviat. I called the Nunavut Department of Sustainable Development about sport fishing licenses. More precisely, I left messages. A couple of days later someone called back and informed me that, no, they didn't take credit cards, not in person, not over the phone, not by facsimile transmission, and not by email. The voice said that the cost of the licenses depended on the exchange rate and that mail, the kind that involves the movement of stamped paper across international borders, was the only way to conduct business.

To account for monetary fluctuations, I made out the check in an amount ten percent higher than the actual price based on current exchange rates and then stuffed it into an envelope with instructions for the Sustainable people, if there was an overage, to keep the change. Then I was off to my friendly neighborhood postal clerk whose out-of-uniform tie featured Looney Tunes characters.

"What's the delivery guarantee on this?" I asked.

"We'll get it to the border in a day, but after that, in Canada, all bets are off." Then he smiled.

"Sounds good. I'll take it." I liked this man with the cartoon tie.

Four weeks later, I received four Nunavut fishing license applications in the mail. I filled out the forms and repeated the cycle with the friendly postal clerk. Another three weeks elapsed. With our departure date drawing near, I finally received the licenses that made us legal anglers.

While I waited for the fishing licenses to show up, I checked out lodging possibilities in Arviat where we would end our trip. With our budget stretched and a growing wariness about Arctic hotel rates, I inquired at the Eskimo Point Lumber Supply Company, which reportedly had a bunkhouse. A bunkhouse, after two weeks of sleeping on the ground, might seem like the Four Seasons in Manhattan.

With some persistence, I got an EP Lumber Supply supervisor on the phone. At first, the supervisor failed to recollect any existence of said bunkhouse. Finally, he said, "Oh that! Well I'm not sure I can recommend your sleeping there. What's that you say? There's a woman in your group? No, I don't think you can bring her into a place like that."

"Thank you for your candor, sir. I think I'll try the local hotel."

"Yeah, you'd be better off there or maybe even sleeping in your tents at the edge of town."

My next call was to the Padlei Inn in Arviat. I asked about room rates.

The clerk said, "One-hundred-eighty dollars a head."

"No, I'm sorry, I meant to ask about room rates for double occupancy, you know, two people per room. How much is that?"

"One-hundred-eighty dollars a head."

"Okay.... How about if all four of us sleep in one room. How much is *that*?"

"One-hundred-eighty dollars a head."

"So, you're telling me that we can have one person each in four rooms or four people in just one room and it's still...."

"One-hundred-eighty dollars a head."

"Well, thank you. I commend you for consistency." Click.

Back at Mel's house, I reported that $720 was a lot of money for one night in a hotel without any stars next to its name. We agreed and decided to make do with whatever arrangements we could find the night of our arrival in Arviat. Contrary to my friends' pet hate for improvisational events, our stay in Arviat would entail that very quality, but at least it was planned improvisation.

"You know what I like about our trip plan, Tom?" I did not wait for an answer. "It's a logistical masterpiece, but it still has the scent of adventure. You know what else I like about it?"

"No, Guy, tell me."

I admitted my eagerness to visit a native village and to learn how the Inuit live on a land that was permanently frozen. I also explained my curiosity about *where* they lived today, concentrated in settlements along the coasts. Mel's previous slide shows had shown Inuit settlements and, if it weren't for the absence of trees, one might say that they resembled southern Indian Reservations—those lacking the dollar infusions from casino money.

South of the tree line, the explanation for current settlement patterns among Native Americans was clear. Our pioneering ancestors occupied their lands—cleared, fenced, grazed, and plowed them under. Then, under the banner of lopsided treaties, we marched their dwindling numbers into impoverished, postage-stamp-sized reservations.

"My point," I explained, "is that whether sub-Arctic aboriginal populations live on 'the rez' or in the cities and whether or not they've preserved any aspects of their culture, they can't return to their traditional livelihoods." That, I explained, was impossible, because nearly every trace of their former homelands was gone. What was once theirs was now someone else's fenced-in private property. It was covered over with farms, cities, roads, and keep-off signs that left only a tiny fraction of the original prairie intact.

"So, Guy, you're saying that in the heartland of the continent, the buffalo are gone, and there's no place for them to roam." Tom had a way of cutting to the chase.

"Exactly."

It wasn't that Native Americans should return to some bygone iconic lifestyle. It was that any *options* for them to return to the prairie and their traditional ways were gone. Knowing what little I knew at the time, the Inuit, on the other hand, appeared to have that choice. After all, the tundra was still there and the caribou still migrated over the Barren Lands as the bison once roamed the Great Plains. Yet, they had abandoned the lifestyles of their nomadic ancestors. "It's a paradox," I said. "I don't get it."

"Well," said Ruth, perking up, "they've got a pretty good welfare system in Canada, housing and health care, too. That's probably better for them."

"Yeah," I sighed, but somehow the explanation for being concentrated in these micro-urban communities must be more involved. "How did Inuit families go from being nomads wandering over the tundra to living in these coastal towns? And then getting entangled in the Canadian welfare system? You know, it's not like transferring from one bus to another."

Mel recounted the travels of John Quaife and Judy Geck, mutual friends who had kayaked the sounds of Baffin Island in the vicinity of Pangnirtung, a small Inuit maritime village that grew up around a trading post. They learned in the 1960s that most of the residents there were still living in tents. John surmised that chasing down seals and walruses in kayaks and stalking them with harpoons wasn't just hard work. It was dangerous, too. Injuries—a broken leg or bad cut—could be fatal. Life in the settlements, according to John, was predictable, easier, and longer. Mel concurred, reasoning that the population growth of these settlements was proof of their benignity.

"Okay, okay," I said, "maybe that's all there is to it, but…."

"I'll tell you what it is," Tom interjected, "It's the McDonaldization of society." The world, Tom stated, was coalescing toward a matrix of indistinct modular cultures, a franchise on every continent.

"Guy," Tom said, cutting to the chase again, "you're the person here with time on your hands; why don't you check it out? Do a little research. Be our official cultural attaché on the trip."

Outwardly, I showed no emotion, but inside my mind was racing. I knew at once that I would rise to meet Tom's challenge. From that moment onward, I was on a mission.

Soon, in addition to pondering the question of, "what's my major in the university of life," I was attending the best institutions of higher learning immediately available to me: the Hennepin County, Minneapolis, and St. Paul public libraries. I found a few interesting books, but the materials, beyond juvenile literature about Eskimos and the Arctic, were thin. It wasn't that the reference librarians weren't doing their jobs, either. They worked with quiet efficiency on my behalf, often with an urgency that seemed to suggest my research might hold the cure for cancer. They retrieved books and articles from storage, rounded up photocopies via inter-library loan, and generally made me feel not so bad about paying my taxes, but I had little time and less patience to wait for my requests to trickle in.

Noticing that many of the inter-library loans came from the University of Minnesota's Wilson Library, I decided to drive down Washington Avenue into the heart of Minneapolis and inquire about direct, nonstudent access to the Wilson's resources. Because I was now in the income maintenance mode rather than the income growth stage of life, I avoided the pricey parking fees in the nearby ramp and opted for a surface lot a couple of blocks away. I further rationalized my cheapness by pondering how many fractions of a second these extra, aerobic steps might add to my life span. This optimism faded when I found myself in what might be charitably called a low-security neighborhood.

I got out of the car and faced five strapping lads seated on the pavement next to the sun-brightened, whitewashed walls of a cinder block building. For early afternoon entertainment, these young men passed around a liter of vodka and blessedly ignored me. I was impressed by how politely they shared this scarce resource among themselves. Just the same, I pushed the lock button on my keyset twice, thus provoking the car's horn, and decided that a self-assured look would serve me best. I did not engage them with small talk. Then I strode past them to my destination—the Wilson Library, which prominently occupied the center of the campus.

Eighty dollars later, I was a card-carrying "Friend of the Library" with a checkout privilege of up to ten books at a time, a privilege that I would often push to the limit. It wasn't just a metaphor about my stage of life; I was literally back at college surrounded by earnest young students whose presence made me feel better about the solvency of the Social Security System. When I retraced my steps to the parking lot, my car was intact, and no one was there to greet me, only an empty vodka bottle and a crumpled brown paper bag on the asphalt.

The Wilson Library, with its six floors and warrens of aisles and stacks, was the cathedral among the various local libraries. Architecturally, it was no more splendorous than a dressed-up high-rise warehouse with IBM punch-card windows, but there was no mistaking the Wilson Library. In size and quiet reverence within, this was a sacred place.

I also scoured the Internet on my laptop and found a syllabus and reading list for Anthropology 284a at Yale, titled "Inuit Past and Present" posted by Michael Kral, Yale Research Affiliate. Thankful that I didn't have to pay Yale tuition or make an onerous contribution to the university's development fund to ensure my admission, eventually I would read most of the required materials and about half of those suggested on my own.

The Wilson Library's inner sanctum was the James Ford Bell Library of rare books, manuscripts, and maps, some dating back to the 1400s. The crown jewels of this library-within-a-library grew from a collection donated by the library's namesake, a local boy who founded General Mills. The JFB library had the feel of a plushly furnished, oversized bank vault, and I had the place virtually to myself. This included the services of an assistant curator, who, after emerging from the archives, presented me with a 1740 reprint of a 1633 edition of Captain Thomas James' travel journal, *The Strange and Dangerous Voyage of Captain Thomas James in his Intended Discovery of a North West Passage into the South Sea*.[1]

Captain James was one of the many early seventeenth century explorers who misguidedly sought the shortcut to Asia, the fabled Northwest Passage, through Hudson Bay. It was easy to see how the seasonally open waters of Hudson Bay were more enticing than the actual passage to Asia, the ice-choked labyrinth known as the Arctic Archipelago. Although Hudson Bay was our canoe party's desired destination, these early explorers found only disappointment in the Bay's unbroken shores.

But these explorers were a brash and confident breed. In addition to expecting to find precious metals, they carried letters of introduction from their kings addressed to the emperor of Japan. None of these letters made it to Asia, and many of the bold souls who carried them, once they entered the Bay, never made it out. These included the Bay's namesake, Captain Henry Hudson, who, in 1612, abruptly found that the controlling mission of his ship, the *Discovery*, had become that of mutiny. The mutineers set Hudson, his son, and a handful of others adrift in the ship's lifeboat. They were never heard from again. For the Europeans who would follow Hudson, Inuit arrows, exposure, and crushing ice took their toll, and disease, notably scurvy, wiped out others, sometimes entire crews.

In 1631–32, Captain James, of *Strange and Dangerous Voyage* fame, spent a harrowing winter locked in the ice of the bay that now bears his name. Roughly the size of Lake Superior, the greatest of all inland lakes, James Bay is the southern arm of Hudson Bay. Captain James began his journal with swagger but with no fault of exaggeration: "Many a Storme and Rocke, and Mist, and Wind, and Tyde, and Sea, and Mount of Ice, Have I in this Discovery encountered withal; Many a despaire and death had almost overwhelmed me." He described cold so severe that it froze their eyelids shut. When rocky shoals and shifting ice threatened to shatter them, he assessed his fate: "If it be our fortunes to end our days here, we are as neere to heaven as in England."

James clinically describes his crewmembers' symptoms of scurvy, the result of Vitamin C deficiency: "The cold was extreme this month [February 1632], as at any time we had felt this year and many of our men complained of infirmities.

Some of sore mouths, all the teeth in heads being loose, their gums swollen, with black rotten flesh, which must every day be cut away.... Others complained of pain in their heads and their breast; some of weakness in their backs; others of aches in their thighs and knees; and others of swelling in their legs."

At the end of May, when the snow and ice finally started to melt, James and his surviving crew members regained their health by eating the "herb and leaf" of green "vetches as they first appeared out of the ground," and they ate them to the virtual exclusion of all other food. I imagined a bucolic scene dotted with human grazers.

For those who have endured the miseries of the North Country's black flies, mosquitoes, no-see-ums, and other insect piranhas, James' description of their torment might provide the vicarious comfort of historical company. "The mosquitoes," he wrote, "upon coming our way, were most intolerable. We tore an old ship's flag in pieces, and made us bags of it to put our heads in; but it was no fortification against them. They would find ways and means to sting us so that our faces were swollen hard out in pimples which would so itch and smart that we must needs rub and tear them. And these flies, indeed, were more tormenting to us than all the cold we had heretofore endured." Torment by black flies or freezing to death in a blizzard—it was a toss-up.

The human effort distilled into the Wilson Library's volumes were both humbling and heartening. Here, in a multiplicity of languages, were millions of books, each a lasting marriage of the conceptual and the tangible, ink and pages, words and meanings, all bound together. Within these stacks, I could reach in and shake hands with any author and, with a bit of reading, know that neither author nor I was alone. Moreover, with the knowledge so acquired, I could become whatever I might choose to be. The allotment of a single lifespan imposed certain limitations, of course, but the possibilities for liberating one's mind existed here, and after that, I reasoned, the soul couldn't be far behind. Someday, this entire body of human knowledge would probably be relegated to buggy-whip status and be contained on a single server secured in a charmless, air-conditioned bunker, but here, in the Wilson Library, I could walk through it. I could touch the body.

While I strove to become a responsible student of the Arctic, I learned that the people of the Far North were an often-studied group. From time to time, I reflected, they must feel like celebrities hounded by a Paparazzi of anthropologists, archeologists, sociologists, biologists, and political scientists. Whether it was the harshness of the climate or its location at the edge of the world, the Arctic was a captivating place. Indeed, there must be as many doctoral dissertations and masters' theses about the Inuit as there are Inuit. The joke that a typical Inuit family has two adults, four children, and at least one visiting anthropologist holds enough truth to be painfully funny. And it must be at least a little discomfiting to have all of these strangers peering at you, like voyeurs at your bedroom window.

Edward Abbey, in *Desert Solitaire*, expressed similar concerns about the Indians of the American Southwest and said that, as for himself, he did not relish the prospect of perfect strangers examining his daily habits and folkways, inspecting his costume, questioning his religion, classifying his artifacts, investigating his sexual practices, or evaluating his chances of cultural survival. Thus, to the people of the Far North, I apologize for my additional pair of peering eyes. I wish to understand, not intrude, but I suppose that's what we all say.

In my search to understand the cultural and environmental changes affecting the Barren Lands, I met a variety of interesting people. I met most through their writings and a few through conversations and correspondence. One of those, whom I could meet only through his writings, was the late and renowned Canadian anthropologist, Diamond Jenness (1886–1969).

Jenness lived among the Copper Inuit of the central Arctic coast for several years beginning in 1914. He became the adopted son of a Copper Inuit couple and their daughter became his sister. With the help of his adoptive family and remarkable patience, Jenness observed and documented the legends and ways of the Inuit. He acquired priceless collections of tools and artifacts, recorded songs, and drew diagrams of more than a hundred Inuit cat's cradle games and other string tricks. To obtain these, Jenness traded rifles and ammunition, metal pots and pans, and other merchandise from the industrialized world. Jenness wistfully recognized that he stood at the threshold of irreversible changes in Inuit culture and that his own barter with them only accelerated those changes.

In his writings and public addresses, Jenness, who served in both world wars, did not succumb to academic quibbling nor did he favor a dense or hesitant style of prose. He was a man of his times, said what he meant, and, without question, could turn a phrase. His seminal academic works, among others, included *The Life of the Copper Eskimos* and *Eskimo Administration.*

In the Cold War era after World War II, Jenness advocated strengthening Canada's claims of northern sovereignty by relocating Inuit families to the High Arctic. He also advocated for Inuit education and job training in *southern* Canada and their voluntary resettlement there. Some might consider these recommendations insensitive or politically untenable. Despite his accolades, Jenness' positions were not universally esteemed.

However, in Jenness' popular work, *The People of the Twilight*, he asks a question, one that was as relevant at the time of our trip as it was in 1928 when his book was published. This is the question: "The tribal bands where each man toiled for all and shared his food in common are resolving into their constituent families … [where] every man vies with the rest in the race of wealth and worldly prosperity … Will history 50 years hence record the same fate for the twilight land where for two years we carried out our mission? Were we the harbingers of a brighter dawn or only the messengers of an ill-omened, portending disaster?"[2]

Jonathan Waterman, who chronicled his remarkable three-year (1997–99) solo trek in a sailing kayak from Alaska to Canada's Boothia Peninsula in *Arctic Crossing*, refers to this question as the "warning" of Diamond Jenness.[3] Whether it was a question or a warning, it still stood in keen relevance, unworn by the passage of time.

Even after my effort to learn about the Arctic and my travels in the Barren Lands, Jenness' question still staggered me: *"Were we the harbingers of a brighter dawn or only the messengers of an ill-omened disaster?"* I could not say, but if I was certain of one thing, by the end of the trip I knew that the answer was not black nor was it white.

Soon the blooms of Minnesota's hurried spring yielded to the green leaves of summer. My days as an ersatz college student floated by, one day quickly dissolving into another. But our departure date drew near and my re-entry into the world of practical matters bore down upon me. Moreover, the truth is that I did not get very far in my studies. Most of my research would be done after I returned from the Far North. The dog didn't eat my homework and I didn't leave it on the bus. I just didn't get it done, and there would be occasions during the trip when my lack of preparedness as our group's cultural attaché would become awkwardly if not painfully evident.

One of those more immediately pressing matters was trip "provisioning." Not being as resourceful as the historical Inuit, Mel and I and the Moores did most of our hunting and gathering at local supermarkets. We filled a couple of grocery carts with beans, rice, spaghetti, summer sausage, cheese, tortillas, dried fruit, coffee, cocoa, powdered milk and fruit drinks, granola, oatmeal, pancake mix, a few small tins of ham and chicken, peanut butter, humus, jam, crackers, trail mix, candy bars, cooking oil, seasonings, prepared dry foods like macaroni and cheese, beef stroganoff, hash browns, soup mixes, desserts, and last, but not least, a couple of bottles of high-proof rum. In addition to the cheese and the summer sausage, the only edible thing that wasn't canned, dried, or powdered was the rum. To reduce the chances of spoilage, we would eat the more perishable items in the early part of the trip.

Back at Mel's house, we added Mel's homemade beef jerky and venison sticks as well as dried vegetables and tomato sauce to the assemblage and then repacked everything into plastic bags. When we finished, we had enough food to feed the four of us and stuff the entirety of it into less than two packs. Pretty amazing and cheap, too. Normally you might rebel against such food, but on the trail, our exercised bodies would savor it like haute cuisine from a four-star restaurant. Nothing enhances the flavor of food more than appetite.

To ensure that we came equipped with the "right stuff," Mel gave each of us a two-page double-columned, single-spaced list of recommended personal clothing and gear. With list in hand, I scurried through my closets to assemble what I could and then darted to camping and sporting goods stores to purchase missing items and help stimulate the economy. But I had to call and question Mel on a couple of them.

"What's with the ear plugs and the eye shades? Why are these on the list?"

"Well, Guy, it never gets very dark north of the 60th parallel in July, so I'm bringing eye shades to help me sleep."

"Oh. And the ear plugs? They must be so that you can sleep while I snore, or vice versa. Right?"

"Yes, but I was thinking that *I* would need the ear plugs, probably nose plugs, too."

"Your flattery, Mel, is misguided as are your fears of flatulence and the assumption of its singular source. Anyway, how're you supposed to be our sentry for polar bears if you sleep with plugs in your ears and blindfolds over your eyes? Are you counting on using my eyes and ears while you pump the shotgun?"

You can't beat the buddy system, but sometimes there are too many contingencies. I had a persistent vision of Mel, ears plugged and eyes blindfolded, shaking off his sleeping bag and waving a shotgun somewhere in the direction of a ravenous bear. We decided to work through these contingency complications during our twenty-one-hour drive to Lynn Lake, Manitoba.

Chapter 3

The Prairie Highways

By the time we pulled away from the curb in St. Paul, the afternoon sun had begun to soften and, by the time we would see our driving destination, the town of Lynn Lake in northern Manitoba, we would see the sun set, rise, and begin to set again. Although we would have plenty of windshield time together, Mel and I never got around to discussing our contingency conundrums about dealing with bears. They would remain unresolved.

At the town of Lynn Lake, we would transfer from vehicle to floatplane, which would fly us across the provincial boundary and drop us off in the tundra of Canada's newest and most northern territory. Compared to the Earth's billions of inhabitants, past and present, we would then be among the privileged few to stand upon the Barren Lands. We would feel them under our feet, listen to them, and breathe their winds into our lungs.

I saw my friends' spirits building. Mel would immerse himself in the great outdoors and, thereby, slip into a temporary state of amnesia about the reorganization of his university department. Tom would bury himself in a milieu of details different from the numbers he crunched at his office, and Ruth would escape from the people who never brought her flowers.

As for my own wanderings in wilderness, I was intrigued more by what I might find than what I might escape. Tempered by a resolve not to become a nutcase, I was wary of expectations of the mystical variety or, for that matter, episodes of divine intervention, for which I was undeserving. I surmised that the secrets of the universe might not be any fun if I found out what they were.

Nevertheless, a change in surroundings, I thought, might help clear some of the ambiguities fogging up my mental windshield. I was open to the possibilities.

We rendezvoused in front of Mel's house and quickly loaded the packs and other stray items from carefully checked-off lists into Tom's rig. We would be rolling across the continent on three axles, one under a trailer and the other two under a beige Ford E150 van powered by a 225 horsepower V-8 engine. The shiny white panels of the enclosed trailer hitched to the van's stern bore the brand name "Wells Cargo," a fitting tribute to its owner's penchant for puns.

Tom's van gave proof to his fastidious reputation. He had waxed and polished the van's exterior to a lustrous sheen and sanitized the interior to operating room standards. Inside this antiseptic vehicular environment, we would recline in the comfort of leather bucket seats and individualized climate controls. Whispers of a phantom car salesman echoed in my ear: "Guy . . . let me tell you, this baby's *loaded*."

Ruth had centered a large cooler on the van's floor and stuffed it with sandwiches, sodas, chips, roasted peanuts, and other road-food temptations. Owing to my wife's nutritional background, this food was the equivalent of dietary contraband in our house. While I knew that these items were addictively evil, their forbidden status made them alluring. Truly, I was unworthy of this vehicle and unable to "just say no" to its catered contents.

Out on the street, we passed cameras around to Marsha and Sue who snapped bon voyage shots. Rather than a celebratory hug, Marsha gave me a polite kiss, which, in its brevity, masked a complexity of emotions. She stood by her man, but the instincts of her heart were pulling her in different directions. Any earlier perceived differential between the act of my departing for a few weeks and her husband's outright abandonment were quickly vanishing.

Changes swirled around both of us. With the demands of childrearing and jobs no longer requiring full-time attention, the question of how we might share this windfall of time loomed before us. We needed to redefine our togetherness, but here I was, leaving for nearly a month.

With canoes strapped to the van's top, we departed into the late afternoon sun of high summer and followed Interstate 94 northwest to Fargo, North Dakota. White-numbered, little green signs along the way measured, in miles, the engineering marvels of the Interstate highway system while our tires hummed the praises of modern industrial technology. It was a splendid way to burn up a couple hundred gallons of fossil fuel to get back to the simplicity of living with nature.

The sandwiches made me think of Charles Lindbergh and the sparse grub that Minnesota's native son took on his transatlantic flight in 1927. Our flight would be on the road, not in the air, and over the North American continent, not an Atlantic-sized ocean, but it had a similar singularity of mission. With the exceptions of refueling and a minor side trip on Friday morning, we would drive the 1,100-mile route to Lynn Lake nonstop.

Tom and Ruth had filled the van's seat pockets with a veritable library of camping and adventure magazines. The ads and articles were mostly alien to me—beyond my experiential comprehension. Knowing that Mel and the Moores kept abreast of these topics and the latest advances in equipment was reassuring but also a little intimidating.

My friends knew all of the paddling strokes and their names, and, frankly, I was lucky to have them as paddling partners. Their fluency suggested the successful completion of continuing education credits in advanced technical canoeing. They spoke of the J stroke, the sweep, the reverse sweep, the pry, the draw, the ever important forward cross bow, the back cross bow, the forward ferry, the back ferry, the basic forward paddle stroke, the back paddle stroke, this stroke, and that stroke, just as you and I might say, "Please pass the jam." Over the years, I had intuitively learned most of these maneuvers, but more in the way that a sidewalk saxophonist carries a tune without knowing the names of the notes.

After carrying us across the Minnesota prairie, which included an imperceptible continental divide, the 225 horses under the hood of Tom's van needed watering. We stopped at a filling station in Fargo, North Dakota, slaked their hydrocarbon thirst, and then led our team onto Interstate 29, a four-lane river of pavement that paralleled the Red River of the North. Like us, the waters of the Red would eventually find their way to Hudson Bay.

Our tires rolled across a bottomland so flat and wide that we could see the curve of the Earth in the rectangular fields of sugar beets, potatoes, and grain that extended without interruption to horizon lines in every direction. The sun, which had long celebrated this summer day, finally slipped below the tabletop landscape. Soon, we passed Grand Forks and East Grand Forks, sister cities that held hands via the bridges that spanned the river's muddy banks and whose residents referenced their timelines to BF and AF, which is to say before and after the flood.

Normally, the Red River wasn't much more than an oversized drainage ditch. Had we blinked, we would have missed it earlier in Fargo. However, this river annually bore a springtime curse: melting southern headwaters often backed up behind unmelted plugs of ice in the colder north—the river's downstream, Arctic-bound destination.

In 1997, when blizzardy accumulations melted beneath incessant spring rains, the Red's timid Dr. Jekyll waters became Mr. Hyde's torrents. Fields of heavy black soil, plowed and tiled, where prairies and marshlands once stood, did little to slow the runoff. When the Red fanned out over the valley's floor, formerly the bed of ancient Lake Agassiz, it left sixty thousand people homeless. Waters, laden with top soil, lapped at the walls of city buildings and then shorted their electrical wires, setting upper, unsubmerged floors ablaze. It was a good example of hell on earth. Some of the area's residents left and never returned. For many of those who did return, the sweet and earthy smells of springtime rains, normally the harbingers of life's renewal, weren't so sweet anymore.

Paying no homage to the flood of '97, we motored onward, paralleling the Red and finally arriving at Canadian customs at the North Dakota–Manitoba border around midnight. Earlier, gathering clouds had snuffed out the last of our twilight. Now they blanketed us in perfect darkness.

The customs agent bore a cigarette-wrinkled face and stood ensconced like a museum specimen behind the glassed-in booth. I guessed two to three packs a day, probably from a habit that had begun in early childhood. The interior light, dimmed by tinted glass, shadowed the creases in his face and accented his stubbly chin with a greenish, fluorescent glow. We had arrived at an off-peak hour. It was just us and the "border services officer."

Tom explained that we were going to Arviat, formerly Eskimo Point, and declared that we had less than four liters of alcohol, a shotgun, firecracker shells, and slugs. And, yes, he apologized for not mentioning it sooner, some pepper spray. Every mother of a daughter would want Tom as her son-in-law, always the polite and articulate gentleman, but none of these qualities impressed the man behind the glass.

The mention of Arviat furrowed the agent's brows. He looked a little puzzled but still sleepy. The announcement of the shotgun sparked some alertness. But the revelation of pepper spray put matters over the top. Bulging, magmatic whiteness erupted from the cratered sockets that held his eyes.

Mel, fully prepared, temporarily appeased the ashen-faced constable by producing his permit and Canadian license to carry the shotgun. The declaration of pepper spray, however, apparently implied the equivalent of international weapons of mass destruction. Tom's entreaty that we had bear pepper spray, not terroristic pepper spray, failed to alter the intransigence of this outpost Canadian officialdom.

Eventually, we were welcomed to Canada with our bear repellant, but only after Tom showed the agent the canisters, which fortuitously sported illustrations of menacing bears. By inexplicable logic, the bear motif somehow assured the agent that the repellant wouldn't be used on humans. Thus, we avoided further delay, not to mention strip searches, latex gloves, extraordinary rendition, and other unknown indignities.

The alcohol, by the way, was mostly 151-proof rum for medicinal purposes, such as, muscle relaxant and, shall we say, mood alteration. As a flammable fluid, it could also serve as emergency stove fuel. Amidst the onslaught of black flies and mosquitoes, we enjoyed the civilizing influences of a daily finger of rum, cut with powdered lemonade, and drunk in the comfort of our bug-free Tundra Tarp.

Crossing the border transformed U.S. Interstate 29 into Manitoba Provincial Highway 75. We droned northward to Winnipeg, Manitoba's capital, largest city, and namesake of the province's largest lake. We had changed countries, but the flatness of the landscape was the same.

Mel and Ruth dozed, but I couldn't sleep, and Tom, a compulsive driver, held fast to the wheel even though he had already driven across two big states and well into Canada. His eyes fixed on the road with a mechanical stare, the kind that suggested a heightened risk of sudden vehicular death syndrome. Owing to my aversions to driving into the ditch or opposing lanes of traffic, I tried to keep Tom alert by engaging him in conversation.

"Tom," I said, "why do people live in Winnipeg?"

"Dunno."

"Because they like to watch Mack trucks and hog barns float by on the Red River."

Tom stifled a yawn.

"It's okay, you don't have to laugh. It's not even my joke."

"Hey, I've got one for you, Guy. You know how Canada got its name?"

"I give up. Tell me."

"Canada's founding fathers were sitting on a stack of beaver pelts in the trading post when they agreed to draw three letters from a hat. The guy says, 'Well, look at that; it's a C, *eh*? And the second letter, why it's an N, *eh*? The third, a D, *eh*?'"

Halfway through Tom's delivery, I recalled having heard this joke before but chose to delay the courtesy of a chuckle until he finished. Then I announced that I knew the real answer.

"Yeah, but is it funny?" asked Tom.

"Maybe so, that is, if you can find any humor in irony."

"How so?"

"Well, apparently, the great modern nation of Canada was named for a word in an ancient and now extinct language." I explained that of the ten native Iroquoian languages in Canada, only seven were still spoken. Of the three that were extinct, only one word still survived. That word, *kanata*, was the word for village and was now the name of the country, Canada.

My little etymological exposition was an interesting diversion but also a conversation stopper, so I steered the discussion to global warming. Tom was well versed in the topic and, for the next hour, we traded factoids and came to the agreement that, even if the issue was debatable, the trends were troubling. Since the beginning of the twentieth century, the Earth's temperature had increased more than two degrees Fahrenheit, a small increase but enough to make the difference between glacial ice and waters flowing into the ocean. The polar icecaps were breaking up and melting away. Atmospheric carbon dioxide (CO_2) levels, the primary greenhouse gas component, were fast approaching 400 parts per million, and all these phenomena—greenhouse gases, global temperatures, and sea levels—were following in lockstep with the earth's exponential population growth. We had taken millions of years to reach the one-billion mark in the early 1800s, but we were now asking the planet to shoulder an additional billion people every 10 years. Heeding Genesis 9, verse 7, we had gone forth, trampled about Eden's garden, and multiplied—mission accomplished!

I suggested that the earth's atmosphere was like a reactor vessel in uncertain equilibrium and then wondered aloud how long CO_2 or any other input could keep increasing before that equilibrium would be upended. Yes, plant life required CO_2 for photosynthesis and, as an industrial gas, CO_2 found many uses, including dry ice, but at elevated levels, by displacing oxygen, CO_2 became an asphyxiant and, at high enough concentrations, it was toxic. The U.S.A. OSHA Permissible Exposure Limit (PEL) for CO_2 toxicity was 5000 ppm. Tom and I blackly reflected that future generations might not have to worry about climate change; eventually they'd be dead from suffocation or toxic poisoning.

I noted that the Arctic, in some respects, functioned like an Earth-sized barometer. When the world heated up one degree at the equator, the Arctic heated up two or three degrees—more than enough to thaw the tundra's permafrost. The explanation for this multiplying phenomenon lay in the fact that as the reflective covers of snow and ice receded or seasonally didn't last as long, effects became causes. Uncovered land and open waters absorbed more of the sun's heat and, in turn, intensified the warming trend. It was a self-perpetuating feedback loop.

The night's darkness colored our shared mood. Tom mused about the loss of heroism associated with treks to a North Pole free of its ice cap, about how open waters would sap the market for North Pole adventure books. Tom suggested that we could forget the dogsleds and forego the temptations of cannibalizing the corpses of fallen comrades in order to survive. "You know," he said, "just book it on Carnival Cruise Lines."

The odometer clicked off a few more miles while the highway's dashed white line hypnotically quieted our chuckles. Worried that this pause might trigger a narcoleptic incident, I turned to the topic of icebergs.

"You know, icebergs are pretty amazing things. Recently I was reading that they're not just frozen, lifeless objects with no other purposes than sinking ships or blocking their passage. And," I said, "I'm not talking about the seals and gulls and the occasional polar bear commonly associated with them. There's a whole cast of lesser known players below." I explained that mats of algae clung to the icebergs' bottom sides, and clouds of plankton and shrimp-like creatures, known as krill, drifted in the shadows. Seafarers from codfish to whales feasted on the plankton-fattened krill, and the fish, darting among sunlit fissures, sacrificed themselves to the seals, which sustained the bears at the top of the food chain. The sinking litter from all these iceberg hitchhikers then became the gastronomical fortune of clams and crabs. To keep these bottom dwellers in check, the Arctic's oversized mammalian vacuum cleaners stood ready. Sensitive whiskers enabled walruses to pick out crustaceans and bivalves and suck them up by the thousands.

"Yeah, yeah," said Tom, "I get it. From top to bottom, one thing feeds off the other."

"And everything," I said, "depends on the ice. That includes the Inuit, too." That, of course, was plainly true.

Nunavut's leaders were saying that their hunting culture was in danger of melting away. The people of the Far North claimed that they and their homelands, due to the Arctic's climatic sensitivity, were like sacrificial canaries in the planetary mineshaft. "Save the Arctic and you save the world" was the catchphrase.

The polar bears, on the top of the predatory pyramid weren't just the Arctic's iconic poster art animals, either. They were the bellwethers. To save the Arctic and thus the world, I deduced, we would do well to save the bears, not by imprisoning them in zoos, but by saving their habitat and thus ensuring our own.

"To re-coin a phrase," I said, "'it's the *habitat*, stupid,' isn't it?"

"Yes . . . but I'm not stupid."

"I know."

"I know you know, and I know," said Tom. "Hey, you don't have to shoot the bears with rifles to kill them off. You just have to take away their homes, you know, wreck the neighborhood."

The homes of Hudson Bay's polar bears, we knew, were under siege. Since the 1980s, later freeze-ups and earlier ice-outs had added four more weeks to the open-water season. The upshot was less time for the Bay's bears to hunt seals on the ice and store up fat. With shorter offshore feeding seasons on the ice floes and longer onshore summer fasts, polar bear litter sizes and birth weights were declining.[1] In a few more generations, these great animals could vanish from the Bay.

On the tundra, new species had taken up residence: caterpillars, red foxes, and barn owls in a place where there were no barns.[2] Spring snowmelts couldn't sustain forage plants through the longer summers. Just before the onset of winter, when the caribou needed to bulk up for the lean months ahead, the vegetation dried up. Earlier ice breakups isolated the caribou on islands, stranding them from grazing and breeding grounds while greater daily temperature fluctuations in spring and fall increasingly encased their food—primarily lichens and mosses—in ice. Unable to dig through to their food, caribou and muskox cut their feet on the ceramic-like crusts and sometimes starved in alarming numbers.[3]

Again, the stimulative effect of my litany, evermore gloomy, waned. Seeking a more cheerful tone, I spoke about the possibilities of ocean shipping through the formerly ice-clogged Northwest Passage and the offshore oil fields uncovered by receding sea ice.

Tom envisioned a perpetual motion machine of human enterprise. The shrinking polar ice cap, he said, would give us more access to more oil so we could fuel more refineries and build more tankers to transport more oil. The ultimate combustion of that oil would further insulate the planet in carbon gases, and, thus, melt more of the ice. The vanishing ice, in turn, would enable access to more oil, until, of course, it was all gone, first the ice, then the oil.

One plan, for new mines in the Far North, I recalled, proposed a deep-water port in Canada's Bathurst Inlet along the Northwest Passage. Jobs were the draw, but the road connecting the mines to the port would cut across caribou migration paths, and the tankers would carry risks of oil spills, which, if they drifted under the ice cap, would be impossible to clean up.

Tom said that he and Ruth had once paddled the Hood, a river bound by spectacular scenery before it emptied into Bathurst Inlet. The Hood's Wilberforce Falls, he said, was the "Niagara of the North," but the spark in Tom's voice was fading. Soon he could say nothing more than a drowsy "mmm."

After eight hours of driving, our erstwhile long-distance driver finally submitted to the forces of sleep. Just outside Winnipeg, Tom pulled over and the two of us did a do-si-do around the van, which put me behind the wheel and Tom immediately to sleep in the passenger seat next to me.

In an instant, it became a truly dark and stormy night. Rain drummed staccato timpani on the van's sheet metal. I put one hand on the wheel and fumbled for the windshield wiper controls with the other. Except for the headlight beams ahead, which were being strafed by fusillades of raindrop tracers, the inky night blotted out everything.

I turned the van with its sleepy occupants and roof-mounted canoes onto Route 6, a two-lane ribbon of saggy asphalt. Heading north, the highway took us around the west side of Lake Winnipeg. What Route 6 lacked in hills, it made up for in abrupt and inexplicable curves. A palsied hand must have drawn this highway's route across Manitoba's paper-flat landscape. Each driving lane had a pair of grooves pressed down and worn smooth by the tires of untold tons of vehicles.

When I approached fifty miles per hour, the van's tires started to hydroplane and bounce like skipping stones on these parallel linear puddles. To maintain control, I edged the van toward the centerline and tried to align the tires on the unsubmerged crowns of pavement. While the scarcity of opposing traffic accommodated my instincts to hog the middle of the road, I was beginning to think that shooting a five-mile run of class-three rapids in an open canoe might be a more relaxing way to spend a few hours.

On previous outings to Manitoba, our group had driven this same highway in the daylight. Highway 6 wound its way through the so-called Interlake Area, an isthmus of land that separated Manitoba's Great Lakes, Lake Winnipeg to the east and lakes Manitoba and Winnipegosis to the west. This land between the lakes marked an area of transition, from the northeasterly Boreal Forest and granite outcroppings of the Canadian Shield to the parklands and farms of the Canadian Prairies, which lay to the south and west.

Ranking as the world's tenth largest freshwater lake, the greatest of Manitoba's so-called Great Lakes was Lake Winnipeg. In North America, only Lake Superior and Lake Michigan were longer and not by much.

The waters of Manitoba's greatest lake, although large, were somewhat cosmetically challenged. The Cree Indians aptly named Winnipeg, which, in their language, meant "murky" or "muddy waters." Depending on the reflected colors of the day, the lake looked like it was filled with diluted pea or bean soup. Because of its combination of long length and shallow depth, winds aligned with the Lake's northwest–southeast axis sheared the surface and created wind tides up to three feet high. Unstable clay soils accounted for the lake's natural turbidity, and the sloshing currents pushed by the tides eroded the shores and stirred up the sediment. Despite its lack of allure as a sky-blue body of crystalline water, Manitobans still valued their largest lake as a commercial fishery and beloved place for recreation.

Somewhere, at an anonymous crossroads, we found an open gas station. Inside, a bundle of newspapers lay on a dusty, plate-glass window sill. The headlines issued warnings. Swimmers were to stay clear of Lake Winnipeg's beaches, including those of the nearby town of Gimli, a spec of urbanization stuck on the western shore of Lake Winnipeg.

Gimli got its start when a handful of Icelandic families fled their island country's crippled economy and, in 1875, miraculously journeyed to the geographical center of the North American continent. In 2004, the town had the largest concentration of Icelandic people outside Iceland and was the home of the world's one and only Royal Crown Whiskey distillery. Later in July, Gimli's Icelandic and International Film festivals would balloon the population, but itinerary constraints prevented our attendance. News of the untimely beach closing probably wasn't the kind of public relations the town's promoters had in mind.

"Good thing we're not canoeing in Lake Winnipeg, eh?" I said, affecting a Canadian accent and pointing to the newspapers.

Ruth raised her eyebrows.

Gimli, Manitoba, and Milwaukee, Wisconsin, although vastly different in size, shared the common curse of polluted lakeshores. Lake Michigan beach closings in Milwaukee were a regular occurrence. I suggested that we might have made a wrong turn somewhere on Interstate 94. Maybe, I chuckled, we were in Wisconsin instead of Manitoba, but my sleep-deprived, zombie-like friends were unresponsive to my feeble humor.

Even in my hometown of Minneapolis, the City of Lakes, the beaches were not immune to closures due to runoff contaminated by goose poop, lawn fertilizers, and all manner of street wastes. But here in Canada, near the end of the road, somehow I thought I'd be getting away from it all, pollution, too. "All," it seemed, was spreading everywhere.

The newspaper article said that the warnings for Lake Winnipeg beaches were due to too much fecal coli form bacteria—a thankful euphemism for a familiar four-letter word. Further reading indicated that people could reduce the risk of gastroenteritis, infections, and rashes if they kept their heads above the water and showered after they swam. How nice.

The pollutants, from points near and far, originated from an international watershed that included runoff from agricultural chemicals, feedlots, hog farms, malfunctioning septic tanks, poorly treated sewage, and the droppings from lowly seagulls. Apparently, seagulls have high concentrations of E. coli in their feces. It was clear that the town's fathers favored the seagull theory. Unlike Gimli's aging wastewater treatment plant that reputedly dumped chlorine and undertreated sewage into the lake, the gulls, as a natural phenomenon, were beyond reproach.

Burdened with excessive nutrient loads and aggravated by Manitoba Hydro's manipulation of water levels, Lake Winnipeg sprouted summertime rafts of blue-green algae that covered as much as half the lake's surface. These toxic blooms clogged fishermen's nets, starved the waters of oxygen, killed fish, and generally fouled the lake for recreation.[4]

With everyone accounted for, I steered us back onto Highway 6. A couple of miles down the road, I glanced into the rearview mirror and saw that my shut-eyed passengers had become oblivious to the world. The darkness ahead, pierced only by the headlight beams, stared back at me unflinchingly. Within it, I saw an apparition of a mother yanking her splashing child from the polluted waves of Gimli's beaches. Below these waves, I saw phantoms of fleeing fish, their gills gasping for clean water.

I looked up to where the stars might appear on a clear night and contemplated the abyss of blackness above me. Maybe, I thought, that was why people were so fascinated with spending billions to build villages on the moon and land a man on the frozen planet of Mars—to get away from the crap we were piling up in our own backyards.

Chapter 4

The Boreal Forest

I blinked. I bit my lip. I thought of singing but kept my silence. My sleeping passengers did not deserve annoyance, let alone cruelty. I wanted to drive until sunup, but nothing I could do could keep my eyes open any longer. Finally, I made a feeble but audible plea for help. Mel took the wheel, and I crawled into the back seat, whereupon I drifted in and out of an unsatisfying, sporadic sleep.

Fortunately, our route was simple: Take Highway 6 all the way to Thompson, Manitoba. Mel, plugged into the driver's seat, didn't have to consult me or even check the map. There was only one road to take and only one direction to take it.

Abruptly, the reassuring hum of the road beneath our tires changed pitch with the effect of a buzzing alarm clock. One of my eyes cracked open, then the other. The eastern horizon, which now held the hint of a new day, had begun to drain away the night's darkness. The light, although pale, was sufficient to reveal that we were on a bridge and that we were crossing the agitated rapids of a large river. These were the cliff-lined Grand Rapids of the Saskatchewan River, and something about them was very strange. It had been a dry summer, but this river appeared to be in full flood stage, aggressively so, and its turbid waters were pigmented with an eerie, almost alien shade of green.

I asked Mel if he knew anything about the peculiarity of this river. Like a mystical guru, he provided a two-word answer, "Manitoba Hydro." Pitying my puzzlement, he drew a breath and started to explain. Mel's words had the effect of revelry, bringing us to attention. Tom, back in the driver's seat, occasionally glanced in the rearview mirror toward Mel, and Ruth, lifting her nose from her paperback, began to listen.

"Manitoba Hydro is a mega utility engaged in mega projects, primarily hydroelectric power dams in the northern parts of the province. Cedar Lake lies just upstream from these rapids. In the late 1960s, Manitoba Hydro built a dam on the lake's outlet, which marks the continuation of the Saskatchewan River." Mel went on to explain that the dam backed up Cedar Lake's water level by more than a hundred feet and submerged nearly a thousand square miles of land. The result was around 500 megawatts of hydroelectricity, about the same as a large coal-fired power plant.

In effect, Manitoba Hydro used Cedar Lake and five other reservoirs on the Nelson River watershed as holding tanks, accumulating and then releasing water flows to meet the load requirements of the power grid. "The greenish tint of the water," Mel said, "comes from the vegetation that gets periodically flooded. Chlorophyll, from the soaked leaves and evergreen needles, leaches into the river and discolors the water."

Like Mel, I hated to see another river buried under another reservoir, but I couldn't see how the damage could be undone. "Mel," I said, "it's *fait accompli*. I mean, blowing up the dam isn't a practical solution, is it? Besides, it's green energy? The water keeps on falling and the turbines keep on turning, right?"

"Guy, some people think that the only thing green about this energy is the color of the water." Mel, in professorial mode, said that the Grand Rapids dam was hardly the largest of Manitoba Hydro's projects. That distinction belonged to the Nelson River Diversion Project whose effects extended up and down the lengths of two major watersheds. The Diversion Project, Mel said, shunted the flow of the Churchill River across the watershed's divide and then dumped hundreds of millions of additional cubic meters of water per second into the Nelson River. This added flow dramatically increased the power output of the Nelson's generating stations.

Replicating this project in the United States would be like digging a ditch across northern Iowa to divert more than half the flow of the Missouri River into the Mississippi. The Churchill River's watershed was large, about the size of Minnesota. The Nelson's basin was even larger, second in North America only to the Missouri–Mississippi. Its catchment area reached from the Canadian Rockies on the west, to Montana, the Dakotas, and Minnesota on the south, and into northwestern Ontario in the east.

It was Eric Sevareid's book, *Canoeing with the Cree*, that steered Mel toward Manitoba Hydro. *Canoeing with the Cree* told how Sevareid and his friend, after graduating from high school in the spring of 1930, traveled 2,250 miles by canoe from Minneapolis, Minnesota, to Hudson Bay. They paddled upstream, struggling against the currents of the Minnesota River, and then slogged through a swampy portage to Traverse Lake at the Minnesota–South Dakota border, the source of the Red River of the North. From there, the pair floated the Red to Lake Winnipeg, which empties into the Nelson River. They paddled partway down the Nelson before veering eastward and meandering through a series of lakes and smaller rivers. This route eventually brought them to York Factory on the shores of the Hudson Bay barely before freeze up.

The book launched Sevareid's career as a journalist. It also piqued Mel's curiosity about retracing other parts of Sevareid's journey, including the Nelson River. The problem, Mel found out, was that the Nelson was no longer a canoe-friendly waterway.

Sent into sudden rages by erratic discharges from seven hydroelectric dams and augmented in flow from the diversion of the Churchill[1], the Nelson River eroded its shorelines, causing them to slump and collapse, and had even washed away entire islands. The fluctuating river levels destroyed waterfowl nests and degraded wetlands, smothering them with rot that released mercury and tannic acid into the water and methane into the atmosphere.[2] Meanwhile, the Nelson's sediment-laden waters had silted over spawning areas, wiping out the river's native populations of sturgeon and whitefish.[3]

"Remember the Bloodvein and Pigeon rivers?" We had all paddled down these rivers together a few years ago, through wilderness and First Nations' communities on the east side of Lake Winnipeg, so we nodded and Mel continued: "Manitoba Hydro wants to build new dams on the Nelson and run the transmission lines across those rivers."

After our return from the Barren Lands, I read more about the history of the Churchill–Nelson River Diversion project and discovered that Mel had understated the effects. They extended beyond the degradations of wildlife habitats and would-be canoe trippers' recreational visits. For the families who call the watershed Nitaskinan ("our land") and who had lived along the Nelson River's banks for generations, it was a more poignant situation.

For the aboriginal Cree, the legacy of Manitoba Hydro was a daily reality. Fishing for both commercial and subsistence purposes had declined due to diminished yields and quality. The fish, locals said, tasted like mud, and nursing mothers were warned not to eat them due to mercury content.[4] Traditional hunting, trapping, and fishing livelihoods had fallen away to joblessness and dependency.

The Grand Rapids Dam on the Saskatchewan River, the tributary to the Nelson that we had just crossed, forced the relocation of Cree and Métis communities to barren uplands. Eviction was required when Manitoba Hydro permanently submerged the homes, gardens, burial sites, and traditional hunting grounds of these communities. The submerged areas included an expansive delta region, formerly world-renowned for its migratory waterfowl habitat.[5]

Instead of an environmental impact study for the Churchill–Nelson Diversion, Manitoba Hydro officials favored a report prepared by the consulting firm of Van Ginkel Associates.[6] The Van Ginkel report described the aboriginal people of South Indian Lake as "anachronisms in the present age of technology." The diversion scheme, according to the report, would "do nothing more than move forward in time the break-up of this community and way of life."[7] This prophecy was fulfilled when the backed-up waters of South Indian Lake inundated the land and shattered the livelihoods of the "anachronisms" who lived there.[8]

Once the wellspring of their resources and their transportation corridor, the Nelson River now flowed with debris and stumps that impaled boats and mangled the propellers of outboard motors. In the colder months, the manipulated water levels and reversals of seasonal flows created slush-covered, unsupported ice sheets. Winter travel on the ice, formerly safe, was now treacherous for humans and animals alike, including the endangered woodland caribou. Native people, who once drank directly from clear waters, now had to treat these sources. Within the span of a single generation, the Nelson was the story of an ecosystem trashed and of livelihoods torn apart.

Proclaiming that the province's hydroelectric capacity was only partially exploited, Manitoba Hydro touted the construction of new dams and generating stations. Their energy output was aimed at the export market in the United States even though Manitoba's internal energy needs had already been met for many years to come. Provincially owned as a Crown Corporation, Manitoba Hydro pointed to the lucrative export market as the key to its success and the reason why Manitobans enjoyed the lowest electrical rates in North America. The Manitoba government, having become addicted to the utility's "water rental fees" and "debt guarantee charges," undoubtedly would also approve more hydroelectric projects.

As a carpetbagger canoeist, my lobbing of stones from the other side of the international border may not have been an endearing quality, but I also struggled with another character flaw. I winced with hypocrisy. I knew that the electricity in my Minnesota house came from Xcel Energy, and Xcel was Manitoba Hydro's single largest export customer. It was a deal of millions and billions. In exchange for a twelve-year allocation of millions of kilowatts (500 megawatts, to be exact) Xcel paid Manitoba Hydro $1.7 billion. Minnesota utilities and their customers were purchasing forty percent of the electricity powered by Manitoba Hydro's dams,[9] and more billion-dollar megawatt deals were underway. Yes, it was true. While I drove a car fueled with gasoline refined from oil imported from the Middle East, I powered my household appliances with electricity imported from

Canada, electricity that was generated by the funneling of Manitoba's rivers to places where gravity alone never would have taken them.

Upon returning home, every hum of my air conditioner reminded me that I was not a bystander in this harnessing of the Nelson's power. When I paid my electric bill, some of that payment went to Manitoba Hydro to operate the Churchill River Diversion and to help keep Manitobans' and Minnesotans' electric rates cheap. Some of my U.S. dollars also paid for multimillion-dollar settlements, settlements such as Manitoba Hydro's long overdue Northern Flood Agreement with the First Nation's peoples of the watershed. The Northern Flood Agreement's monetary compensation to the Cree came more than thirty years after the building of the first dam, the Grand Rapids Dam, the one whose outflow we had just crossed.

For the Cree, whose land and waters were linked to their livelihoods and to the core of their identity, the money fell short of justice. The delay in compensation only made this shortfall worse. The Cree's land, the land that cradled the formerly free-flowing currents of the Nelson River, was not fungible. It was unique, and the Cree knew and we all knew that no amount of money could ever make them whole again. The money might have compensated for some aspects of the damages, but what, if anything, could ever compensate for defilement?

With visions of defoliated transmission right-of-ways and power lines casting shadows over our former canoe routes on the Bloodvein and Pigeon rivers, we became a somber group. Miles flicked by like the countless steeples of spruce trees that flanked the highway and crowded each other for a share of the sun. Tom held the steering wheel in one arm and stretched with the other. Ruth returned her eyes to the pages of her novel. Mel issued a silent benediction by tilting his head back on the seat's headrest. I looked out the window and watched the morning sun inflate like a fat, yellow balloon.

The brightening day saw us deep into the heart of the Texas-sized province of Manitoba and also into construction delays, which were not surprising. Highway 6's frayed conditions, after all, truly needed some mending. Flag-waving construction workers, typically covered in mosquito head nets, motioned us to stop at various points. They kindly explained the work being done and the types of equipment we might encounter travelling through the construction zones. This they did individually to the occupants of each and every vehicle in the queue. Wishing us a good day, the workers politely requested our cooperation and caution. They were so nice that I almost asked for their names and addresses so I could send them Christmas cards.

We stopped for breakfast at a tidy roadside café near the junction of Highway 6 and Highway 39. The uninhabited character of Highway 6 made the presence of this newly built café something of a spectacle, a regular tourist attraction if you will. Inside, we filled up on omelets and then eyed the candy bars lined up like precious jewelry in a glassed-in display case. By the brand names, we knew that we were in a foreign country. One, the Cadbury "Mr. Big," was the size of a brick, and another, the "Wunder Bar," was truly wondrous in size. With our bellies full, we resisted these obesity enablers and exited to the gravel parking lot. Sunny breezes, which had swept away the rain, inspired us to see one more tourist attraction, Pisew Falls.

Fifty miles up the road, we took a right turn and began following a curving driveway that led us to a large and empty parking lot near the Falls' trailhead. A short walk then put us at the banks of Grass River, a well-known canoe route. Rising mists slicked the boulders and framed the scene with a rainbow and, although the drop was modest—only forty feet, the sheer volume of water pumping over the edge was impressive. The park's managers had installed warning signs that advised us, for our safety, not to insanely leap over the handrails of the overlook.

Although pretty, the ease by which we accessed Pisew Falls made the place seem like a theme park. All it needed was a water slide. Had we paddled for miles and come upon these falls, I'm sure that it would have been a moment of awe, but we were in the motorized look-and-run mode. I wondered what a portage-weary canoeist nearing the end of a two-week trek on this river might think if he were to look up at this boardwalk and see a gaggle of tourists in tank tops and flip-flops, popping snapshots and cracking bad jokes. We returned to the parking lot and left it as we came.

By midday, we were nearly five hundred miles north of Winnipeg, and my appreciation for the size of the Boreal Forest was growing with each mile. From Alaska to Newfoundland, this granite-studded forest of rivers, lakes, and wetlands spanned the continent like an immense emerald crown. Trees were everywhere, but only a few species, mostly evergreens—black spruce, white spruce, balsam, jack pine, and tamarack—and occasional scatterings broad-leafed aspens and birch, were hardy enough to survive here. Eight times the size of Texas, the scale of this forest enabled it to function as one of the world's great carbon sinks. Together, the Boreal Forest and the adjoining tundra served as North America's lungs, breathing in carbon dioxide and exhaling oxygen, thus slowing the buildup of greenhouse gases.

What the Boreal Forest lacked in the diversity of its tree species was offset by the wealth of animal diversity that it sheltered. During a few hours of driving, we kept track of the wildlife observable from the highway: three foxes, five sandhill cranes, Canada geese, ravens, eagles, and a woodchuck. Named for the Greek god of the north wind, Boreas, this forest was also the last refuge of the great mammals that once ranged over North America. Had we been luckier, we might have seen bears, wolves, wolverines, lynx, moose, and North America's largest land mammal, the 2,000-pound endangered wood bison. Billions of birds, as diverse as spruce grouse and white pelicans, also made their seasonal or permanent homes here, as did hundreds of species of songbirds, some migrating from as far as the Amazon.

Coursing through these webs of life were the continent's last free-flowing rivers of any significance. Some, like the Nelson and the Churchill, had surrendered their wild character, but most had evaded the locks, dams, diversions, and channelization schemes that had shackled North America's southern rivers. Here, in the Far North, the rivers were bound only by the unyielding bedrock of the Canadian Shield, which sent them seaward along routes so contorted that they appeared to follow the tracings of deranged mapmakers.

The vastness of this forest suggested a resource of inexhaustible magnitude, but, in fact, it was finite and fragile. On our way back to the States, we flew into Thompson and landed in the haze of forest fires. Global warming and increased forest use had increased the prevalence of wildfires, both in acreage and in frequency.[10] Acid rain stressed the trees, leaving them vulnerable to insects, and surging populations of worms and beetles, pampered by warmer winters, invaded the forests and worked their destruction. Left as standing tinder, the skeletal remains of these trees were readily ignited, whether by lightning or careless humans.

Our vehicular voyage through this sea of increasingly charred forest finally landed us on the urbanized island of Thompson, Manitoba, population 14,000, and self-proclaimed "Hub of the North." The town had sprung to life when prospectors discovered nickel ore here in 1956. Thompson's integrated mining and smelting complex was reputed to be the largest of its kind in the world. Having come of age abruptly and uniformly, the town had a worn 1960s and 1970s feel. We didn't tune in, but I wondered whether the local radio station might have played oldies from that era.

Our first priorities in Thompson were to refuel the van and then to debug the windshield. We found a convenience store surrounded by a circle of sunbaked asphalt and fronted with a row of gas pumps to serve our purposes. Inside the boxy little building, the clerk asked us where we were headed.

"The Thlewiaza River in southern Nunavut," Tom replied.

The clerk sympathetically pointed to the containers of bug dope on the shelf and then, with a smirk, urged us to stock up. Tom stood in feigned shock with his hands on his hips.

"No! You mean there are mosquitoes on this river? Wait 'til I get a hold of my travel agent! He never said anything about bugs. This is *totally* outrageous!" Tom slapped his credit card on the counter and then scribbled his signature with a disappointing flare. Regrettably, my inability to keep a straight face undermined the credibility of his performance.

We poked around town, which didn't take long, and then stopped at the Heritage North Museum, a proper log cabin structure dedicated to the preservation of Thompson's natural and cultural history. We glanced inside but didn't enter, opting for the free picnic tables in the yard instead. These we had for ourselves, except for an intense midday sun, which bleached the landscape and drove us to a thin lacework of shade from the canopy of a parched birch tree. We finished our sandwiches and reflected on how the town's flora was struggling to hold up under a second year of drought.

The sights of Pisew Falls and the Grass River triggered memories of our prior outings down the Kopka and Gull rivers in northwestern Ontario, Manitoba's provincial neighbor to the east. We reminisced how, on the Kopka, our canoes glided past cliff-lined pools separated by waterfalls that stair-stepped down the watershed. Mosses and lichens painted the Kopka's cliffs with splashes of saffron, ocher, and lime, and our portage routes often required us to rappel down these colorful crags. By the way, if you are ever interested in some fun, try rappelling down a cliff with a canoe.

One afternoon on the Kopka, amidst spritzes of glistening rain, we paddled our canoes in the direction of departing rain clouds, which, looking like dark wet earth, had piled up above the eastern horizon. Meanwhile, the sun, behind us and now beaming through clearing western skies, began to transform the forest around us with heaven's brilliance and to frame the scene with the crescent of a magnificent rainbow. This fantasy land of prismatic colors and river-borne reflections was so captivating that I lost any sense of sitting in the canoe let alone paddling it. The world it seemed, with dark above and light below, had turned upside down, and the only sense I had was that of being there, enveloped by the glory of the earth.

Our next trip, down the Gull River, just south of the Kopka, was also memorable but for all the wrong reasons—continuous rain, overflowing banks, un-runnable flood-swollen rapids, impassible portages, broken canoes, wrenched backs, and intolerable bugs. But the Gull was special beyond these customary difficulties. It also included attacks by terrestrial and aquatic predators and ended with a medical evacuation.

The only time it didn't rain on the Gull was the afternoon that Mel and I decided to enhance our menu of dried and dehydrated substances by jigging for some fresh fish, walleyes to be exact. We paddled to a promising pool and quickly started filling our stringer when a northern pike, the size of my leg, decided that our stringered walleyes would suffice as a tasty serving of hors d'oeuvres.

When this freshwater version of Jaws blasted through the water with the stringer of walleyes dangling from its mouth, I nearly jumped overboard. I quickly recovered my composure but also felt violated by the theft of our supper, so I yelled to Mel, "Get the net!" But Mel, with a puny landing net for the task, was ahead of me. Somehow he had managed to wrestle the fish into the canoe, where, still full of life, it continued to thrash about with great vigor and loud thumping that shook the canoe.

We then debated the fate of this ultimate freshwater predator. It was an odd situation. We had taken this jack fish, as Canadians call them, with live game fish as bait. As such, Mel's catch was technically illegal. Not only that, it was much too big for supper, so we pardoned our barracuda-like intruder—despite its crimes of theft and disorderly conduct—and released it to the river, but only after extracting the slightly worse-for-wear walleye, which we retained for our supper.

This little adventure pumped my adrenaline and sparked my curiosity about whatever else might be lurking in this pool. I was thinking that maybe we should have brought a landing gaff when Mel announced he wasn't feeling well and insisted on heading back to camp. Mel, you're a spoilsport, or so I thought.

Later, I knew Mel's complaints were serious when fresh filets hot off the skillet failed to lift his spirits. He announced the onset of a urinary tract infection, the first in many years, and explained that he had no medicine to treat his condition, which he knew from experience could grow rapidly worse.

A normal recreational pace would have put us three or four days away from our take-out point. Instead, we paddled out in a two-day marathon of rain-saturated portages and flood-enraged rapids. Along the way, I downed half a bottle of ibuprofen to keep my shoulder capable of stroking a paddle. The last portage was a mile-and-a-half long, which, I must say, is a bit of a hike when you have to carry a seventeen-foot canoe on your shoulders. By the time Mel got to a doctor, his fever was just shy of 105 degrees and the possible onset of convulsions.

As we sat beneath the birch tree's stingy shade and retold these stories, Mel reassured us that, yes, he had his UTI medicine with him this time. We expressed gratitude for his preparedness and concurred that convulsions and canoeing shouldn't be mixed, especially on this trip.

In addition to Mel's medical emergency and the attack of the predator pike, I recalled that the Gull was where I became acquainted with the leading edge of modern logging equipment, a different sort of predator. Until the night following the northern pike attack and the onset of Mel's UT infection, I didn't know what a feller-buncher was.

Initially, this unidentified whining, grinding, groaning thing was a mile or more away from our tents, but it woke me up. Then these menacing noises grew louder and closer. It sounded like a nightmarish, mechanized ogre coming to get us. Its real aim, I learned, was not us, but the forest.

A feller-buncher is to the Boreal Forest what a rotary mower is to a suburban lawn. Around twenty-five to thirty feet long and weighing approximately sixteen tons, these mechanical behemoths moved about forest on metal tank-type tracks or huge rubber tires compacting the soil and creasing it with enduring ruts. The operator, in a sound-proofed and climate-controlled cab, used joy sticks to clasp massive metal jaws around the trunk of a tree and to maneuver the whirling saw blades that severed the tree from its roots. The grand finale was to lift up the whole tree, still in the hold of the feller's jaws, and drop it on a bunch of previously cut trees, hence the name, feller-buncher. Advanced models manipulated the amputated tree, measured the run of the trunk, de-limbed it, and then cut logs to standard lengths prior to dropping them on the bunch pile. In this manner, a spruce that may have taken a hundred years or more to reach the size of a small telephone pole could be stripped of its limbs and plopped on the ground in a matter of seconds. This efficiency was a true marvel of industrial technology but perhaps a less than welcome outcome for the creatures—red squirrels, ruby crowned kinglets, gray owls, and the like—that heretofore might have been residing in the tree's crown.

The investment for a new feller-buncher, of course, was more than that of a family sedan. This significance of this capital outlay obliged logging companies to order feller-bunchers with headlights and operate them 24 hours a day. That night on the Gull River, I learned firsthand about the optimization of this 24/7 duty cycle.

It was also in this part of Ontario, during our floatplane flight to the Kopka River, that I became aware of the scope of industrial logging in the Boreal Forest. Once aloft in the plane, our hawk's eye view staggered us with an image of the world laid bare. I had seen clear-cuts in the Rockies, the Pacific Northwest, and in my home state of Minnesota, some of them disheartening, but nothing compared to the clear-cuts in northwestern Ontario. Here, individual cuts were as large as forty square miles, an area nearly twice the size of Manhattan.[11] Loggers left buffers of forest along most shorelines, but the visual effect while floating down the river was eerie as the sunlight sometimes shone through these thin ribbons of trees from their naked backsides.

Apparently, Ontario officials rationalized these mega cuts on the basis that they replicated the effects of forest fires. Logging that mimics natural losses, I supposed, had merit, but something was fuzzy about the logic that allowed the cutting every tree within human sight simply because it was the same as burning them down. Even Mel, our forestry professor, agreed.

Clear-cutting a forest might emulate aspects of a fire, but the two were not equivalent. Granted, a forest fire did not produce useable wood products, but it was kinder to the regenerative prospects of both forest and wildlife. That was evident when we looked down from the floatplane and saw heavy equipment moving about like ants across an environment suggestive of an endless anthill. Rutted with roads and pocked with borrow pits, this raw and decapitated land was littered with the debris of a forest that was no more as far as we could see.

Pushed by the boom in landfill-bound junk mail, paper mills and industrial logging had crept farther and farther into Canada's North Country each year. Pulpwood extraction converted large swaths of mixed forests into monocultures. As wood became scarcer and technology improved, the size of the trees used for pulpwood decreased. Once passed over, loggers now took the scrawnier trees from the swampier and more northern reaches. We had seen some of these little logs, not much bigger than baseball bats, stacked by roadsides for pickup by the mill trucks.

"I'm not saying that I want to live without toilet paper. Someday," I said to my companions, "I'll probably get around to reroofing my garage and a few sheets of OSB (oriented strand board) might come in handy. Heck, everyone needs a roof over his head. I don't expect clear cuts to end either, and I'm not inclined to protest them, say, by lying down in front of a feller-buncher."

"Or," Tom suggested, "by living on a platform on the top of a tree."

"No, not that, either. I just wish everything could slow down a bit."

"And be a little more balanced?"

"Yeah, whatever that means."

"So, you want to be unbalanced?"

"You know," I said, ignoring the vacuousness of our words, "everybody's going gaga over the Amazon Rainforest, but the Boreal Forest has been keeping the planet alive and breathing for thousands of years. It's right here in North America, too, right under our noses, but nobody seems to care whether we cut it down, flood it over, burn it up, or pollute it to death."

"It's all moving pretty fast, isn't it?" said Tom.

I nodded. Then we packed up, put the van in gear, and drove off in search of Highway 391, the 150-mile spur off Route 6 that ended in Lynn Lake.

Hoping to find a local map of Thompson, I thumbed through a stack of travel brochures that we had picked up along the way. There was "Friendly Manitoba" and "Manitoba—Doorway to the Wilderness." I wondered how Manitoba, which was still allowing logging in its provincial parks, would continue to honor her reputation as the "doorway to the wilderness." If we were to come back this way again, how much of North America's great lung would still be alive and breathing?

Just outside Thompson, the signs at the beginning of Highway 391 warned travelers that there were no services or gas stations for the next 320 kilometers, the distance to Lynn Lake. Other signs said "Warning! Winter Survival Equipment Recommended." It was a lonely road of occasional pavement, patches of gravel, potholes, and long clouds of gritty dust marking the wakes of other vehicles. Thankfully, for the sake of our lungs, our encounters with other vehicles were few and far between. Incredibly, people could take a public bus between Thompson and Lynn Lake although we saw none. Four hours after leaving Thompson and nearly twenty-one hours after leaving Minneapolis, we had finally arrived in Lynn Lake in northwestern Manitoba.

Fishing and hunting lodges as well as several First Nation communities dotted Lynn Lake's outlying areas. The town functioned as a service center for these, but it was hardly a tourist trap, clearly not a stop that people would make impulsively while casually driving down the road. Granted, NASA favored the town's remoteness for launching high-altitude research balloons and thereby occasionally inflated the local population with PhDs, but overall the town's fortunes, unlike the balloons, were not soaring. Visitors had to be intent on getting here and, if they were so inclined, they had better make it fast. The town looked like it might not last much longer.

Prior to the shuttering of local mines in 2001, Lynn Lake claimed as many as three thousand inhabitants. Now, with only seven hundred remaining and not enough jobs to go around, it was nearly a nascent ghost town—a tough-looking place with a lot of boarded-up buildings and abandoned houses, some blackened by fire. The last public ATM had been pulled out a month before our arrival. Lynn Lake was also home to the Marcel Colomb First Nation, an aboriginal community within the geographic community of Lynn Lake, and the relationship between the two had not always been trusting. Fortunately, the Lynn Inn was still in operation and we had a place to bunk for the night.

Prior to checking in, we followed a gravel road that took us to the outskirts of town and the Transwest Air floatplane base. The base featured a gravel-filled pier, an assortment of garage-like buildings, fuel tanks and pumps, and an expansive view of the lake but with no floatplanes in sight. We introduced ourselves to the supervisor, a cordial man of significant physical and authoritative presence, and then asked about flying out early that same afternoon. He explained that the plane hadn't left La Ronge, Saskatchewan, where it was being held for service. We would have to wait until the next morning, our originally scheduled departure date.

We drove back to town, checked in, and then entered our room through a pair of two heavy, solid core doors, one opening onto the other. No lollygagging around with lightweight Minnesota-style storm doors here. Lynn Lake was a place that had real winters.

After repacking our gear for the next day's floatplane flight, we walked down the block to the Esso Station where Tom and the station manager arranged to have the van shuttled back to Thompson. Sporting a frayed flannel shirt, the station manager forsook the professional mechanic look—embroidered name on dark blue uniform and the like. For all I knew, he could have wondered in from the bush and found the prospect of taking our van on a joy ride to uncertain destinations appealing, but this far north, trust was our only option.

Then, with plenty of light left in the day, we took a self-guided walking tour. The homey mining museum had closed earlier, but the abandoned mine buildings on the town's outskirts tempted us to explore. We hopped in the van and a few minutes later found the mine's ruins in the middle of a mutilated landscape. Absolutely nothing was green or growing on these escarpments of mining spoils. The scene was surreal, otherworldly. I kept thinking that the town might be able to reinvent itself for the motion picture industry, maybe as a backdrop for movies about alien planets or the aftermath of atomic warfare.

Back in town, later that evening, I bumped into the Transwest supervisor as he exited the Legion Hall in an effusive mood. I would have accepted his offer to go back inside for a drink, but I didn't have any Canadian money, a predicament that might have required him to buy, and I didn't want to impose, however appealing his offer. Before we parted, I mentioned that my friends and I had been cavorting around the abandoned mines and, gosh, weren't those piles of mine waste tailings huge?

Following a slight pause, my newfound friend's eyebrows lifted, and then he explained. The ominous looks of the mines' moonscape environs did not deceive. Our quartet of wayfarers had inadvertently strolled across one of Canada's most notorious hazardous waste sites. Yes, right here in Manitoba, the gateway to the wilderness, lay one of Canada's "Toxic Thirteen."

For more than twenty-three years, Sherritt-Gordon Ltd. extracted millions of tons of zinc, copper, and nickel ores from its Lynn Lake mine and then, in 1976, they pulled the plug and left behind a mountain's worth of tailings. Spread over a square mile of land, the tailings leached sulfuric acid wherever gravity took it. Some of the tailings also found their way into local streets and residential areas as bargain backfill. The run-off eroded the town's water pipes and discolored the drinking water. During the summer, when the stuff wasn't buried under the snow, the wind blew polluted dust everywhere. The Manitoba Provincial Department of Environment identified eleven contaminated sites within the town's boundaries, and the town's residents claimed excessive instances of cancer.[12] First Nations communities downstream of Lynn Lake were worried that their commercial and subsistence fishing operations could be affected.[13]

After the Sherrit-Gordon departure, another company, Black Hawk Mining, opened the Keystone goldmine nearby and constructed dams and covers to contain the goldmine's tailings. Most likely, according to MiningWatch Canada, these tailings contained cyanide. Meanwhile, the run-off from the Sherritt-Gordon tailings were starting to infiltrate Black Hawk's new containment facility and thus had jeopardized its capacity.

Black Hawk closed its mine in 2001 but neglected to pay the Town of Lynn Lake C$3,000,000 in back taxes. In an encounter that included armed police to ensure a peaceful transaction, the town seized the last helicopter load of gold as security, and then released it after Black Hawk posted C$250,000 bond. According to Lynn Lake's mayor, Audie Dulewich, the cash-strapped town obtained a settlement and avoided bankruptcy but recovered only about twenty-seven cents on the dollar of its original claim.[14]

Canada classified the mines in Lynn Lake as "orphaned," which was worse than being abandoned. For whatever reasons—dissolution of the original companies or grandfathered exemptions—orphaned mines' former owners were not held legally accountable for damages and cleanup. Of the hundreds of abandoned mines in Canada's tundra and Boreal Forest, many were orphans, including a uranium mine in northern Saskatchewan, and only a fraction of these had undergone environmentally acceptable closures.[15]

The Manitoba government, which collected royalties from mining operations and would have to pay for Lynn Lake's remediation, issued a report that gave the town's residents a clean bill of health. Distinguished by omissions, this rather rose-tinted assessment failed to sample the human population for metals, conducted no medical tests of individuals, and undertook no epidemiological studies.[16] The town got federal help to upgrade its water treatment and distribution systems, but the mines and their spoils still stood.

That evening, as I walked back to my room, I watched Lynn Lake's main street come to life with her residual souls and influx of summer visitors. A First Nation artist from Thompson, who had grown up in Lynn Lake, was putting the finishing touches on a large mural depicting an idyllic camping scene that covered a two-story building's outer wall, and much of the population, in a sort of Mardi Gras mood, strode down the sidewalks and crisscrossed main street. The townies turned out at the Legion Hall while the First Nation people favored the more integrated scene at the Lynn Inn's bar, but the street welcomed all, and, at least for this evening, the town's toxic environs held no sway.

The midsummer sun, now only a few days past the solstice, lingered on the northwest horizon. It gilt the gables and held back the night. All around, the crowns of trees embraced the silent glow. And here, in northern Manitoba, a hollowed-out town would hang on for another day.

Chapter 5
The Flight Over the Tree Line

The next morning, we walked across the street to the Lynn Inn to share in the rite of the last breakfast: a decent meal served on a table with the added luxury of being seated off the ground. It would be more than two weeks before we would use a table and chairs again. Fed and packed, we drove to the Transwest floatplane office, snapped some group pictures on the dock, and then performed a variation of a bucket brigade to nest the canoes and packs into the fuselage of the Twin Otter.

The DeHavilland Twin Otter and its smaller brother, the Beaver, were the workhorses of northern air travel, whether equipped with oversized wheels for tundra landings, skis for snow, or pontoons for open waters. With two turboprop engines and a sixty-five-foot wingspan, the Twin Otter was what might be called proven technology. The first of 844 Twin Otters came off the assembly line in 1964 and the last in 1988, a fact that made Transwest's plane between sixteen and forty years old. Seeing that our plane looked like it was one of the more mature models, I began to ponder the tradeoffs between proven technology and metal fatigue. This was not just a plane. It was a collection of individual rivets, hinges, and thousands of other stress points of unknown integrity.

Reassuringly, the pilot and the copilot each looked old enough to vote. They moved about with a touch of swagger and handled the plane like an extension of their bodies. These young men must have played the key skill positions on their high school athletic teams. I wondered if they had thought much about the maxim concerning bush pilots, the one that states there are old bush pilots and bold ones, but no old, bold bush pilots.

The buoyancy of my confidence started to list when we motored to the middle of the lake and then bee-lined toward the opposite shore, parting a huge wake, but *not* lifting off the water. The engine's noise and the spray from the wake made it impossible to hear anything else. In a couple of roaring minutes, the details of trees on the once distant shore began to approach with alarming clarity.

But I, as an unflappable, all-knowing man of the wilderness, was able to retain my composure. However, if truth be told, beneath my skin of confidence, a rash of anxiety was starting to itch. Were we loaded too heavy? Would we clear the trees? Of course we would, I hoped. If not, there was enough of the lake left to stop, right?

Finally, with little distance to spare and as though someone had thrown an anchor overboard, the plane halted and pirouetted on its pontoons. Then, I understood. It was all about the angle. The Twin Otter's aerodynamic assemblage of predestined scrap metal, with us in its belly, instead of running with the wind and the waves, now opposed them, and we popped up like a kite on a string.

It took us about two hours to fly the 290 miles to Seal Hole Lake in southern Nunavut. One hundred years ago, that journey from Lynn Lake, by a tortuous canoe route replete with back-straining and boot-chewing portages, would have taken much of the summer. Now the encroachment of utilities and roads had chipped away at the Canadian wilderness. While we left no disfiguring slashes on the land, our sortie by airplane was no less of an intrusion, one that was commonplace these days. In fact, helicopters crossed over our path twice when we paddled down the remote Thlewiaza River a few days later.

Our pilot traced the contours of the land, sometimes flying at elevations only a couple of hundred feet above the ground. Below our flight path, we scattered loons, ducks, geese, gulls, and eagles and watched their shadows race along the ground. A bull moose, startled by our plane, leapt up from a willowy bank and exploded the water. As our mechanical annoyance flew northward, the cover of trees receded, revealing a barren, tawny landscape laced with lakes.

Then, our pilots nosed the Twin Otter even closer to the ground. The modest ridge of land to the west was now higher than our wings. Truly, we were just skimming over the brush. Maybe the pilot was trying to mimic the manner of ducks when they try to get some extra lift by flying no higher than skipping stones across a lake. Maybe he wanted to give us a more intimate view of the Land of the Little Sticks below.

P. G. Downes, a wilderness trekker who paddled, poled, and portaged his way through the heart of northern Manitoba in the 1930s, assessed the limitations of floatplanes when their rarity was still akin to today's space missions. An airplane, whether one hopped from lake to lake or jetted across continents, delivered a magnificent view but one that was isolated from the land and its textures. Flying, from Downes' perspective, provided no better understanding of the land than cruising across Idaho in the family sedan on Highway 12 explained whatever was going on in the minds of Lewis and Clark when they crawled over the Bitter Root Mountains and ate their horses to keep from starving.

Close to the Manitoba–Nunavut border, the Twin Otter regained some altitude and then continued to climb. Soon, my view extended from one curve of the Earth to the other. As far as we could see, no trace of human life could be seen—no buildings, no camps, no trading posts, no roads, no human beings. We flew by the northeast side of Nueltin Lake, a huge, meandering body of water whose shores once hosted an outpost of the Hudson Bay Company's trading empire.

Jurisdictionally, this transitional area of taiga and tundra belonged to Nunavut, the land of the Inuit, but it appeared to be empty, the home of no one. Of course, our chances of spotting anyone from a plane, even if we had flown here a hundred years ago, would have been slight. In the Far North, people had always been scarce and scattered. Yet, small bands of native people, originally from Siberia, once roamed here, and they had entered these lands well before Columbus anchored off the shores of North America, even before the ancient Greeks had suggested the possibility of a spherical Earth.

As I scanned the Barren Lands below me, I wondered exactly how and when the First Peoples of Canada earned their status as "first." The full truth of this controversial topic, I surmised, would remain locked in antiquity. When I returned to the States, I continued my reading and became acquainted with archaeologists whose explanations pointed to a plausible consensus. I learned that, rather than being a foreboding place, it was the Arctic's wealth of resources that enticed the earliest humans to make their homes here.

The story of the first human presence in the Far North begins seven thousand years ago, when the last of the continent's mile-thick glaciers finally retreated. Free of its ice age mantle, the land greened, herds of caribou and muskox followed, and flocks of birds darkened the skies. The emerging coastlines attracted seals and walruses, and the free-flowing rivers welcomed schools of fish. These wildlife populations, while widely dispersed, aggregated in great densities and, when found, could be efficiently harvested.

However, before humans could avail themselves to this emerging bounty, they needed special skills to survive the Arctic's cold and treeless habitat, skills that had eluded North America's earlier, more southerly inhabitants. To build shelters and make fires without the benefit of trees, to maintain a balanced diet despite the absence of vegetation, and to stitch skin garments so they wouldn't leak or let in the cold—all these things required great ingenuity.[1] It was not Indians to the south who had arrived earlier; rather, it was the Siberian hunters, the Paleoeskimos, who had mastered these necessary technologies.[2] Four to five thousand years ago, these new North American hunters, the first ever equipped with bows-and-arrows, migrated eastward. Following the movements of their favorite prey, the shaggy and vulnerable muskox, they began to push the margins of human existence across one of the last unoccupied regions of the world.

Around 500-800 BCE, the climate cooled and either a new wave of immigrants from Siberia or remnants of the earlier Paleoeskimos reinvented themselves as the Dorset culture.[3] The Dorset people shifted their focus from the Barren Lands' interior to the coasts where they found marine mammals and achieved a richer, less precarious existence, including larger shelters, which they heated and lit with smokeless soapstone lamps.[4]

For the next 1,500 years, the Dorset lived in virtual isolation until the climate changed again, this time during the Medieval Warm Period, which began around 1000 CE. Areas of open waters expanded, but the loss of ice also meant the loss of the seals' habitat on which the Dorset depended. The Dorset also knew nothing about harvesting the large whales that had migrated into the increasingly open waters. However, whalers from the Bering Strait, known as the Thule, did. Soon, the Dorset were no longer alone. The newly arrived Thule whalers used drag floats, harpoons with detachable heads, and other specialized weaponry to hunt their huge prey.

Bowhead whales, which conveniently swam and slept near the surface and floated when harpooned, were the Thule's favored catch.[5] A single bowhead whale could sustain a Thule community and its dogs for months. The people ate the whale's layers of nutritious skin (muktuk), extracted the mandibles and rib bones for shelter framing and sled runners, and burnt the melted blubber in their soapstone lamps.

In the summer, the Thule families paddled onto the Dorset's shores in large, open skin boats, called umiaks, which were escorted by hunters in kayaks. In the winter, they arrived overland in sleds pulled by powerful teams of dogs. For the Dorset people, whose locomotion was probably limited to their feet, these mobilized strangers must have been an ominous sight.

Within three centuries, the ice-adapted Dorset people disappeared. Although some of the Thule may have taken a Dorset spouse or adopted their children, there is no evidence that the two cultures mingled or that the Thule killed off the Dorset. Most likely, the Dorset withdrew to fewer and more marginal lands and then faded from existence.[6] By 1200 CE the Thule had spread eastward, encompassing all of the Canadian Arctic and much of Greenland. Archeological evidence from two islands near Arviat, our canoe party's destination, indicated that by 1100 CE the Thule people were active along the shores of western Hudson Bay.[7]

Although the Thule were well equipped, the richness their culture would not endure. A colder period returned and culminated in the Little Ice Age of 1550–1850 CE. The increasing coverage of year-round ice impeded both the whales, which had to surface to breathe, and the Thule hunters who required open seas to pursue them. The resources needed for healthy teams of whalers dwindled. Later, European diseases further fragmented these societies, all of which fell away to a more nomadic and frequently hungry existence.[8]

Many of the remaining Thule bands took to sealing in the winter, building clusters of igloos on the ice, and hunting seals through their breathing holes. In the spring, they stalked seals basking on the ice floes along the coastlines. During the brief summers when the open waters and waterfowl returned, the people snared molting geese and ducks, arrowed them with bows, and gathered up their eggs. On the land, they caught ptarmigan and arctic hare. As summer advanced, groups divided into their constituent families. Children and parents trekked over the tundra to pick berries and jig for trout. When the char migrated upstream, they corralled them in weirs of stone and willow wood, speared the fish, and feasted on the catch.

In early fall, women and children, howling like wolves, drove the caribou toward river crossings and pitfalls. Along the way, the Inuit built stone figurines in human likenesses, called *inuksuit*, which augmented the apparent number of hunters flanking the caribou trails. The hunters, often close enough to touch their prey, ambushed the caribou with lances and bows and arrows. It was virtually hand-to-hoof combat.

Some of the so-called Caribou Eskimos, who lived in the area that we would travel, reversed this pattern. They stayed on the coasts during the summer and headed into the Barren Lands during the fall and winter, sometimes staying inland year round. Here, near the tree line, they eked out a marginal existence following the migrations of their prey.

Whether inland or coastal in orientation, families tended to scatter during the summer and then reunite in a winter village where they would share their caches, sew clothing, tell stories, chant songs, play games, and dance to the beat of their drums. These modified lifeways of the Thule became the cultural basis of the historical Inuit who traded and sometimes skirmished with the likes of Martin Frobisher, Henry Hudson, and all the other Europeans who would follow.

The steady, deafening hum and vibrations of the plane required us to yell to hear each other's voices, so nothing much was said. With casual conversation precluded, each of us, save for our respective thoughts to keep us company, was alone. I kept my face pressed to the window of the Twin Otter and gazed at the seemingly endless tundra below.

I was no more the rightful discoverer of these Barren Lands than the early European explorers were, but that sense lodged within me. I wondered what the authentic, early finders of this place felt when they first entered this untrammeled region. For the Thule hunter beaching his kayak on some unknown shore—as he stood there with his family and looked to the horizon—I wondered what they might be hoping for? What did they see and say to one another? Was their motivation to strike anew a matter of survival or the universal hunger to seek and discover?

Then I looked to the Twin Otter's cabin where our young pilots sat and pondered their motivations. Were they passionate about flying, interested in the business of it, or just doing a job and trying to make a buck? For many, I knew, flying was a dream, whether it was the everyday chap who saved up for lessons in a small, piston-motored propeller plane or the professional who captained a jumbo jet. It was, in many respects, the same kind of dreamy derring-do that inspired hobbyists to build and fly ultra-light planes, aircraft akin to winged patio chairs. Even if it was a life-foreshortening experience, I understood the seductive possibility of an ultralight aircraft—that of hovering aloft like an oversized bug or bird. To be sure, a plane, any kind of a plane, was more than an airborne bus or taxi. In *High Flight*, the pilot poet breaks the Earth's surly bonds, climbs through sun-split clouds, and, upon windswept heights, touches the face of God. Okay, okay, I admitted it. I was jealous of those who found answers so pure, whose passions grabbed them so squarely in the gut.

My thoughts drifted to the nature of things. I recalled reading something about Epictetus—the ancient philosopher who said that things do not affect men, only the principles and notions we attach to them do. Things and activities—whether we flew airplanes, networked computers, festooned our homes with curios, or haunted the pool tables of dimly lit bars—they and their associated notions defined our existence. It was curious. Here I was, enveloped by a spectacular and, one might say, even alien scene, one that should have detached me from introspection. Instead, it intensified my reflective mood.

Fast Eddie, the "loser" in the movie *The Hustler*, who, in his search for character, struggled with all kinds of demons, many of his own making. But he understood something about doing his thing. "You know," he says, "like anything can be great . . . I don't care, bricklaying can be great, if a guy knows. If he knows what he's doing and why and if he can make it come off . . . it's a great feeling, boy, it's a real great feeling . . . It's like all of a sudden I got oil in my arm. The pool cue's part of me. You know, it's a pool cue, it's got nerves in it. It's a piece of wood, it's got nerves in it. Feel the roll of those balls, you don't have to look, you just know . . . I can play that game. . . ."

Fast Eddie's sweetly inebriated girlfriend, Sarah, responds: "You're not a loser, Eddie, you're a winner. Some men never get to feel that way about anything."

I thought of my great-great uncle Ernst, a violinmaker, who shared some of Fast Eddies' traits. He kept moving westward until the ocean stopped him at San Francisco. For Fast Eddie, it was the clicking of colored balls on a green-felted table. For my great-great uncle Ernst, it was the logs whose veneers gave voice to his violins. Those trunks of maple and walnut had traveled with him from Wisconsin to the Pacific Coast. After the 1906 earthquake and fires, he sent a letter home. Despite some property damage, he had survived. Life, he reported, could continue. He still had his logs.

As for me, I didn't know whether my "logs" were missing. I didn't know what they were anymore.

I thought about an acquaintance, a train buff. His job had been an hourly wage, not much more than a way to put food on the table. He was retired now, but he still loved his trains and palled around with a bunch of iron horse fans. They collected model trains and kept their schedules on locomotive-illustrated calendars. On the highways, they chased trains to their crossings and emptied their coin jars to take train trips. They knew everything about trains and railroads since the first steel rail was spiked to a wooden tie. Would I be collecting wilderness canoe trips as my friend collected locomotive prints or as European travelers filled their closets with photo albums?

In essence, travel was just another activity, another "thing" that one could do. However, among the wise and wealthy it seemed to hold a high position on the altar of meaningful endeavors. Indeed, this was my present activity, too, but I wasn't sure. I wasn't sure how it panned out as the presumptive panacea. Did we self-actualize by squeezing our butts into oxygen-deficient jumbo jets or by inhaling the diesel fumes of motor coaches on the way to Disney-fied meccas jammed with pointy-elbowed tourists? And what, pray tell, made a bus a motor coach? Did we gain anything by planting our bottoms on palm-lined beaches, melanomanizing our epidermal surfaces, and flipping our mental switches to the "off" position? What happened if the switch *stayed* off? Even in the more rarefied forms of travel and endurance—from scaling mountains to swimming the English Channel to canoeing the rivers of the Barren Lands—was the consummation of wanderlust a life-fulfilling quest, or was it another form of insanity, like the insanity a rat finds in a cheeseless maze?

A friend of mine dreamt of traveling alone in the solitude in northern Ontario. Eventually, he found a slice of time to nourish his longing and paddled his solo canoe into the two-and-half million acres of the Wabakimi Wilderness. At the end of the second day, he camped on an island and watched the sunset paint an inverted image of itself on the lake's stilling waters. Ripples fanned out from the wakes of beavers swimming back and forth. There he sat, soaking in the view and savoring pan-fried filets from freshly caught fish.

Then he decided that there was only one thing left to do. That was to get the hell out of this place. On a southbound highway, he pulled over and called his twenty-two-year-old son. It was an SOS of sorts. His son took leave from his work and responded in the manner of a Good Samaritan. A couple of days later, both were out hiking somewhere, beneath the Big Sky but within the folds of consanguinity.

No doubt, activities and things brought order, structure, and sometimes adventure and beauty to our lives, but what one man finds engaging another might see as pointless and dull, maybe even a fast track to madness. Perhaps we're inclined toward our talents or instincts, but what of the man who finds no easy home in activities or things, who sees them as passive or shallow distractions—mere interferences for drawing in the real stuff of life and community? What of the man who seeks these connections but feels that they may be slipping away or who may even be haunted by doubts of their existence? Such a man, I can tell you, is vexed.

Suddenly, the pilot corkscrewed the Twin Otter into a sequence of ascending turns. The forces working on my body mass became the resolution of multiple vectors and surges of gravity. Fortuitously, this crescendo of noise and movement flushed the lugubriousness about "activities and things" from my mind. At the same time, the breakfast-filled contents of my stomach began to protest their confinement.

Our lofty position enabled the pilot to search for the best landing axis. Treacherous ice still jammed the distant northern reaches of Seal Hole Lake. Luckily, the lake's outlet to the south held no ice, only open waters. The pilot then sighted an approach clear of boulders and reefs.

Just beyond our watery touchdown, the tundra, like a tourniquet, drew the lake's outflow through a funnel of rapids. Even from our sky-high position, I could see these rapids' individual waves. Their immense size made we wonder whether they might be causing the earth to tremble, and then I knew. They could belong to no other river than the Thlewiaza, the Big River.

Moments later, the Twin Otter's pontoons sliced through the waters of Seal Hole Lake. The pilot nudged the plane onto the beach just upstream from the lake's outflow whereupon we did the bucket brigade routine in reverse, quickly freeing the plane of its burden.

I tipped the copilot, instructing him to share the money with the pilot. I'm not sure whether my tip was insultingly low or a worthy gratuity. Whatever it was, the pilots showed their appreciation by flying so low over us on take-off that we all ducked to avoid getting propeller haircuts. Probably not enough of a tip, I thought. In a couple of minutes, the plane and its noise disappeared, as did we from the pilots. Surrounded by rocky land, sky, and water, the emptiness of this place engulfed us. It was as though we had landed on a different planet.

A journey that took ancient Asian hunters generations and iron-willed Europeans in wooden ships a year or more had taken us less than forty-eight hours. We had crossed the continental threshold into the edge of the Arctic, to the shores of the Thlewiaza River in the Barren Lands of Canada. Now, with the whining of tires and the drone of engines behind us, our travel would be by the pull of paddles, the currents of wind and water, and nothing more.

Part II
Down the Big River

Chapter 6
The Land of the Little Sticks

A sea of tundra lay ahead of us. Tom, Ruth, Mel, and I would navigate it, not in search of the Northwest Passage, but the mouth of the Thlewiaza River, some 200 miles to the east. Each of our two unnamed red canoes would be powered by a pair of paddles and the arms that gave them force. Each paddler had two paddles, a bent-shaft paddle for flat water and a straight paddle for the rapids, although, in a pinch, either was functionally sufficient as a spare for the other. Like a string quartet, there was elegance in the simplicity of our endeavor.

Our course down the Thlewiaza would be like sight-reading an unknown score of music, live at the concert hall. Various interpretations were possible, but we'd have only one chance to get it right. There would be no do-overs, no chance to take it over from the top again. Dumping a canoe during a weekend of recreational paddling might entail getting wet and hitchhiking back to the car, but this was not a weekend trip. Our vehicle was five hundred roadless miles to the south. Our finale, if harmonious, would depend on each person's contribution in proper balance and rhythm.

Despite harmonious intentions, we began on a few sour notes, the first being Tom's footwear flop. When it came to footwear, we canoeists were an unsatisfied lot. Our feet were in the water as much as out, and we trudged over all manner of obstacles: slippery slimy rocks, snares of intertwined roots, and boot-sucking muck. From the French Canadian voyagers, who suffered chronic foot rot and subjected their feet to draconian cures, to modern-day trekkers, the ideal canoeing boot had proved elusive. Mel and I used felt-soled angler's wading shoes, which provided traction on water-slicked rocks but required the use of stinky neoprene socks. These wading shoes weren't ideally suited for abrasive upland terrain either.

Tom thought he had found the ultimate combination: rubber boots pulled over the top of Gore-Tex hiking shoes. Eager to try his layered footwear innovation, he pulled on his new black rubber boots only to rip one wide open on the first tug. For the rest of the trip, Tom walked around with one wet hiking shoe and a black, rubber prosthesis on the other leg, or so it appeared. Later that day, when one of his tent poles broke, we feared that Tom must have angered the spirits.

These evil spirits then decided to spread their wrath when we looked for, but could not find, Mel's portage pads. They were somewhere, back home or in the floatplane, but they weren't with us. We would have to improvise with life jackets for padding or deal with pinched shoulders against bare canoe thwarts during the portages. Although these setbacks tempered our moods, excitement prevailed.

I sat in the canoe's stern, and Mel took the bow, a position that allowed him to scout the rapids, beginning with those that we had spotted from the floatplane. We donned life jackets, lashed our necessities of food and shelter to the gunnels, and then freed the canoes from the gravelly shore. Our packs of red, blue, tan, and shades of forest green filled the hulls like multicolored peas in split-open pods. A slight tug of current seduced us toward the rapids whose muffled roar we could hear but not yet see. Despite the docility of our push-off, the first stroke of my paddle felt like a boldly decisive act. The wind stirred, but no one spoke a word.

We followed a finger of land that separated the lake from the river and then pivoted our canoes around the point. In an instant, the waters forming the Thlewiaza River peeled away from the lake and swallowed us into her throat. As if to genuflect, Mel and I simultaneously knelt down to lower our centers of gravity and improve our paddling leverage. The transparent water below revealed a montage of rocks and boulders that passed by in a blur.

The volume of water flowing here rivaled that of the Mississippi River in Minneapolis, and the Thlewiaza, nicknamed the "Big River," was water Arizonans would covet, but this river held to an opposite destination. It was slipping and sliding to the opposite side of the continent, to Hudson Bay.

We had committed an irreversible act. The Thlewiaza had the force to crush a canoe and shred its contents, whether lashed in or not. The heavily laden canoe's scant freeboard also afforded little margin for error.

I flashbacked to my childhood memories of the "Cyclone" rollercoaster that nudged the shoreline of Lake Minnetonka. Prior to my baptismal encounter with these sinusoidal whitewashed wooden scaffolds, the "Cyclone" had already reputedly launched several souls to their screaming deaths. When the safety bar clicked over my pintsized lap, I knew. There was no way to back out. My parents, relieved of their charges, watched from solid ground while my neighborhood buddy and I, in honor of my tenth birthday, ratcheted to the top. Ominous clickety-clack noises and shared wide-eyed glances confirmed the mutuality of our doom.

Now, just like the rollercoaster ride of my distant youth, Mel and I, a couple of middle-aged men, were going to ride down the Big River, and . . . there was no going back.

I was also struck by the fact that I hadn't held a canoe paddle for more than a year. It was like the moment of trepidation one encounters before hopping on a bicycle for the first time in the spring. I had hoped to shake hands with this river and get comfortable with my paddling grip before entering these swifts. Instead, we dropped into a mile-long sluice-like run.

I avoided a panic attack, but I began to focus on a singular fear, one that I allowed to fester, mainly because it was rational. No one asked me if I wanted to talk about it or check into a thirty-day, twelve-step holistic process to restore my self-confidence. I had to confront the cold reality of my condition: I was fast becoming a hypothermophobiac. It was high summer, but this river's water ran numbingly cold. It poured off the lip of a lake still packed with ice. The Thlewiaza was close to a quarter mile wide, and we were in no place to be casual about dunking a canoe.

In calm, cold water, a typically clothed fisherman could last about two hours before succumbing to hypothermia. In the fast moving waters of the Thlewiaza, heat would transfer quicker. If we wiped out, I wondered: How many minutes and seconds would it take for this water to strip away our body heat and cause us to shiver uncontrollably? Before our speech slurred and our muscles stiffened? Before delusion and then unconsciousness took hold?

Would we be better off holding onto the canoe and its contents or letting them go in order to concentrate on saving ourselves? Would we lose more precious body heat and thus make matters worse if we tried to swim to shore? If we couldn't make it to shore, Mel and I could hug each other to conserve warmth, but that would only postpone our fate. Besides, I wasn't sure that I wanted Mel hugging me as my last rites. I thought of these things. Impressively, I did not whimper.

Steering clear of the frothing haystacks of water in the center of the river, we clung to the less turbulent edges. If we dumped here, only a short swim now separated us from the shore. Just ahead, a prominent ledge threw off a curl of water large enough to catapult us and our canoe into aquatic orbit.

"Pull over—by those rocks," Mel barked. When it really mattered, in the rapids, the bowman, Mel, became the skipper.

Only a couple seconds now separated us and our canoe from the point of instantaneous lift-off, but we were able to stop short of it and scrape to halt along the rocky shoreline. Gingerly, we stepped among the jagged rocks and held fast to the canoe, which was still in the water. I looked to the Moores who followed several hundred yards distant, too far for me to either hear their calls or see their expressions, which was too bad. I had a pitiful desire to see the face of human fear. Then Mel yelled again, instructing me to help him line the canoe.

To "line" a rapid was Mel's canoe talk for neither portaging nor shooting the rapid, but walking the canoe around the ledge, in the manner of a leashed dog. The canoe stayed in the water while its masters, on the bank, controlled the lines tied to the canoe's fore and aft. We scampered over the boulders and held tight to our leashes, keeping the loaded canoe at heel while coaxing it around the ledge. The trick during lining was to keep the upstream end of the canoe tight to the shore to prevent the stern from sweeping uncontrollably outward into the full force of the river's current.

Ledges like this became everyday occurrences, but the interplay between motionless rock and fluid current always captivated me, if only for a moment or two. Some ledges, ground down by eternities of erosion, were worn as smooth as whalebacks. Others, heaved up by colossal forces, revealed the planet's fiery origins in mysterious veins and layers.

After sidestepping the big curl, we maneuvered the canoe into a backwater eddy and then waited for Tom and Ruth to catch up. Above us, fast moving laser beams of sun pierced the wind-driven clouds. They penetrated the chilly waters and then, to our surprise, illuminated a school of glistening fish gathering around us in the pool below.

Thinking that these fish might be small lake trout, Mel rigged his rod and immediately hooked one. I fumbled with my newly spooled line while trying to overcome a bout of fish fever. I took a breath and finally joined in the fun of seeing fish attack my jig in waters as clear and cold as chilled vodka.

These feisty fish, which were around 18 inches long, however, were not lake trout. They were arctic grayling, an exceptionally handsome member of the trout family. They flaunted a pinkish iridescence over silvery gray sides and a swordfish-like dorsal fin, polka-dotted with rose and turquoise. Were it not for the instant death that warm saltwater would cause them, these grayling would be in proper fashion among their flamboyant brethren of the oceans' coral reefs. Bulging eyes added a homely touch, but this attribute improved the grayling's peripheral vision to strike at surface insects, which we often saw them do, as well as to flee from eagles and seals. In truth, I found these eyes more appealing than repulsive. When it came to the lasting attributes of beauty, fish and otherwise, in my mind, character and function trumped prettiness.

We gave the grayling a break from their involuntary aerobic workouts at the end of our fishing lines and then accelerated our own heartrates as we steered through more rapids. Finally, the rapids dissipated over the fan of an alluvial outwash where they emptied into the calmer and inviting waters of an expansive pool. We took a break, allowed our pulses to return to normal, and then re-rigged our rods for some shore fishing at a more leisurely pace. The river quickly rewarded us. Within spitting distance, a monster of the Loch Ness variety charged my line. Saving me from the burden of incredulous friends, Tom's camera work corroborated the landing of a fence-post-sized lake trout before I released it.

It was here that I began to see how these Barren Lands, "The Land of the Little Sticks," earned their name. Sparse groves of evergreens, reaching no more than ten or fifteen feet in height, straggled up and down the hills. Winter's erosive ground blizzards had stripped away their lower branches, laying bare their trunks, most of which weren't much larger than the fat end of a cue stick.

From a distance, these wind-scoured trees, many a hundred years or older, portrayed a human likeness, naked trunk as legs and upper boughs as torso and head. Where they stood apart from one another, they looked like Giacommetti statues—gaunt, alienated, alone. In occasionally isolated clusters, their silhouettes outlined images of forlorn refugee families, searching for homes on the endless tundra after having mistakenly wandered north of the tree line. I wondered, in the Barren Lands' ripping blizzards, whether one might hear their cries.

A few miles later, the river widened and the shoreline wandered, producing a convolution of boulder-studded bays and points. A gentle bowl of tundra formed one of these recesses and welcomed us to camp. We rigged our tents with neat lengths of white parachute cord and anchored the cords with lichen-covered rocks gathered up from plentiful supplies. Against a backdrop of muted tundra textures, our taught geometric domes of red and blue nylon declared their presence, whether crassly or cheerfully, I couldn't quite decide.

We put the campsite in order and followed up by lobbing fishing lures into the river's backwaters. Mel caught an eight-pound lake trout, a timely catch and perfect in size for supper. I watched him flense the fish and wondered how many practicing surgeons could rival Mel's speed and skill with a filet knife—flesh removed without a bone and scaly skin slipped off with a swipe of the blade.

Well-fed and equally tired, we crawled into our cocoon-like tents and squeezed into our mummy-style sleeping bags, pulling them up like body-sized socks. Despite the dawdling of the twilight outside, sleep came quickly inside our cozy quarters. Mel didn't use his eyeshades or his ear plugs that night or any other night. Either he was so tired that it didn't matter or, in the case of my ear plugs, my snoring didn't live up to his apprehensions.

During our first couple of days on the river, fishing for both lake trout and northern pike was good, so good that I envisioned catching huge fish at will. Oddly, a mild apprehension eclipsed my mood. Would the repetitive reeling-in of lunkers debilitate me with muscle fatigue or carpel tunnel syndrome? Would my supply of fishing lures expire due to the inevitable break-offs in the jaws of these heavyweights? Would the predictable consistency of good fishing lead to monotony?

Fortunately, worry did not consume me. Besides, our interest in angling was more than sporting. We were counting on fish to supplement our food supply, and the culinary convenience of dripping-wet fresh fish was hardly worth any complaining. We might be doing some catching and releasing, but we wanted to do some keeping and filleting, too.

However, our luck with these larger species fell off and, farther downstream, only the grayling proved reliable. The river lived up to its formal name, the Thlewiaza, the "river of little fish." It was the "Big River," but it was full of little fish.

The next morning, we partook of oatmeal breakfasts liberally supplemented with ibuprofen tablets—the miracle drug for middle-aged joints and muscles. The Thlewiaza's tranquility, unruffled by wind, and flawless blue skies enticed us to break camp. Back out on the river, Mel hooked a lake trout of a dozen pounds and then labored to land it. After he released his catch, we paddled to a steep run of rapids and decided to pick and line our way through them along the river's banks. Near the rapids' run-out, a larger ledge, about the height of a canoe, required us to portage.

This outcropping's downstream side held a perfect sun-washed place for lunch, and the shelf of ice along the bank became our picnic table. This expanse of ice also kept our cheese and sausage chilled and, to our further delight, the bugs at bay, even while the sun's intensity coaxed us to shed our jackets. After lunch, I stood on the ledge's promontory and worked my jig along a current seam and retrieved eager grayling, one after the other.

As much as the navigating of rapids and the angling for fish engaged me, the enormous catchment of tundra that united the Thelwiaza's waters began to draw more of my attention. Without the clutter of buildings or the cover of forests, the tundra exposed itself, boldly revealing its shaping by the sheets of ice that once bore down on the continent. Just a scratch or two beneath this tawny surface lay the permafrost, the remnants of the last ice age, still intact.

The newborn skin of this land, neither scarred by roads nor pricked by power poles, suggested that the last ice age may have been a more recent rather than ancient phenomenon. The tundra, in fact, at only ten thousand years old, was the Earth's youngest biome, but it seemed even younger than that, like a place whose creation someone's granddad might have witnessed.

Paddling mechanically, I lost myself in a preposterous daydream in which I entered an imaginary, cave-like tavern. Inside, I bellied up to the dimly lit bar and generously ordered a round of beers for a covey of old-timers. I was about ready to ask my new-found acquaintances how it was hereabouts when the last glaciers pulled back and how deep the permafrost was when I heard Mel's voice.

"Guy, where in the Sam Heck are you steering the canoe?"

"Huh? Oh, yeah . . . I was wondering." I turned the canoe back on course. "Mel, I was wondering. If you drilled down through the permafrost, at what depth would you penetrate its base and, owing to the heat from the Earth's molten core, find unfrozen ground?"

"Beats me . . . but don't let these 'deep' thoughts, distract you, okay?"

"Okay."

While these underground mysteries intrigued me, they lay buried beyond my sight, so I shifted my focus back to the land that cradled the Thlewiaza. Granted, no mountain ranges shouted at us to snap their pictures, but the vastness of this place asserted its own dominance. The hills, like ocean swells, rolled on endlessly, finally vanishing beneath an even bigger sky.

On a more localized scale, conical mounds, teardrop hills, and winding ridges, known as *eskers*, punctuated the landscape, all of them the marks of departing glaciers. The eskers, seemingly the works of ancient railroad builders gone wild, served as the tundra's meandering elevated transportation corridors. Artic travelers, both past and present, human and animal alike, had favored them for their firm footing and bug-deterring exposures.

Birch and willow, dwarfed by climatic brutality, framed the water's edges. Whether in defiance or desperation, these shrubby trees thrust their pencil-thin trunks sunward through skirts of sumptuous moss. On higher ground, isolated pockets of stunted trees followed the folds of hills—the tamarack in lacy lime, the darker spruce, and the bristly jack pine—all of them willing to take root in the thinnest of soils. These coniferous oases were scattered among the tundra's ubiquitous weave of sedges, prostrate shrubs, lichens, mosses, and sundry cushion plants. Finally, outcroppings of sand, gravel, and rock defined the steeper slopes and ridges. This transition of bonsaied flora and park-like landforms evoked images of classic mountain scenes except on a smaller scale, almost like a museum diorama.

By mid-afternoon, our canoe-bound legs begged for a stretch, so we beached the canoes and took a hike. We bounded over a cobbled shoreline rimmed with brooms of stunted birch and then up a grassy incline to the top of a hill, which rewarded us with views all around. While my companions retraced their steps to the canoes below, I stood still and fussed with my digital camera's innumerable settings.

When I looked up, an antler-less caribou appeared on the ridge. Living up to its species' reputation for both myopia and curiosity, this solitary "deer" wandered within a dozen paces of my position. Conveniently, it stopped, posed for a photo shoot, and then sauntered away, showing little concern about my presence. Maybe this junior *rangifer tarandus* mistook me for one of its kind, maybe even its mother. Poor child, I must have been such a disappointment—wrong species, not enough legs, and no udders.

With legions of black flies invading the territory, I felt sorry for man and beast alike, but more for the latter. By day's end, I would dive into the sanctuary of a screened-in tent. For this caribou calf, the only refuge from these terroristic swarms would be to keep moving.

We capped off our second day by cruising through a shallow, five-mile long lake. Despite our forward motion, a tailwind allowed the black flies to trail us and pester us at their leisure. Near the end of this flat-water, an esker appeared that explained the presence of the lake. This ridgeline had crossed the river's path and dammed it from one bank to the other. Two spillways, one at each end of the esker, allowed the river's continued flow.

The band-like island between these two rapids, which turned out to be an interrupted land bridge braided by caribou trails, beckoned us to camp and so we did. The Moores applauded the concept of fresh fish for supper, so Mel and I tried our luck at the fishy-looking outflows of the spillways, but we caught nothing. On my way back to camp, I flushed a pair of ptarmigans from a patch of brushy bottomland. Still in possession of some of their snowy winter color, they flaunted plumages of mottled brown, white, and rust.

We would regularly stumble upon these chicken-like birds, often in the same kind of brushy cover. To distract us from their eggs and hatchlings, they ran madly around in circles or feigned broken legs while moving away from their nests. They took to flight but only with reluctance and then with little grace, which, I supposed, was the way a chicken would fly.

The buggy and muggy afternoon left us feeling itchy and grimy. There would be no greater luxury at this moment than a bath. All we needed was the courage to immerse ourselves in a river that still had chunks of ice floating in it. An inviting beach awaited us down by our canoes.

I plunged in and took a few invigorating strokes, proving my virility while simultaneously shrinking key attributes of my manliness. Mel took a sponge bath and then dunked himself for a rinse. Our dripping vanilla bodies accented by sun-reddened faces and hands bore rude resemblances to strawberry sundaes. Refreshed and re-attired, Mel and I joined the Moores for rum cocktails and dinner on the ridge top, which afforded excellent views both up the lake and down the river.

"You know," I said, "I didn't get a chance to read about the permafrost before we left. How thick do you think this stuff is?"

Tom pondered the matter and then jokingly spat out a random number: "One-hundred-and-eighty-three feet." He stood by his answer, asserting that this thickness must be true somewhere on the Earth's surface.

Later in our trip, we would meet two southern construction workers who served as surrogates for the crusty old timers of my daydream. To the question about the permafrost depth, one of them said, "Really thick, I mean, like kilometers," and from his coworker came the proverbial, "All the way to China."

Tom's answer, which implied variability, was correct, at least in that regard. The thickness of this perennially frozen ground varied depending on surface temperatures, soil type, drainage, snow cover, and vegetation. Soil compaction and the transfer of heat from buildings also affected the depth to the boundary shared by the seasonally thawed surface layer above and the permafrost below.

The construction worker, who answered "kilometers," wasn't far from the mark, either. The permafrost extended only a few feet in its discontinuous southern regions and, in the continuous areas farther north, between 800 to 2,100 feet, just a bit short of one kilometer. From the standpoint of the permafrost's challenges for building roads, utilities, and buildings, however, "All the way to China" may have been the best answer.

After supper, I walked along the strands of caribou trails that followed the ridge and then disappeared over the horizon. Slants of mahogany and indigo crept up the hillsides. Within these deepening hues, a sense of movement prevailed. Uncountable caribou—walking, trotting, and running—all in single-file columns over uncountable years had carved these narrow, neatly furrowed trails, which I now borrowed for my own footsteps. The pounding of herds of caribou hooves, their snorting and gasping, and the telltale clicking of their slapping leg tendons must make a wonderful racket, but tonight all was calm. The only thing larger than the sky was the silence of this place.

The enveloping calm contrasted with the evidence of movements. These movements had preceded us, and they would outlast us. Along one axis, we paddled the same river that fish, seals, and hunters in their pursuit had followed for millennia. Along the other, the caribou's migratory instincts led them in Texas-sized circles of unfathomable endurance, season after season, year after year.

I was little more than a tourist on a one-night stand, but I sensed a belonging, a sort of honorary membership among the distinguished predecessors of these crossroads. Together, our imprints here left no more than a trace, but we passersby, whether tangibly or intangibly, had defined the character of this place. This landscape, the continuum of its beauty, was now a part of me. Was I now a part of it? This place and I, were we somehow immortally intertwined?

A faint breeze bent the grasses toward my overlook. Each blade cast its own waving and lengthening shadow and then dusk eclipsed the day. Consciously, I drew in a breath. For over thirty years, whether owing to my hardwired nature or hard-driven nurturing, I had immersed myself in work, yet a day seldom passed that didn't torment me a little and sometimes more about paths not taken.

Good old Robert Frost, he took the trail less traveled; I took my father's. Had I wandered differently, whether a path worn more or less, at least I would have dodged the innuendos that nipped at the SOBs of the world, those with "son of the boss" as their unofficial job titles. There was nothing of substance to regret, but the New England poet's prophesy was right, not that I wallowed in discontent, but there was a sigh now and then, because the question, about the paths not taken, well, that question had never gone away.

Separated from my mold of twenty-five years, one that I hadn't expected to be poured into in the first place, Thomas Hardy's words echoed, "nothing bears out in practice what it promises incipiently." All things, as they did for Hardy, now seemed more tentative. I sensed that I was now more the humble recipient of my destiny than its artisan, that the strength of my will lay not so much in how I shaped my fate, but in how I might respond to it. To be sure, I had not spent down my endowment of volition nor had I exhausted the reserves of my youthful obliviousness and naiveté toward risk, the absence of which could be incapacitating. I would move forward, but where I might stray along this splintered path was unclear.

If the wind did not bring me clarity of passage, at least at this day's end, on this arctic ridge, epiphanically, it furrowed my brow: There was a time for everything under the sun, from being to becoming, but at this moment, I breathed in the air of being. Soon enough, I would reckon with "becoming," with chiseling some new form of myself. I would not and could not avoid this, but maybe this was the time and place to let it be.

This insight led to a confession—a premise for the conclusion that would follow. Regardless of how I might polish it, my resume was a humble affair. With or without me and despite my efforts to master it, the world, with its seven billion people, had seen fit to keep on turning on its own accord. Granted, this wasn't much of a revelation, but it was an admission that spoke to other triumphs, triumphs as ordinary as they were miraculous, like the ones embedded in the ancient campsites along this river and pounded into the ruts of these caribou trails.

These great circles of effort drew their force from nothing more than a raggedy old cliché, but the truth of it struck me deeply. Maybe it was the climb more so than the summit that mattered. Likewise, for the ether of true love, maybe the real truth of it lay right before our eyes in the daily art of trying to reach it. Yes, maybe it was our reach more than the dubious prizes we seek, the rhythm of pounding hooves along the trail that comforted, the grit of each day's effort that alone was worth the endeavor.

Standing at the intersection of passages within me and about me, my eyes traced the horizon line. This land understood in a way that was greater than its vastness, greater than its silence. I answered back in kind. Silently, I gave thanks for being alive. For nothing more than life itself.

Chapter 7

The Singing Hills and the Quiet Stream

Bracing winds and unobstructed sun heralded our third day on the Big River. We broke camp, filed down to our beached canoes, and along the way crossed over wolf tracks, which had been left in the sand overnight. Our stealthy nocturnal visitors apparently chose not to alert us to their presence, only to leave their footprints. In the smooth wet sand, the depression left by their paws looked as perfect as newly minted fossils. We then creased these sands as we slid our canoes into the waters of the Thlewiaza, a river that Canadian author Fawley Mowat aptly described as "rapid riven."

Indeed, it took us only a short paddle before we reached our first set of riving, sun-sparkled rapids, replete with tsunami-sized waves. They were significant enough to justify an actual name on the map—Portage Rapids. Despite their appellative caution and interminably long funnel of seething, spray-crowned waves, we decided to skip the portage but also exercise enough prudence to avoid a suicidal run down the middle. Consistent with our established pattern of peaceful non-engagement, we picked our way down the tamer slick-water edges and then lined the major vertical drops.

The ultimate test of a paddling relationship, of course, is the running of rapids. Like husband and wife hanging wallpaper together, paddlers may still be friends after their canoe, with them or without them, washes out of the rapids' fan, but a few days' passing may be required before they like each other as much as they did when they started the task. If true sublimity in a canoeing relationship could ever be attained, it would be when the paddlers of bow and stern maneuvered the canoe as one, as from a single mind.

Granted, Mel and I never quite arrived at this inner peace of perfect paddling unity, but we were getting closer. Nor can I say that our paddling karma, such as it was, resulted from meditation. Neither of us tried that, but being middle-aged and thus somewhat levelheaded probably helped. Clearly, neither of us was out to prove anything. However, when difficult stretches of the river required skippering duties to be shared and thus to dilute Mel's authority, he could become grumpy, and when criticized, I could become defensive. It was a recipe for tension and, as the reader will see, there would be occasions when these tensions surfaced.

Beyond levelheadedness, we also relied on a lexicon of paddling terms. In the corporate, techy vernacular of the time, we might have said that this terminology enhanced the reflexes of our man-canoe interface. Boulders that pushed up and accelerated the river's current without breaking the surface, for example, were pillows. The river's clear waters made it difficult to discern their depth, whether the pillows were safely well below the hull or close enough to slice it from stem to stern. Terms, such as, *Vs, drops, rooster tails, eddies, headwalls, boils,* and *whirlpools* peppered our speech.

I paddled the stern, normally the skipper's position, except when it came to shooting the rapids, when our roles reversed. Then it was Mel's job in the bow to set the course, which is to say, when it really mattered, Mel was the boss. Actually, he was always the boss. To safely zig-zag through the rapids, my jobs were to keep the canoe aligned with the direction set by Mel and, in tight turns, to pivot the canoe like a firefighter steering the back end of a hook-and-ladder truck.

In the running of rapids, we measured our success by the amount of water we shipped and the size of the scrapes from the canoe's red polyethylene hull we left on the rocks. If we made it through the run without too many scrapes and avoided drenching ourselves, we exchanged celebratory compliments. Occasionally, we pumped our paddles high in the air and behaved like touchdown-crazed football players.

Communication, though, is an imperfect art, and Mel and I had some stylistic contrasts. Mel's shout of "left," for example, sometimes energized my dyslexia. Were we to go to the *left* of the boulder or were we to stay clear of the boulder on our *left* and go to the *right* of it? If I was confused, Mel shouted "left" again and louder, spelling out the letters L-E-F-T. I don't have to tell you who the straight man was in these Abbot-and-Costello "Who's on First?" exchanges, and yes, sometimes, the severity of the situations tempered their humor.

After Portage Rapids, we dropped into the sunny embrace of a small, crater-like lake haloed by a thick shelf of ice that was high and wide enough to accommodate us and our canoes below it as we floated by and cooled ourselves in the dripping shadows. This craggy, ice-rimmed lake did not last long though. Shortly ahead, another line of whitewater, divided by an island, danced on the horizon.

Hypothesizing that a longer run would entail a more gradual descent, I favored the more roundabout route to the left. Normally, we'd scout the rapids, but the island blocked our view. The channel's length also meant that we might be scouting all afternoon. The initial drop, what we could see of it, looked more inviting than intimidating, so we decided to throw caution and reconnaissance to the wind and shoot the dogleg rapids to the left with ride-'em-cowboy abandon. Joyously, I was in my element.

At the rapids' outflow, the channel splintered into more channels, which in turn sliced through immense cakes of ice that stood slightly taller than my six feet. With summer-greened flora everywhere else about, occasional ledges of grainy ice had startled us, but these plateaus of ice, sculpted with opalescent alcoves, were absolutely magical and worthy of a pause.

Accordingly, we stopped and idled within one of these umbrageous, pearly blue grottos and then watched the sandpipers scurry along the gravel bars out on the river. More so than silliness, their frenetic pace suggested an understanding of the necessity, not just the joy, of *carpe diem*. Their days of prancing with wetted feet beneath the sun, just like ours, were numbered. Were there any doubts, all our bobbing friends had to do was to look up and see these walls of ice, standing like arm-crossed schoolmarms and reminding us that summer's short recess would soon be over.

A few more bends in the river brought us to a bench of land on the right-hand bank. We beached the canoes, climbed to the top, and discovered a meadow with a small lake whose shoreline held several piles of fresh bear scat. I gave little regard to the bear droppings and instead pointed to the taller hills that rose up from the opposite shore.

"Hey, look, mountains!" I shouted.

These hills, topped with rocky promontories, presented a classic alpine scene with a mountaintop lake in the foreground. Of course, we were only a little above sea level and these peaks, at only couple hundred vertical feet above the river, were no mountains. They could be scaled in minutes, not days, which is exactly what I did.

I rambled around the lake to the bouldery top, caught my breath, and then beheld the tundra in glorious tawny green below. It was dotted with sparkling lakes while the river, like a silver ribbon, meandered and then narrowed to a vanishing point under an infinite sky. Involuntarily, my arms parted and my lungs filled to sing out the title song from a 1960s musical about a young Austrian nun. Yes! The hills were alive, but my voice, like the proverbial tree falling in the woods, could be heard by no one but me. Effectively, I was invisible and inaudible, but I do vividly recall being there—celebrating the sense that I was on top of the world and singing in triple F. With neither burden of oxygen tanks nor pain of amputated, frostbitten limbs, I had conquered this "peak"!

Climbing over these hills and ridges was a bit like stepping into a time machine that transported me into the past. Except for its imperceptible wearing from wind and weather, I reasoned that this Land of the Little Sticks hadn't changed much over the years. These views could have been the same that Samuel Hearne saw in 1770–72 when he walked across the Barren Lands with little more than the clothes on his back and adopted the ways of the Chipewyan in order to survive.[1]

Hearne's mission was to find the legendary Metal River, which held the promise of precious minerals and the missing link to the Northwest Passage. He and his native Chipewyan guides started at Fort Prince of Wales, a citadel-like trading post on the western shores of Hudson Bay (near present-day Churchill, Manitoba). A year-and-a-half later, after trudging across the tundra, they had reached the mouth of the Coppermine River at the top of North America and discovered that these lands truly were barren, more precisely, barren of everything Hearne had sought.

Hearne's disappointment in finding mostly picked-over rubble, one measly four-pound chunk of copper, and an unnavigable cataract-strewn river was preceded by horror when, along the way, his opportunistic Chipewyan guides gratuitously ambushed an encampment of unsuspecting Inuit families. The Inuit, who had never seen firearms before, stood in confusion as slugs from the Chipewyans' muzzleloaders tore through their bodies. Those still breathing or fleeing were quickly run down and hacked to death. European mapmakers later consecrated the site of this butchery with the name "Bloody Falls."

Hearne returned to Hudson Bay where he eventually served as Fort Prince of Whales' factor and married Mary Norton, the "mixed-blood" daughter of the fort's former cantankerous chief who had died from natural causes during Hearne's absence. The couple, along with a small zoo of pet animals taken from the wild, lived there contentedly, that is, until some ten years later when the French, who were allied with the thirteen colonies during the American Revolutionary War, sent three war ships to capture the fort. Although he had forty-two cannons and a fortress at his disposal, Hearne knew that he was still outgunned and outmanned and, from his travels with the Chipewyan, he also knew of the grisly effects of violence. Promptly, he surrendered. The French then imprisoned Hearne and his employees and sent Mary Norton and the fort's Indians fleeing. When the British finally regained control of the territory and reinstated him as the governor, Hearne found that the love of his life was gone. Having grown up in the manner of a delicate European, Mary had starved to death in the wilderness.

Compared to Hearne's incredible two-thousand-mile roundtrip journey and his tragically ended marriage, our little Barren Land trek was nothing. Mel and I would be travelling a tenth of the distance sitting in a canoe made of Space Age plastic and paddling downstream in the middle of the summer. As for our Euro-American wives, fortuitously, they were safely awaiting our return in Canada's now-friendly neighbor to the south where each of them could easily reach any one of several grocery stores in a ten or fifteen-minute drive.

As I stood on my little mountaintop musing about Samuel Hearne, my eyes scanned the immensity of the landscape. Eventually they fell upon Tom, Ruth, and Mel who were now specs in the distance. Then it dawned on me. Their reluctance to join my "alpine" quest may have been a sensible aversion to the depositor of the scat. Luckily, I experienced no grizzly encounters, but I took precautions in my descent. I made noises, tried to look mean, and kept my fingers crossed, precautions which, judging by the absence of any large mammal molestations, possibly proved effective.

A few miles downriver, we saw our first seal, which we guessed was a ranger (or "harbor") seal. Perfectly at home in the river's swifts, it bobbed its head to scrutinize us and then leapt through the air like a two-hundred-and-fifty pound salmon before disappearing under the water. We learned that ranger seals swam upstream as far as Seal Hole Lake, our starting point. How they managed to get upstream through places like Portage Rapids was difficult to fathom. Indeed, they must be powerful and determined swimmers.

With enough mileage logged for the day, we chose to overnight on a ridge that paralleled the right-hand bank and overlooked the river below. For the first time, we erected the tundra tarp and thus found relief from the infinities of flies and mosquitoes that sought our intimate company.

After supper, we hiked along a windswept sandy ridge that angled away from the river. Our tracks now mingled with those of wolves, fox, and caribou, and the reposing sun began to immerse the hills with dusky shadows.

Within those distant shadows, I imagined a single-file line of people. It was Hearne and his squad of Chipewyans steadily inching their way to the northwest. In a year, they would be at the mouth of Coppermine River and the ice-encrusted shores of the Arctic Ocean.

An instinctive rhythm measured our days. We arose in the light and fell asleep before dark. In some sliver of time, darkness came and went, but more as theory than observed phenomenon. Without alarm clocks, we routinely woke up around 6:00 am, broke camp a couple of hours later, and found ourselves at work on the river, early enough to garner a salary man's respect.

Despite this discipline, the nearly nightless days disoriented me. Everything needs a reference, just as hot needs cold and black needs white, so it is that a day, to be understood, needs a night. Without their separation by darkness, I occasionally lost track of the days and paid even less attention to the arbitrary construct of time. What, after all, was 6:00 am? Who needed clocks or calendars? Thankfully, Mel's journal entries kept track of the days and thus mitigated the risk of falling behind and missing our pickup at Hudson Bay. With Mel's log reliably accounting for their numerical succession, I let one day flow into another, remembering the days for what they were, not their calendar identities.

After a breakfast of canned ham and reconstituted eggs, supplemented with hash browns and ibuprofen, we said good-bye to our ridge-top campsite, waddled to the riverbank, and thereupon placed our bodily burdens into our obedient canoes. Swiftly, the waters of narrow channels carried us down the Thlewiaza, which, with ledges of bedrock, chose to interrupt us only occasionally. These we navigated by lining. By midday, we came face-to-face with a battery of sand hills, one layered up upon the other. They looked like an immensely tiered wedding cake frosted with lofty dollops of sand.

We beached the canoes along a brushy shore skirting these hills and then claimed a nearby grassy clearing for a picnic lunch. The clean ring of stones in the center of this cozy meadow indicated the presence of recent campers. It was all rather intriguing, and we might have lingered had the droplets of a cloudburst not hurried our pace. We unpacked and then re-packed our picnic in a matter of minutes, only to see the rain stop as abruptly as it had started. Sometimes, the weather was rude prankster.

The quick return of clemency inspired us to hike up the face of the dune, which was a modest trek, about the length of an airplane runway. Along the way, we walked by animal dens, burrowed under occasional tufts of grass, and then intersected the curious lines of tracks connecting them with those of our own. Assorted skeletal specimens, the sun-bleached, weathered remains of predators' meals, also marked our summit-bound course.

"Mel," I said, "You'd think that porcupines or some other creatures would make a meal of these caribou bones, you know, that they'd clean up this litter."

"They have to be fresh bones for porcupines to eat them. Besides," Mel instructed, "I've never seen porcupines this far north. Acid decomposes bones, and this sand could be more neutral than acidic. Also, it's comfortable now. It's high summer, but the climate here for most of the year is like putting stuff in the freezer. Other than the erosion from blowing sand, these bones are going to be here for a long time."

"They're like a Georgia O'Keefe painting."

"Like a what?"

"Never mind. . . . Hey, Mel, what do you think? Is a skeleton the evidence of life or death?"

"Both."

"And death, is that the end of life?"

"Dunno. Haven't crossed that bridge, yet."

"Do you think that humans are the only living things with souls? Do you think that caribou carcass over there had one? What makes us so special?"

"Guy, I'm not musical and I'm not religious, either, okay?"

As we reached the top, the winds, which had gone about the task of forever building up these dunes, now, in an instant, split apart the clouds above. A shaft of sun shone through and moved across the valley floor below, but I heard no celestial voice accompanying this heaven-sent beam. No rumbling voice bellowed to answer my questions about souls or, for that matter, to berate me for anthropomorphic lunacy. What did impress me was the psychosomatic thirst I was developing. Distantly, water was everywhere, but the barrenness of these dunes, which would have put them at home in any worthy desert, say the Sahara or the Kalahari, attested to the aridity of this place.

Sunny breezes joined us on our return to the river and stayed with us during the rest of the day. After seventeen miles of paddling, we drifted along an outside bend in the river and spotted a promising hilltop campsite above the crescent of the curving shoreline. I hauled my pack up the incline and then felt the accumulated fatigue from the day's efforts sink in. I was hot, tired, gritty, and grimy. I wondered whether it might have been better to wash my clothes or simply burn them but then rationalized the continutation of their intensifying foulness as a possible deterrent against mosquito and blackfly attacks, never mind that the actual effect most likely was the opposite. Issues of personal hygiene notwithstanding, visions of lemonade cocktails danced in my head and watered my mouth. Seated in the bug-free luxury of our tundra tarp with drink in hand and inspiring views in every direction, I would have no better place to bid this halcyon day adieu. Truly, in terms of campsites, this one would have to rank among some of the world's best places to kick back and relax, especially after a long day of paddling.

Remarkably, I would disallow myself of these hedonistic pleasures. I was struck by the realization that the Big River was no longer yielding big fish and that the absence of this supplement would impair our collective dietary experience. Despite the lure of a leisurely drink, primeval instincts lifted me to higher pursuits. I sensed a duty to provide for the tribe. Perhaps it was not a duty but only a desire. Either way, the mission was simple. It was time to catch some fish and, if not big lake trout, maybe a few grayling.

A nearby tributary stream called to me. With fly rod in hand, I strode down the hill and began my march across a bottomland of Arctic meadow. I fixed my eyes on the point where the stream cascaded over a ledge of broken boulders just before losing its identity in the widening waters of the Thlewiaza.

The tundra, as it often did, encumbered my progress with grass-tufted muskeg hummocks. These curious, rooty mounds of vegetation, somewhat in the shape of a camel's humps, crowded the low-lying areas and seemed to be intent on growing upward so as to escape their moisture-saturated environs. I threaded my way around them and, with each step, the soggy, boggy ground from which they grew gave way and yielded as my footfalls sought firm resistance. One might duplicate this effect by walking through deep snow or over a double layer of water-saturated foam rubber mattresses. There was also the added obstacle of the hummocks themselves, which, at perfect ankle-sprain height, required a bit of dodging and changing of strides.

I also walked across areas of patterned land—vegetative mosaics that resembled hexagons and other polygonal shapes, from a few feet to thirty or more paces across. Their perimeter crevices captured rain and melt-water, which, in the winters, expanded into wedges of ice that widened the cracks and pushed up rocks and soil to the surface. The result was a distinct variation in microhabitats across each polygon. Seen en masse from an airplane or the top of a hill, this quilting of the Earth's surface was both appealing and otherworldly. As these polygons also provided excellent cover for bugs, I quickened my pace to stay ahead of the parade that marked my trail.

Finally, I reached this unnamed tributary. It was hardly a river, but certainly a comely and ample stream, even navigable by canoe for paddlers with sufficient intent. I stood a half mile upstream from its confluence with the Thlewiaza. I wondered whether I would be the first person to wet a fly line here, but I had my doubts. I couldn't count the times I had previously reached a seemingly inviolate, God-given place only to find a discarded beer can or an indestructible piece of plastic collecting silt on the bottoms.

But no such industrial debris marred these environs. The stream, in the manner of all streams, rolled on endlessly, drawing life from the land and giving it back again. Along the banks, each leaf and blade drank from the stream's waters and captured its share of the sun. The stream, itself, lay like a strand of diamonds across this verdant breast of arctic meadow. The diamonds danced down the riffles and tumbled into pools of sapphires. Diamonds and sapphires cradled in iridescent green—I wanted to hold this moment, to own this intersection of time and place, but I knew my possession of it would be no longer than the lifespan of the mayfly *ephemeroptera*, which when born of the river lives but a day to flutter in the breeze.

People said it was time to slow down, relax, and even meditate. Maybe that's what I was doing—meditating—but I wasn't ready to tilt my life's balance in that direction. Not just yet. And, with due respect to the power of mediation and the genius of Albert Einstein, all the wanting of the world wasn't going to slow down the pace of time, either relatively or absolutely. I was no different from anyone else. The game had started with my first desperate breath and the clock had never stopped.

Time slowed down only when you were stuck in traffic or your boss subjected you to a performance review with exhortations to be more "proactive" or to abide by the most newly rediscovered traits of highly effective people. Aside from such circumstances, time's ticking didn't slow down any more than the twitching of a twig stuck in the stream's unyielding current. If anything, it accelerated. This tenuous bubble of existence just kept floating along, glistening in the sun, distending into all manner of unwieldy forms, ready to pop at any instant.

Unlike humans and other earthly ephemera, rivers—at least within the intervals of tectonic shifts—were timeless. They did not reign in time's flight; rather, they reminded us of our inconstancy. *Time, like an ever-rolling stream, bears all who breathe away.* Isaac Watts obviously favored the symbolic potency of rivers when he penned those Psalms-inspired lyrics three centuries ago.

Several millennia earlier, the authors of Genesis determined that primordial birth had begun in a void of darkness when God's spirit swept over the waters, thus creating the heavens and the earth. Whether these ancient chroniclers intended us to interpret their work metaphorically or literally, I could not say. For me, in the case of water, separating symbol from substance was difficult.

Ancient Greek philosopher and purported father of science, Thales of Miletus, professed that water was the original source of all life, both mortal and immortal, which is to say the human soul itself. A rather fantastic claim, to be sure, but not entirely unlike Charles Darwin's suggestion a score of centuries later when he said that the earth's original pioneering organisms might have emerged from a "warm pond."

More recently, scientists suggested that life's origins might have begun in the chemically rich waters of volcanic pools or the hot springs bubbling up from cracks in the oceans' floors. Meanwhile, astronomers searched for water's evidence on distant planets as proof of life's existence there. Thus, from ancient to modern and from the sacred to the secular, life begins with water, a stream, if you will.

Whatever the flowing of waters told us about life's origins, they also spoke to us about life's yearnings. And to its contradictions. Rivers that lashed out to swamp our canoes or rush beyond their banks to flood our cities were the same waters we could not live without. Our blood coursed with this universal solvent and, for many, the spirit hungered for it. Pilgrims sought out healing springs. Christians washed away their sins and baptized their followers with water, the "vehicle of the Holy Spirit." Jews immersed converts in the purifying waters of a spring-fed stream or "mikvah," and in Islam, as in Christianity, water was God's gift, not only the source of life but the substance from which man was made.

The transformation of water to gas—from parent to child—and then back to water again cycled as endlessly as the Earth's rotation. The molecules of the Thlewiaza's waters could have been among those that existed since the beginning of time, bonded from the same atoms of hydrogen and oxygen that were born with the first crack of the Big Bang. Indeed, these were molecules worthy of being named to Canada's Register of Historic Places, but here we were, nonchalantly dipping our paddles into them, swallowing them into our bellies, and sweating them out our pores.

Keats said that beauty is truth. If so, the stream now beside me flowed with absolute truth or at least the hope its existence. Its intimacy was intoxicating. The present instant for me, it seemed, had almost become a dream. This trinity—the source of life, the beauty of it, and the truth of it—had converged as one.

For all streams, a single seaward destiny held both their end and beginning anew. Truly, they revealed the sentient stuff of life, but in their riffles there were winks. Masked within their gurgling swirls were giggles that flirted with the soul. Just as its truthful beauty, molecular origins, and unending renewal hinted at some understanding of all this alpha-and-omega business, the stream stole away its secrets.

How were we to measure the infinity of space? What lay behind our irresistible urge to discover and explore, to create and be creative? What explained the human will, which, while distinguishing us from purely sensing or vegetative species, endowed us with powers both terrifying and redemptive? How did we come equipped with this often broken compass we call morality? What accounted for this brief flicker, this astonishing theater of life, where we, as actors, struggled with unscripted lines? But the answers slipped away from me, silently beyond my reach. They floated away with the currents and drifted into the shadows of the deepest pools.

To the place where the streams flowed, they would continue to flow, and I knew that my life was as trifling in this universe as my search for answers was in vain. I was grudgingly impressed by those who found clear and certain insight in the inerrancy of Scripture, the Big Bang, or the bottom line that more was always better. Their expressed opinions, however, also tended to trigger an impulse in me to flee. I found more affinity among the seekers of truth than among those who claimed it. I freely admitted it: I didn't have the answers. I wasn't even sure what all the relevant questions were, but I was bold enough to ask one. Could a life stripped of uncertainty and cleansed of mystery find any happiness? Might we even be happier if the mystery in our lives increased?

I was also bold enough to claim that a little grace might be possible now and then. I was no Pollyanna. Life might be as horrific as a leap from a burning skyscraper, but for the couple who held hands on the way down, there was grace, just as there must have been some kind of grace, in the manner of the twenty-third Psalm, that led me here. Beside this quiet stream.

This un-named tundra stream prompted childhood memories. The raw, newly sprouted suburb where I grew up had pushed up against the banks of Bassett Creek. Our neighborhood, like all the others at the time, was populated by the dividends of post-World War II peace: baby-boomer kids, dozens of them on every block, and I was one of them. Years ago, the wonderful free-range kids of my neighborhood were together, often united by the simple joys of water in motion and the curious creatures living along the banks of this modest stream.

At the same time, my father read *The Adventures of Huckleberry Finn* to me. I am pleased, by the continuing calls for its banishment by smallminded people, that this masterpiece of literature has achieved even higher acclaim. As a child, Twain's words filled my head with the magic of the Mississippi. It was a place where Jim and Huck transcended racial barriers and reached out to touch each other's hearts. I would understand more about these latter aspects when I got older. All my youthful mind could comprehend at the time was that Bassett Creek had become my little Mississippi. It was the place of my own childhood adventures.

In the winter my childhood pals and I skated on Bassett's tenuous ice, and in the spring marginally buoyant log rafts took us down her rain-swollen waters. We had no idea why we were making these pitiful vessels that got stuck on every bar of mud or gravel or where we were going, except down the creek, but it all happened with soaked shoes, muddy clothes, and great exuberance.

Not much had changed since then. Currents still swirled around us and drew us toward unseen, uncertain destinations, but who among us knew? Even forty or fifty years later, who among us could truly say that they knew where they were going? In the end, Huck didn't know either, except that he was going "West."

I snapped out of my nostalgic gaze, stripped a length of line off the reel, and then threaded it through the eyelets of the rod. Fly-fishing, I knew, could never be anything more than an activity for me. Yet, among all possible activities, it might have been the most appealing. If all was vanity and striving after wind, just as one might dance to celebrate life or to defy its absurdities, I could go fly-fishing. It was, after all, a patient and contemplative endeavor that united one with the decency of nature.

To be sure, fly-fishing had altered my worldly outlook. Formerly repulsive life forms had become admirable riparian friends. Words like *larvae* and *pupa*, which I once hesitated to use in polite company, for fear of some unfortunate mispronunciations, had become entomological wonders. Creepy things stuck on the sides of rocks were actually the tiny mobile homes of caddis flies, marvelously constructed of minute bits of stone and twig. Horny head, skinny whip-like antennae, hairy legs, threads for gills, mottled tent-like wings, segmented body, gelatinous eggs—these attributes of the caddis were the essence of beauty, their presence the assurance of a healthy, unpolluted stream. Clouds of these fluttering moth-like insects, synchronously emergent from their underwater homes, were not nightmarish swarms. They were dreams come true for trout, dreams that drove them madly toward the surface.

Owing much to its simplicity, I felt that fly-fishing was the more elegant form of angling. It didn't require the expense, noise, or stink of a boat and motor, or the complexity of their storage. A pair of waders hung over a peg in the garage was sufficient. It was just that simple.

However, it wasn't all that simple. Complexities arose. These occurred when the fish began to feed in a frenzy and matching the hatch became the fly angler's obsession. Were the fish sipping tiny midges or the fork-tailed mayflies, and what exact insect stage was triggering their appetites—nymph, emergent, or dun—not to mention the color: olive, tan, or sulfur?

Yes, I had been challenged by these complexities. On many occasions, while standing in a stream in my hip waders and despite my dogged efforts, untold numbers of trout had encircled me with gluttonous, mocking splashes all the while displaying not the slightest interest in my offered fly. Then, by the time I had frantically tried every imitation critter in my fly box, including the idiotic fake mouse, the fish, having had their fill, vanished. They vanished to the shadowy depths where all life's secrets were hidden, into the deep and mysterious pools and behind the winks of the giggling riffles.

We fly anglers were constantly being reminded that "all men are equal before fish." These words, attributed to Herbert Hoover, may have been among the most profoundly truthful words ever spoken by a U.S. president. If further truth be known, fly anglers, myself included, sometimes inferred that we were more equal than others. The worst of this activity, therefore, was probably the smugness of its practitioners.

However, redeeming qualities of fly-fishing abounded, and the best part of fly-fishing, from my perspective, was drifting a dry fly on the stream's surface. The lie of one's line, in this context, was a double entendre, bespeaking not only of position but also of deception. With respect to position, the fly line couldn't appear attached; it couldn't drag nor could it have any slack.

With respect to deception, the fly itself was fashioned to look like a bug that may have fallen from a nearby overhead branch. It wasn't an oversized, murderous, trebled-hooked crank-bait that you winched through the stream nor was it a poor worm impaled on a hook and subjected to the additional simultaneous tortures of both drowning and hanging from a bobber underwater. It was an imitation fly, often no bigger than a pencil eraser, just skittering or peacefully drifting on top of the current. That is, until the water exploded, and a trout, like a sprung jack-in-the-box, burst into the sky with your tiny hook in its jaw. Although unmistakably unpleasant for the fish, which instantly became an involuntary acrobat, the deception was perfect, the piscatorial entertainment unrivaled.

With fly rod rigged and ready to go, I continued my walk along the banks of this Barren Lands' stream with no name and came upon a long, elbow-shaped pool. I was alone, beyond the sight of our distant camp. It was just me, the sky, and the stream-rent tundra. Taking a position at the inlet to the pool, I drifted a dry fly down the entering riffle. Then the water erupted. A grayling, desperately trying to shake my hook free and skipping above the water's surface on its tailfin, flashed the full kaleidoscope of its colors in the evening sun. And then a smile drew across my face. Fresh fillets would soon fill our skillet and then our bellies.

At moments like these, euphoric anglers elocuted in predictable ways. Hackneyed phrases abounded, but "it doesn't get any better than this" dominated all others. Despite the First Amendment's guarantee of free of speech, this oft-repeated phrase probably ought to be declared illegal, and I confess I was about to mutter these exact words to no one but the wind, but by not releasing this beautiful creature or the four that followed back to their pristine world, I began to feel like a reluctant mercenary.

Allowing only a moment to admire their luminous good looks and lengths, which exceeded my forearm and outstretched hand, I dispatched the five grayling with efficiency. More so than finding myself on the luckier side of nature's unification of life and death, I had become an arbiter of fate, a feller-buncher of fish. The river's contradictions of destroyer and provider flowed within me.

As I began my march back across the polygons and muskeg hummocks to our campsite, so did the evening's shadows. The diamonds faded, and then I looked back and saw that they had disappeared. The grayling dangling from my stringer flipped and flopped for a while, but soon their life and color, like the diamonds, were gone, and the end of the day was at hand.

Chapter 8
The Black Flies

From the tundra's vastness to the alpine azaleas' tiny pink buds, to be in the Barren Lands is to be smitten with its beauty. In his book, *Sleeping Island*, P. G. Downes quotes a passage attributed to a Dog-Rib Indian. The Indian replies to a Catholic missionary:

> Tell me, Father is (Your Heaven) like the land of the little trees when the ice has left the lake? Are the great musk oxen there? Are the hills covered with flowers? There will I see the caribou everywhere I look? Are the lakes blue with the sky of summer? Is every net full of great, fat whitefish? Is there room for me in this land, like our land, the Barrens? Can I camp anywhere and not find that someone else camped? Can I feel the wind and be like the wind? Father, if your Heaven is not all of these, leave me alone in my land, the land of the little sticks.

Had I been at the priest's side, I might have tugged on his frock and whispered an idea for improving his proselytic success. "Psst, Father, tell him there are no black flies in heaven." An afterlife that promised not just salvation but also no black flies might have closed the deal. I believe that it would have been an offer difficult for most Barren Landers to refuse.

Of course, I had heard about black flies before. I'd even shared my flesh with them a few times on prior sub-arctic trips, but it was among the trekkers of the tundra that I heard the real horror stories, tales about demonic gnat-like creatures driving people to the brink of gibbering madness. I tended to be more puzzled in my response than sympathetic. What was all the fuss about? I had now followed them into the tundra and had come to realize the truth. Their horror was real.

Compared to black flies, mosquitos were single-A minor leaguers. If you covered yourself with loose, light colored clothing and lathered exposed skin areas with DEET, mosquitoes weren't much of a problem. Sure, even if they didn't land on your skin, the discordant drone of these little vampires swarming around your head and sounding like a violin section tuning up without end could be annoying, but black flies were in a different league altogether. In the tundra they inspired fear among man and beast alike.

Beginning with ice-out, the tundra's black fly larva populations start escaping from cocoons that cover thousands of square miles of river bottoms. Each larva hitches a ride through the currents on a small air bubble, emerges into the atmosphere as a winged adult, and thereupon joins an infinite force of airborne terrorists. To me, the black-and-white stripes on their legs and abdomens looked like war paint, and their humpbacked bodies gave them a muscular look, as though they had been pumping iron in preparation for our torment. If I ever saw one under a microscope, I surmised that my nightmares would entail hot sweats and trembling.

Black flies reportedly had bled livestock to death in Canada; and, with the help of mosquitoes, no-see-ums, warble flies, and other airborne pests, they regularly debilitated the caribou herds in the tundra. Caribou burned through calories trying to escape and, in the process, being unable to forage, they often became emaciated. In some parts of the world, their bites caused river blindness (onchocerciasis) in humans. In Canada, the transmission of diseases to humans by black flies was unknown, but it was not uncommon for their bites to cause skin infections, headaches, nausea, fever, swollen glands, and serious allergic reactions. They could also plug the nasal or bronchial tubes, potentially suffocating their victims.

On the Thlewiaza, the black flies worked in tandem with the mosquitoes. The mosquitoes had the morning and graveyard shifts while the black flies took the swing shift, especially on warm days. Sometimes their shifts would overlap, with each species feasting upon us simultaneously. In Minnesota, we joked about our two seasons, winter and road construction. In the roadless tundra, it was winter and bugs.

The black flies didn't just bite us, either. They were sadistic thugs who delighted in our torture. They were smart, too, or seemed to be for bugs. When they weren't biting, they were buzzing around, taking off and landing repeatedly. During our first night on the Thlewiaza, I was lulled to sleep by the pitter-patter of a steady rain on our tent, but the tent's roof the next morning bore no evidence of rain. It was dry. In fact, the pitter-patter wasn't precipitation; it was a rain of black flies repeatedly dive-bombing the tent.

When they tired of their dive-bomb gig, they sought an annoying intimacy with our bodies, especially the orifices of ears, mouth, nose, and eyes. Nothing quite compared to the coughing spasms that the inhalation of a black fly triggered. Black flies also liked to attack us where clothing fit tightly, such as the ankles above the socks, waist just above or below the belt, or forearms between the slits in a long-sleeved shirt. A stiff breeze kept them away, but if we were paddling with the wind or the breeze was light, they were inescapable. They would follow our canoes for miles across open water.

Only the females bit, but when they got around to carving up our flesh with their multiple cutting, sucking mandibles, we couldn't feel it. Cleverly, they excreted an anesthetic with their toxic saliva and then, even more cleverly, they injected an anticoagulant to keep the blood goodies flowing. Because we couldn't feel any pain, the first indication of a bite was visual only, beginning with a small trail of blood and then a reddening and swelling of the skin. This was followed by incessant itching and then, if we scratched the itch, which was nearly impossible to resist, hideous scabbing.

If cruelty was unending gratuitous pain, what was unending annoyance? From my perspective, it was something close to pure cruelty. If so, what kind of divinity was it that created this cruel, evil life form? Perhaps the Cree word *Manitou*, which was used interchangeably for *God, spirit,* and *devil,* had something to do with it—the Great Spirit in a devilish mood.

Maybe the plant kingdom's union steward confronted God and pleaded on behalf of his fellow plants: "Lord, we respect your omniscience, but these bugs are bad. They're perforating our leaves, boring holes in our stems. They're eating us alive. It's vegacide! Why don't you have some of these insects eat the mammals, so both of them can leave us alone for a while?" Maybe God tried to make amends and then went over the top by unleashing the terror of black flies on the planet's blood-filled organisms. No matter how you looked at it, it was hard to reconcile intelligence or compassion with the design of black flies.

During my trek to the no-name tributary, I was awestruck by the scenery and the catching of fish. Apparently, I was also oblivious to the hits that the black flies tagging me must have scored, because soon afterwards my forearms were tattooed with welts. The reddened bites on my right forearm spelled out "MOM," and those on my left arm formed the outline of the devil's horned head complete with evil eyes and sinister smile. Finally, I had caught up with our modern culture's fashion trends of body mutilation. I wore those tattoos for the remainder of the trip and displayed them with a sort of masochistic pride. Besides, there was the vicarious honor of being bitten by black flies that were probably among the descendants of those that had persecuted the likes of Henry Hudson, Thomas James, and Samuel Hearne.

Sadly, we didn't know of any effective repellants for black flies. The available defenses ranged from the disappointing to the ridiculous. The most practical defense, but less than ideal owing to its claustrophobic envelopment, was the head net, the equivalent of an Arabic woman's burqa but made of mosquito netting. The head net could also be combined with a meshed, DEET-soaked bug shirt. Toughened locals and trekkers of authentic stature, of course, spurned head nets. They saw them as the telltale marks of an easily agitated greenhorn.

However, humiliation required an audience, a phenomenon absent in the tundra's isolation, and I was willing to trade a little claustrophobia to gain relief. Interestingly, when black flies were somehow able to sneak inside my head net, they apparently sensed entrapment and thereupon focused on escape rather than biting. While darting around inside the confines of the head net they were still damn annoying, but it was better than having them take my blood.

Public health departments recommended that people avoid areas prone to black fly infestations or stay indoors. On the tundra, this meant staying indoors until there was hard frost, but there was no "indoors" in the Barren Lands interior nor would it be practical to go canoeing after the first hard frost when the lakes and rivers would be sheeting over with ice. Because black flies were daylight creatures, we could go outside after dark, but this solution also had its limitations—the hazards of canoeing in the dark and the fact that, in the land of the midnight sun, darkness was unavailable.

There were, of course, various folk remedies. One of these entailed placing a sheet of dryer fabric softener on top of your head. I've never tried this but maybe I should have. Others called for tying pieces of string to corks and then suspending them from the rim of a hat, smoking a stinky cigar, or wearing a fuel-oil covered aluminum hardhat to which black flies supposedly would be attracted and then trapped by the oil. A combination of all of these repellants —oil-coated metal hardhat festooned with cork dingles, topped with fabric softener sheet and enveloped in cigar smoke—would have been quite the spectacle, maybe enough to simply scare the black flies away.

Dragonflies were one of the black fly's natural enemies. As a child, I was petrified by them. They looked like the genetically engineered hybrids of a micro-sized B-24 World War II bomber and a butterfly and they flew like the nimblest of helicopters. Once I learned about the eat-and-be-merry missions of their brief, four-to-eight week lives—procreating while gorging on black flies and mosquitos—respect and gratitude replaced my childhood fears.

Ruth was thrilled when one of these eat-and-be-merry creatures seized a black fly mid-air and landed on her to finish the meal. It was a personalized Wild Kingdom episode of prey and predator, eat or be eaten, carried out right on her lap. This episode made me wonder if dragonflies could be domesticated in some fashion. A squadron of companion dragonflies to escort me through the bush would have been a delight and, as far as pets go, much more useful than, say, cats.

Finally, there were solutions that relied on industrialized culture to take its course. In this regard, polluting or damming up the river would be most effective, because black flies can only live in the clean, oxygen-rich waters of fast-flowing unpolluted rivers and streams. One evening at our campsite, I suggested on future trips we might consider hiring a crop-duster pilot to precede us.

Tom then recollected that, when he was a kid, his father had access to some surplus DDT canisters and dispensing valves. His dad, according to Tom, would fog the whole neighborhood with this now-banned insecticide made infamous by Rachel Carlson's *Silent Spring*. Then he'd line up Tom and his siblings and, for good measure, fog them, too. "Yeah, I kid you not, that's what he did!"

"Tom, after getting fogged, do you recall getting bitten by black flies?" I asked.

"As a matter of fact, I don't. Not a single bite."

When I got back to Minnesota, I called my sister, Ann, in Seattle. I asked her whether Dad had ever sprayed or fogged us with DDT. Ann asserted that we were in no way underprivileged in this regard and claimed that we, too, were fogged. It was a matter of status as well as faith in progress. "You know," she said, "better living through modern chemistry."

Ann's account of these events reeked of confabulation. Seeking a closure on the matter, I called Mom in Iowa. Despite the trendiness for adult children to blame their parents for their faults, I assured Mom that I wouldn't sue for damages, but she said no. To the "best of her recollection," neither she nor my father had ever sprayed us with DDT. That "best of her recollection" qualification sounded a bit waffly, but she was insistent. They may have wanted to spray my sister and me with DDT from time to time, but that, she claimed, was one line they didn't cross.

Reluctantly, I accepted Mom's answer, meaning that I could claim no purple hearts in this regard. I lamented this lack of distinction. Being doused with DDT, after all, could account for at least some of the deficiencies of my physical and mental character. In the end, all those things I hadn't accomplished, that dual MD-JD degree from Harvard, for example, would still have to be attributed to less convenient truths.

Chapter 9
The Birds Above, the Peat Below

Dip, pull, lift. Each stroke of the paddle voiced its three-part rhythm. Their succession, one series following the other, overlaid this rhythm with yet another. These rhythms kept count of our work and measured our labor. Except for occasional interferences of unruly currents of wind or water, paddling produced predictability between effort and outcome, a verification that, indeed, every action had one that was equal and opposite, just as Isaac Newton said.

Despite my reverence for Sir Newton and his laws of physics, I occasionally wished that we could increase our pace with less than equal effort. Tom claimed that a canoe, at most, could be human-paddled at no more than about six miles an hour. A reasonable cruising rate on flat water, he said, was only a little over half that; and, so, within these limits, I came to terms with our measured pace. Patience was possible as was its derivative, perseverance.

Eventually, these rhythms evolved into a repertoire of music. I heard Gavottes in minor keys and, from cathedrals of clouds and sky above, the echoed cadences of Gregorian chants. In deference to humanitarian concerns, Mel never sang. Because I did not wish to be a soloist, we usually paddled in silence, but the music still played on in my head, and each piece complied with the metronome of dip, pull, and lift.

Patience and perseverance, to the extent that we possessed them, put us in good stead for our fifth and longest day, twenty-five miles and most of them on flat-water lakes. We would have little help from the current, but we would also be free from the lining of ledges and the navigating of rapids. With less focus on our instantaneous movement, my senses were released to receive the world around me, to marvel at the interplay of clouds and sky and, because they could hardly be avoided, the birds.

They were our constant companions. Nearly a sixth of North America's avian species migrated to the Arctic. Here they bred and raised their young.[1] Most of our feathered friends had arrived via journeys from origins much farther than our own distant homes. Ptarmigans, robins, and other little birds, whose names I didn't know, entertained us.

On the river, throngs of waterfowl families, adults and their hatchlings, acknowledged our arrival: Canada geese, whose molting feathers rendered them flightless, the fish-eating and Mohawk-crested mergansers, loons, common herring gulls, black-capped and truly long-tailed jaegers, pacifistic eider ducks whose females held to their nests no matter how close we approached, short-billed dowitchers with straw-shaped beaks whose males take care of the young, the perky sandpipers, the nearly all black and clownish scoters, and the elegant tundra or "whistling" swans that mate for life.

By midmorning, we came upon these aristocrats of the river, the tundra swans. They swam in dignified matrimonial pairs—perfect photo ops if they would have allowed us to approach. We were never able to get close enough or, for that matter, to hear their whistling, the sound their powerful wings supposedly made as they cleave the air. By our observance, this whistling phenomenon was more fiction than fact. One fact was indisputable: the enervating labor they required to become airborne. Like loaded seaplanes, tundra swans' takeoffs required serious runway clearance, a hundred yards or more, during which their black webbed feet cycled across the crests of waves like ridiculous windup toys.

Birds that nested in the Arctic had only one chance to hatch and rear their fledglings. Those in the south, in contrast, with the luxury of longer summers, were able to lay several clutches of eggs and improve their species' survival prospects. I could see how the breeding success of Tundra swans, which were reputedly vulnerable to human disturbances, could become the casualty of too little time to procreate and too much energy diverted to escape.

Occasionally, instead of pairs, we saw just a single swan, most likely the male defending the nest while the female incubated the eggs or tended to the cygnets. These solo swans also might have been the lone survivors of a migratory mishap, maybe a collision with a power line or wind turbine. Suffice it to say, the sight of a solo swan reminded me of Marsha and added to my guilt about leaving her in Minnesota. Splendid male swan, protecting the nearby nest; shabby human husband, nowhere in sight.

With neither tailwinds to aid us nor headwinds to oppose us, we paddled into Edehon, a lake of some twenty miles in length. The lake's becalmed waters, cloaked in a deceptive skin of sun-infused warmth, suppressed our worries about becoming windblown. Yet, it was hard for me not to notice the resemblance of Edehon's shape to a similar segment of the Upper Mississippi River near my home known as Lake Pepin, a lake originally named *Lac Des Pleus* or "Lake of Tears." The tears alluded to the Indians who, on the shoreline, wept over the loss of their chief's son but also to the lake's unpredictable winds, which had an amply earned reputation for capsizing boats and drowning their occupants.

Upon entering Edehon Lake, we intersected a raft of large black ducks and incited them to flight. Yellow-billed and black-feathered, they flew closely over the water, repeatedly rocketing around us in tight but unruly formations, like dozens of children playing tag. Their ring-around-the-rosie flights and large sloping bills inclined us to refer to them as "those goofy ducks." We did not wish to rile them, but they were most excitable and seemingly curious, too. I suggested to Mel that we and the ducks may have had something in common.

"Yeah?"

"Sure. Maybe eons ago we shared an evolutionary path with them, and they're now sensing some kind of kindred relationship with us."

"And these merry-go-round flight patterns, Guy?"

"They're probably just happy to see us. You know, kind of like a long-delayed family reunion." But not likely, as the ducks quickly tired of orbiting around us and then flew straight away.

As the ducks left, fluffy cumulous clouds started to creep up behind us. My forward paddle stroke fanned an arc of water droplets that sparkled and bounced over the water's surface tension like tiny skipping stones before melding back to their source. The lake, so perfectly calm, became a mirror, and our canoes, two little drips slowly running down its polished surface.

The mirror reflected a perfect inverted image of sky and clouds above, creased only by the subtle wakes of our canoes and the dimples of our paddles. This vertiginous double image of both sky above and reflected sky below was disorienting, as though we were not on the water itself, but drifting, floating, and sometimes even falling through the sky. The sensation was that our wingless craft might soon crash to the Earthly surfaces below, but no such surfaces appeared in sight.

When we started, the distant end of Edehon lay hidden beyond the lake's horizon. Now, nearer to the middle, neither shore of origin nor shore of destination could be seen. It was just our two canoes, the plane of the blue lake below, and the bowl of blue sky above.

I looked at Ruth and Tom to our left and watched them glide over the curve of the Earth, their paddles flashing in the sun. They alternated sides, port, then starboard, after every ten strokes. Ruth dutifully counted but admitted to occasionally losing track of the ten-count cue that would prompt her and Tom to change sides. Mel and I, in contrast, paddled on one side until our arms wearied, probably forty strokes or more, but it was never a matter of counting. For us, the traditional shout of "hut" signaled the shift to give one set muscles a rest and employ the other.

The clouds, once joyfully white and far behind us, rose up in a towering line of darkening anvils that outpaced the speed of our now frenzied strokes. In an instant, the mirror on which we paddled broke into millions of pieces. We sprinted for the nearest shore, but slanting sheets of rain were hard upon us before we could beach the canoes and scramble for our raingear. The thunderstorm blew by in less than an hour, but it left the weather foul and chilly. We returned to our canoes and steered them into choppy waters skirted by ice floes piled up on the distant, windward side of the lake.

Mid lake, on the south-facing shore, a gentle slope of land held two recently erected pyramidal structures, each made of four wooden poles lashed together at their apexes. The curiosity of this scene enticed us to investigate. Could they have been the frames of small human shelters? We didn't know. Mel thought they were more likely the frames of smokehouses for drying fish. We also found food-packaging litter nearby, a Frisbee, and a rectangular hole dug into the frosty peat, which probably served as a natural refrigerator for the catch.

Two miles from the end of the lake, we rounded another point, this time into an ambush of northeast headwinds. The world turned metallic: pewter skies, gusts of wind that cut like blades, and waters steely dark and cold as iron. We battled the waves with our paddles, but it was nearly a draw. Eventually we inched our way forward, finally reaching the protective shores of the river's narrowing channel and a well-earned reprieve from the wind. Had we started crossing this lake the way we finished it, Edehon might have been our own Lake of Tears.

Downriver, a campsite-sized island caught our attention, but a congregation of terns had already colonized it and went about screeching their objections to our arrival. Between the racket from the agitated terns and gulls and the guano that peppered the island, we agreed that this was no place for human habitation.

This little island was our first introduction to Arctic terns and, as we got closer to the ocean, their presence would become more common. These graceful swallow-tailed birds were smartly styled with black caps, bright orange beaks, and pearly white bodies. In flight, they glided effortlessly on the winds while occasionally stopping to hover like humming birds in slow motion. It was clear that they preferred life on the wing. The only time we saw them touch the water was when they swooped down to pluck up a minnow, and the only time they perched on land was to tend to their nests.

With an exceptional wingspan-to-body length ratio, the Arctic tern's airplane analog would be the Cold War's U2 spy plane, an aircraft of similar proportionality and extraordinary flight range. Arctic terns, in fact, migrated between the ice shelves of Antarctica and the Arctic, an annual round trip distance of about 25,000 miles, roughly the circumference of the Earth.[2] Just before the start of their semiannual planetary flights, the normally noisy terns, in the manner of an invocation before a great event, briefly engaged in moment a silence or "dread."[3] Then they would be off to the opposite end of the Earth. Living in excess of thirty years, they could log nearly a million miles of flight, enough to earn them, were they human frequent flyers, dozens of first-class upgrades.

These migratory patterns allowed terns to stay in a perpetual succession of summers and nearly continuous sunlight. What better way, I thought, to avoid the effects of SAD, the Seasonal Affective Disorder caused by winter's bleak days. Among humans, SAD was known to trigger symptoms of binge eating, lethargy, reduced libido, social withdrawal, upticks in episodes of cardiac arrhythmia, and general cabin fever. The arctic tern's migratory modus operandi, as such, was the perfect antidote for maintaining a "sunny" outlook, and, indeed, this appeared to be true, as the terns' behavioral attributes included high levels of sociability, bravery, and community service.

Terns not only guarded their own nests, they zealously guarded the nearby nests of other birds. At various points along the river, we became the inadvertent objects of the terns' fearless scorn. They would dive at us and any other intruders until we got out of their space. This fearless vigilantism made them worthy of the rookery's good neighbor award and attracted other birds to nest in the same vicinity.

We left the terns and gulls in peace and escaped to a nearby island, one of larger size and less avian congestion but moated with dense thickets of flooded dwarf birch and willow. We plowed our canoes through the thick tangles, disembarked to shoulder our packs, and then—after a little bushwhacking—emerged onto a modest ridge of open tundra that would serve as our campsite. On the mainland, across the channel, an expansive, boulder-cluttered slope gently rose up from the river's edge.

For us flatlanders from the Midwest, where the black loam of plowed prairies prevailed, the Barren Lands' bouldery geology was a fascinating study. In the distance, the weathered and lichen-covered rocks and boulders strewn about the hillsides faded into vignettes of grays and muted pinks. Individually, they displayed all manner of shapes and sizes, from grains of sand to bread loaves to some as large as Buicks and boxcars. Piled up and polished clean along the river's banks, their distinctive colors and identities became revealed—granite, basalt, quartz, and others I could hardly guess. The slope across the channel from our island campsite displayed the full gamut of this geological diversity—a veritable junkyard of glacial deposits.

To help our cooks, I grabbed the collapsible water bucket and sought a place along the shallow shoreline to fill it and then finally chanced upon a mossy, cobblestoned beach suitable for the task. To return to our mid-island campsite, I had to scramble up the six-foot bank that I had just slid down and still keep the water in the bucket. I was partially successful.

The entirety of this eroded bank was comprised of rusty brown swaths of exposed peat. It was oozing off the edge of the island, in sloping layered mounds, mounds that looked like Paul Bunyan-sized dollops of a coarsely textured ice cream, maybe flavor Number 34, "Partially Decayed Vegetation." Farther downstream, we saw more of these peaty banks laid bare by the river's erosive currents.

These exposed cross-sections revealed the tundra's upper stratum of soil, the so-called "active layer," which, at an imperceptibly, glacial pace, was moving with a fluidic character, not unlike the river itself. Summers' meltwaters lubricated these active layers, causing them to slip down the slopes and "flow" like slow-motion rivers across their rock-hard permafrost substrates. P. G. Downes, the early twentieth century Barren Lands trekker, observed that everything migrates in the tundra—the fish, the caribou, the birds, even the soil.

These active layers of the tundra held virtually no mineral content, neither sand nor silt nor clay, only a few inches of seasonally thawed peat. Due to short, cool summers, they failed to decompose while the "deep freeze" of nearly constant winter preserved them year after year. Locked in the permafrost below, plant remnants thousands of years old bided their time. The tundra's ageless accumulation of peat made it one of the Earth's major carbon dioxide sinks, a mega bank for greenhouse gases. In the land of the midnight sun, summers' photosynthetic marathons had made uncountable carbon dioxide deposits but withdrawals during the rest of the year were literally frozen to a standstill.

The Earth's increase in heat-trapping emissions, however, portended the collapse and ultimately the reversal of this process. Global warming was beginning to thaw some of the permafrost each year. Once out of the permafrost freezer, the vegetative material decomposed, releasing carbon dioxide and methane—greenhouse gases—back into the atmosphere. With this feedback syndrome of causes and effects set in motion, the tundra could soon change from carbon sink to carbon source.

Might these withdrawals trigger a run on the tundra bank, a sort of ecological panic, taking the planet from simmering to scalding? Indeed, the match of irreversibility in this process may have already been lit.[4] I did not know whether the thawing of these continental peat lands would entail the final forfeiture of the French Quarter of New Orleans to the Gulf of Mexico's rising waters or the march of badlands into the continent's prairie heartland, but if the charring of northern forests and the melting of polar ice caps were any indications, our mother Earth could soon bear far less resemblance to her current self.[5]

After supper, I asked Mel to join me in exploring the boulder junkyard across the river, but he did not share my enthusiasm. Mel was right; we probably had engaged in enough exercise for one day. Instead, we took an easy stroll along the island's perimeter and, from the brushy edges, flushed a couple of ptarmigans into reluctant flight along the way.

When I headed back to the tent, a small bird fluttered in front of my nose. Though I was hundreds of times its size, this tiny gray-feathered creature startled me. I looked down and saw that the crush of my boot had landed only an inch away from her trio of thimble-sized eggs, all of which lay in a nest no larger than a teacup. To protect her progeny, this diminutive mother had put her faith in nothing more than a bed of frozen tundra and, as her cover, an arctic meadow abloom with Labrador tea, ankle high and speckled white.

Chapter 10
The Mists of Time

The river's current returned and brought us to a long run of rapids that fanned out into a sweeping rightward curve. The backwater pockets in these tumbling cataracts enticed us to cast our jigs, but we had too few arms to manage both fishing rods and the paddles needed to hold our anchorless canoes in place. Fishing from shore would be easier and bivouacking on the bench of land above, an added convenience.

The bank's faded pink and dusty orange boulders served as both stair steps and obstacles as we unloaded our canoes and climbed to our campsite. Atop the bench, we discovered that our selected campsite had been chosen many times before us. In real estate, it is location, location, location, and from time immemorial, good campsites have always been good campsites.

Scattered about were the impersihable leavings of those who long ago took their rest and made their livelihoods here. These included piles of white quartz chips and ancient-looking sun-bleached tamarack poles, probably the remnants of shelter frames or fish-drying pyramids. We did not move these nor did we scavenge the piles of quartz chips that may have held the temptations of arrowheads and tool blades. One piece near the surface, in fact, looked like a scraper tool. We derisively joked about the trekkers whose apparent motto is "take all the artifacts and leave only footprints.

he Big River had guided us through a great library of places. We were merely among some of the most recent patrons to visit and to borrow. Lacking the hutzpah of Christopher Columbus, we could not claim these remote places of ongoing occupancy as our own discoveries. Our tents were pitched among rings of stone, some of them sunken and covered with lichens, others clean and high and thus more recently placed. We also stumbled across artifacts of more recent vintage. Yesterday it was the Frisbee on Lake Edehon. Farther downstream, we found discarded oil drums, snarls of wire, even a pair of women's panties! In aggregate, these findings were scattered about like the discarded remnants of ruptured time capsules, and each remnant had a story and a history that we could only imagine, because, save for these random excerpts, the pages were missing.

Mel and I worked the shoreline with spoons and jigs to catch the now elusive lake trout, but our only success was the exercise of our casting arms. Mel gave up, changed tactics, and started fishing for grayling. I stayed with the lake trout agenda and got skunked, but Mel quickly caught ten grayling and kept five for supper. Back at camp, courteous conduct compelled me to acknowledge Mel's fishing prowess and compliment his fish chowder, which was gourmet fare whether on or off the trail.

After supper, incessant waves of rain began to wash over our camp and prompt Tom, Ruth, and Mel to seek refuge in their tents. Everything was dripping wet and, on the outside, so was I, but inside my bug-proof rain gear, I was still dry and comfortable. Despite the slight chill and the cloud darkened skies, enough of the summer's lingering light shone through to persuade me to forego sleep and wander about the tundra extending beyond our camp.

With no prominent views to command my attention, I contented myself with the more intimate scenes around my feet. Pathways of wind-rippled sand and gravel alternated with ground-hugging plants: mats of prostrate rhododendrons and willows, silvery gray mounds of caribou moss, tufted cotton grass, and evergreen heaths ornamented with tiny burgundy berries. I wondered whether landscape architects could achieve effects as agreeable as these. Occasional deposits of rocks and boulders accented the scene. Austere and precise, their abstract composition reminded me of a Japanese Zen garden worthy of soulful meditation. Indeed, my footprints through these swaths of sand stood out like the discordant marks of an irreverent act.

Sodden clouds continue to roll across the tundra and drench the land. I turned my head away from the pelting rain and walked back to camp. On the way, I stopped by the ancient tent poles and the piles of quartz chips that we had seen earlier in the day. Archaeologists might sift through these and decipher some meaning, but the real stories—those of the families who, centuries ago, stayed here, the stories of their joys and sorrows, their tears and laughter—would never truly be unearthed. If they were to be known, it would have to be from the pages of one's imagination. Farther downstream, a gloomy tongue of boulders as big as an Iowa farm field protruded into the river.

Abruptly, the windblown patter ceased and was followed by a hush of stillness. I lifted my eyes and saw that the rain had thinned to a drizzle that was nearly dry and that shafts of wild rose had begun to slip through the clouds and make the river blush. Free of their gloom, the boulders glistened in the delicate light. Then I smiled at the question I asked myself: Was I not standing in the mists of time?

Later that night, the rain took the redeye special, straight out of camp, and left us with a bright and bracing morning full of dewdrops. They clung to everything, reflecting tiny images of the whole world about them while soaking my pant legs to the skin. Down by the river, black, coin-sized spiders, munching on a cornucopia of web-snared bugs, danced the eight-leg quickstep over sun-warmed rocks while a river of shimmering sequins awaited us.

It was a day of easy rapids and fishing played before a growing audience of seals. I spotted the first seal in the morning. Far from our canoes, it looked like a black bear. Fifty paddle strokes closer, the black bear silhouette affirmed its real identity—a ranger seal basking on a bolder. It then slid into the water and disappeared.

Downriver, a large island divided the river. We chose the narrower channel, which provided a delightful mile-long run as well as some grayling fishing along the way. At one stop, I charged ahead, reeled in a half-dozen fish, and then, feigning a bit of gentlemanly conduct, yielded this fished-out position to Mel. The channel then emptied into a small lake where we came upon another seal. The seal, seeking assurance of our departure, bobbed its head behind us several times before we finally parted company.

Eventually, faster currents and sandy channels defined our course. We shot through a narrow chute crowded by willow scrub and pools stacked with fish. Pulled too quickly by the current to stop, we left the fish alone in their underwater world.

Whether serene and becalmed or roiled by the winds and rapids, the water's surface was never out of sight, always on our minds, and in some ways quite mysterious. Ubiquitous and tangible, our paddles sliced through it thousands of times, but it also functioned as a nearly impenetrable membrane, magically dividing things aquatic from things terrestrial. From my primitive-man-in-the-canoe perspective, it wasn't the precise taxonomy of kingdom–phylum–class–order–family–genus–species–variety that made scientific sense. In the boldly delineated tundra, it was the starkly divided "kingdoms" of water, land, and sky that ordered my worldview and it was this thin curtain, the "surface," that separated them.

The classification scheme, of course, had no place in modern science, but it seemed to fit my present experience. The siksik, the Arctic's version of an oversized striped gopher (without the stripes) knew its terrestrial place, and so did the fish, which is to say, in the water. Even the migrating arctic char behaved. Unlike their more acrobatic salmonoid brethren from the south, arctic char did not jump into the air. This aversion not only kept them in the water, it prevented them from ascending cataracts, not to mention the weirs built by native peoples intent on trapping and spearing them.

Granted, my conceptual construct suffered from defects in logic. Some arctic animals migrated between these "kingdoms." Those pesky black flies, born in water and menacing us in the air, for example, came to mind. Clearly, these miscreants did not know their place. Others, like the common loon, were adept in two or more realms but endured compromises in function. The loon's solid bones, heavier body, and shorter wingspans enabled it to swim underwater and catch fish, but on land, it was a clumsy creature.

The traditional Inuit also sensed this boundary between the terrestrial and aquatic. Inuit taboos focused on keeping objects from the sea and objects from the land separate. Some bands forbade the cooking of caribou meat, a product of the land, on the sea ice. Similarly, caribou skin clothing couldn't be made or mended on the sea ice even though they would be worn there. I wasn't interested in reviving any ideological irrationalities, but I empathized with the universality of this orientation—the prominence of boundary between land and waters—that living in the Arctic seemed to foster.

I was also fascinated with the depths below the water's surface, which, in part, stemmed from a bit of squeamishness. Even in clean waters, like those of the Thlewiaza's, the depths could not be fully seen, and it was the unseen that sometimes beset me with mild cases of the heebie-jeebies. Just as Inuit folklore focused on the underwater world, namely the legend of Sedna who lived at the bottom of the sea, I, too, was intrigued with this realm.

The story of Sedna was about a young woman who was spurned by a fraudulent lover and then horrifically betrayed by her father even though he had come to save her. The lover turned out to be a raven, and when the raven's flapping wings caused a storm, the father, fearing that his kayak would sink, threw Sedna into the icy sea. When Sedna futilely tried to pull herself back into the kayak, the father chopped off her fingers. Sedna sank to the bottom where her spirit now resided and her chopped-off fingers, according to legend, became the seals, walruses, whales, and fishes that nourished the Inuit. Depending on her mood, she or her dwarf companion, Unga, held the power to withhold or release these sea creatures and thus determine the fate of the Inuit. Clearly, one must not incur Sedna's wrath!

Somewhere near the bottom of the Thlewiaza's deepest pools, I knew that Unga, or one of Unga's cousins must have been waiting for me, to turn me into a seal or a duck. Maybe even into a black fly!

Always in flux, the Thlewiaza's wind-ruffled surface and reflections tended to occlude the depths. However, when the wind softened and the sun was backside, the textures and reflections of the surface vanished, and the surface became a window. In today's calm, the river flowed with windows, and we knew the river's mood not only by the complexion of its surface but by the composition of its depths. In swift waters, the river's rocks, stripped clean by the current, flashed their colors. In the deeper pools, like the ones we had just passed, slippery and silty mosses carpeted the bottoms. Beneath the midday sun, flickerings of tiger-eyes and addled shafts of amber enlivened these tea-colored underworlds.

We emerged from this funnel of slick water pools onto an expanse of sand flats through which the river struggled to find a channel. The river, now transformed into a shallow moving lake, slipped over shoals of rippled, sun-glimmered sand. In the distance, a large dune rose up to contain the end of the lake. Plowed up and dumped there by springs' debacles, the top of this sandy escarpment held the possibility of a campsite.

We put ashore on a beach as smooth and nearly as level as a billiard table and then ascended the ridge. Sharply peaked like a gable roof, the dune abruptly fell away to a bug-infested bog on the backside, which was crowded with thickets of willow, stunted tamarack, and sad little spruce trees. Camping here merited little consideration, but it was a curious place.

A few paces later, Mel found a four-inch-thick slab of slate stuck in the ground like a tombstone. The slab stood roughly three feet high, a foot wide, and bore the engraved inscription, "Here Lies Wilderness MMI." Other than MMI probably referring to the year 2001, we didn't know what the rest of message meant or how the stone got there, but it made me think that Mel and Moses might have had something in common. Had Mel found a heaven-sent, fifth stone tablet, a sequel to the unbroken pair that Moses kept after breaking the first two? Despite the innumerable shortcomings of his companions, Mel chose not to smash the tablet in anger. He left it intact where he found it.

While Mel and Tom marched back to the canoes to retrieve cameras to photograph the enigmatic unilogue, I stayed below, leaned back on the packs, and caught a catnap—one of my exceptional skills. In a few minutes, I awoke and then walked about, examining the gold-speckled rocks dotting the shore.

When Mel returned, he saw no treasure in my geological finds. The golden flecks? Just worthless bits of mica, according to Mel. But why not a little whimsy, like the young geologist on our flight home who humored me and said that I should have packed out some of these rocks. The abandonment of my prospecting finds might have been one more missed opportunity in life, but gold or no gold, I would not have been keen about burdening my pack with rocks or repeating Martin Frobisher's embarrassment of transporting fool's gold over long distances.

On the river's opposite side, a boulder as tall as a house appeared. It looked like a gigantic fossilized buffalo standing alone on the open tundra. Tom scaled the colossal bison. I took a picture of him riding it, one hand grasping the creature's hump, the other waving above his head in rodeo fashion, and the giant stone beast going nowhere.

After paddling through another small lake, we spotted a hilltop campsite, which overlooked the lake and its outlet to the river. Football-sized rocks dotted the finely textured mats of evergreen bearberry that clung to the hill. Once again, scattered, weathered wooden poles verified that we were only the most recent visitors at this site. The silvery white wood made a pleasant contrast with the bearberry's carpet of deep and glossy green.

After a bath in the river, a civilized round of cocktails, and supper in the tundra tarp, we watched the sun slowly sink. It coppered the tundra and lacquered the river in gold, but there was emptiness in this panorama. The scene spread out in the manner of Africa's Serengeti at sunset, but where was the wildlife? Birds and waterfowl had been frequent companions, but we lamented the rarity of other animals, especially the caribou. If they had any decency, they would make an appearance, right? After all, we had paid the price of time and effort to get into this remote theater. Just when would the caribou show begin?

We, of course, had no reason to complain. We were only acting out our roles as impatient tourists, unappreciative of the fact that the Arctic's animal populations are concentrated in large numbers but in widely scattered locations. This just wasn't one of those times or places.

As dusk approached and our grumbling continued, a couple of ranger seals popped into view. Not caribou, but still decent consolation prizes, especially for oceanless Midwesterners like us. The seals bobbed their heads, promenaded their way downstream in the river, and then disappeared around the bend.

Chapter 11
The Last of the Little Sticks

The cheery alpine scenes were gone. The river widened and the terrain flattened. Cloud-filled easterly winds grayed the tundra and dampened the air with scents of ripening muskeg and imminent rain. The river, in some respects, had become routine: flat-water intervals punctuated by rapids, one sequence following another. I caught a few grayling and a couple of lake trout, but my enthusiasm for angling, like the diversity of the landscape, was diminishing.

To sidestep a stretch of nasty rapids, we hauled our canoes across a ledge and stopped for a break. Preferring to move and stretch rather than sit, I walked onto a prominent spit of granite and thereupon repeatedly cast my jig into the downstream waters. Out and back, out and back—I played my jig-tipped line like a yo-yo—movements of habit more so than purposeful endeavor.

The outcropping beneath my feet stood with granite resolve. It was, after all, literally granite. Impressively, it convulsed the river's currents and threw it into fits of turbulent madness, but the worn-down spine of this ancient, igneous stone foretold its fate. It had stood here as testament to the earth's creation, since the beginning of time, but there would be a day when the river would eventually take the last trace of it. In the duel to define eternity, the river would win.

Then a pesky lake trout took my line. I reeled it in, but with only an undersized set of forceps for the task I struggled to remove the hook. Mel, like a gunslinger, reached for the needle-nosed pliers holstered on his belt and relieved me of my frustration. He clamped down on the hook with the pliers, gave them a twist, and quickly released the fish, which eagerly splashed back into the river.

Fishing made sense as a release from something else. Without the "something else," it was like a plunge in a bracing lake or a naked roll in the snow without the heat of the sauna beforehand—an invigorating but unwelcome experience. Apart from the other, neither black nor white had meaning. My interest in fishing was beginning to gray.

I recalled a fellow who cashed out his company and then built a cabin next to a small pond stocked with fish. I was told that he was as content as a duck in water and probably had caught every fish in his pond three or four times over. He probably even knew some of those fish by name. Whatever lay ahead for me, I hoped that it would not be this kind of ducky contentment.

The day progressed, and the dull, gray world turned darker, giving the river an industrial feel. Jammed with Class I and II rapids, the Thlewiaza bore a vicarious similarity to New Jersey's Interstate 95 during rush hour, clogged not with cars but stacked with one standing wave after another. Meanwhile, stiff headwinds swept up the river and, despite the swift currents, opposed our forward motion. Bouldery escarpments, to a height of fifty feet or more, formed the river's banks and funneled its flow in the manner of an Army Corps of Engineers' channelization project. I wondered whether the Corps' engineers might concede that the riprapping laid up here by Mother Nature might be as good as their own design.

Somewhere along the way, Mel, in the bow with his back to me in the stern and without the benefit of visual observation, accused me of "lily dipping," which is to say that I wasn't putting much force into the pull part of my dip-pull-lift rhythm and thus letting him do the heavy paddling work. Perhaps I was uninspired by some of the zig-zag courses he was selecting for us, but I was no lily dipper! No sir. Then, to needlessly prove the point, I returned his grumpy attitude in kind by taking two paddle strokes for every one of his. This response prompted him to ask me if I were crazy. No, I said to myself, just an occasionally childish man in need of confession.

Thankfully, it was time to call it a day, but the steepness of these escarpments and the swiftness of the currents prevented us from stopping. The unseen campsites above, if any, held uncertain promise. Even if we could find a way to disembark from our canoes, daunting climbs over tall boulder-lined banks awaited us. Indeed, we felt as though we might be stuck on the river indefinitely, swept downstream like tiny twigs in a rain-filled gutter.

Finally, we arrived at a welcoming skirt of sand. Rather than holding out for better options downstream, we took this bird-in-the-hand location and decided to make camp on top of the tall sandy bank. With packs strapped to our torsos, we marked our trail up the incline with deep divots from our footfalls and then floured our wet boots with grit along the way.

Just as we reached the top, the skies broke down and began to weep uncontrollably. We donned raingear, hurriedly pitched our tents, and then stood about in a state of soggy idleness. Rain poured off the visors of our rain-jacket hoods like sheets of water falling from the edge of an un-guttered roof. The entertainment value of these personal waterfalls was minimal and short-lived. After a period of aimless loitering, Tom and I left the campsite and walked toward the river. The downpour passed and the lighter rain that followed restored some visibility to the scene. As we stood at the edge of one high bank and scanned the opposite shore, I remarked that the distant ripraped bank looked like a classic civil engineering project.

"Tom," I asked, "Do you what the mission statement of the U.S. Army Corps of Engineers is?"

"Don't know, Guy"

"Straighten it, widen it, drain it, dredge it, pave it, lock it, dam it."

Tom smiled.

Then Tom and I embraced an engineering mindset and tried to estimate the Thlewiaza's water flow in gallons per minute. Conceptually it was straightforward: Velocity multiplied by the cross-sectional area equaled volumetric flow, which could be converted into gallons per minute. Following this approach, we estimated the river's width-by-depth cross-sectional area and then multiplied that product by our estimate of the current's speed. However, sans calculator, I got bogged down somewhere between converting miles per hour to feet per minute and cubic feet into gallons.

Tom came to my rescue: "Guy, I don't care how you calculate it; it's a shitload of water."

Later, back in the States and with calculator in hand and data from Environment Canada, I arrived at a more precise answer: 80,000 gallons of water per second, and this was only the water flowing at the outlet of Seal Hole Lake. It excluded the Thlewiaza's numerous tributaries from the watershed downstream from Seal Hole Lake. This disgorgement, roughly seven billion gallons a day, was more than enough water to meet the daily needs of the entire Phoenix metropolitan population if it could somehow be piped there.

Our perambulations eventually led us in different exploratory directions, the Moores around the campsite, Mel in an upstream direction, and I, with fishing rod in hand, downstream along the riverbank. I felt restless and needed the physical activity to which I had become accustomed. Maybe, I thought, if I hooked a monster lake trout, I could recharge my enthusiasm for fishing or anything for that matter. This was an amazing trip, but oddly it was beginning to feel a bit routine.

The top of the bank gave me an eagle eye's view of the shoreline below. Wherever I saw a "fishy" looking spot, I scrambled down the boulders, planted myself for a few casts, and then crawled back to the top for easier walking. In repeated descents and ascents, I must have climbed a mountain's worth of vertical elevation. Occasionally, the weather broke, which increased the presence of bugs and prompted the grayling to surface, but I took a pass on these fair-weather fish. The objects of my desire, the lake trout, on the other hand, snubbed me and all my lures, nor, for that matter, did I see any lake trout, despite my eagle-eye view.

Accepting the fact that I wouldn't be partaking in any lake trout versions of the *Old Man and the Sea*, I took a two-mile beeline back to camp across the rain-soaked tundra. By the time I returned, I was wet around the edges but mostly dry and toasty inside my rain gear and also tired. I plopped down, used a boulder for a backrest, listened to my breathing, and then, in a few seconds, fell asleep. When I stirred, harmless sprinkles had turned into a miserably cold rain.

Each of us dug through our packs to find every possible wrap of clothing. The temperature, according to Mel's thermometer, had fallen to 48 degrees Fahrenheit while the wind and rain made it feel colder. After supper, we burrowed into the warmth of our sleeping bags.

As my shivering slowed, my thoughts drifted beyond the walls of the tent and beyond the end of the trip. The river knew where it was going, but I didn't. I knew where I had been and where I was now, but my dream tonight would not help. It would confirm only the known. Like fortune cookies that disappoint with platitudinous proverbs and no real predictions, my dream tonight would not foretell my future.

Owing to our minimalist camping mode, which included the thinnest of commercially available sleeping pads, my sleep entailed a rotisserie quality. Throughout the night, I would relieve the weighted side of my torso by rotating and then pressing the other side into duty. Then the cycle would be repeated. I felt a kinship with those endlessly turning hot dogs at the corner mini-grocery store. For better or for worse, the partial wakefulness caused by these twists and turns—this hovering between consciousness and unconsciousness—yielded an abundance of dreams.

Most were just the silly stuff of dreams. I dismissed them, rolled over, and went back to sleep, but on this rainy night, things were different. My dream took me on a business trip to check on a branch office. I drove down streets lined with odd buildings and stopped to enter one, but instead of an industrial warehouse, I found a retail strip mall that fronted a labyrinth of dead-end hallways. Instead of a functional business décor, oddly ornate wooden moldings hung in the hallways, almost like stalactites in a cave.

In this dream, my search extended into the evening. Then my father appeared. Together, we burst through a door into a bright, gymnasium-sized room. This was our business's branch operation, but, in my dream, it had been converted into a nightclub with flashing disco lights, thumping music, and dancers seeking a good time. I stood speechless before the spectacle. Our branch manager, who appeared to be in charge of the shenanigans, approached me. He stood in a pitted-out white shirt. Breathing heavily and with more than a touch of indignity, he explained that what he did on his personal time after hours with the business property should be of no concern to us.

Dad pulled me aside. "This is crazy," he said. "You have to clean house. Fire them. Fire them. Give them their walking papers."

"Dad, we don't own the business anymore. You don't own it. I don't own it. Someone else owns it now. We can't make personnel decisions. We can't go back." When I woke up, I wasn't sure whether I was the father or the son in this dream or somehow both. I rolled over but stayed awake.

The next day we hibernated in our sleeping bags well into the morning. By midday the rain had stopped and we were back on the river, whose rapids heaved our canoes up and down like rocking horses. Finally, the clouds frayed and seams of sun crept through, but the winds persisted and spit the canoe's bow spray into our faces, especially Mel who sat forward and shivered from the effect.

By mid-afternoon, the last of the littlest sticks were gone. We were truly in the open, treeless tundra, the real Arctic. The environment was distilled down to a trinity of land, sky, and water. We started our trip above the tree line at Seal Hole Lake but then had dropped down along its indistinct edge when we paddled through the Land of the Little Sticks. Now, even the little sticks were gone.

At the mouth of a minor tributary, several small northern pike took our spoon-shaped fishing lures for spirited runs, but we declined their sacrifices. We released them to grow larger for someone else's lunch. A few miles later, we beached our canoes on a crescent of sand and eyed the adjoining swayback hill for tent sites. As we landed, a startled ptarmigan retreated into the invisibility of the brush, sparse though it was. A few steps later, our saddle-top campsite revealed that it was an isthmus that attractively divided the river on one side and a lake on the other.

After supper, Tom trained his camera on the big solar flare and giver of life. It ignited the skies and ravished the river with fiery reflections. With plenty of light left in this land of slow-motion sunsets, Tom and I walked toward the bowl of land that held the lake on the other side of the isthmus. The lake's placid waters, sitting at an appealingly higher elevation above the river, were dimpled everywhere by rising fish. The scene inspired me to muse about the possibilities of building a vacation cabin here and the absurdities of weekend commuting to the Thlewiaza.

Soon, we discovered that we were not the only mammals fond of this place. A large, gray wolf escaped from the willow thickets, no more than a hundred feet ahead of us. Looking askance, it loped over the open tundra and vanished in the twilight.

The next morning rewarded us with dividends of heavy dew, clear skies, and warming breezes. We broke camp early and paddled around a bend into a river channel that transformed itself into a shallow, slowly flowing lake peppered with islands and crowded with shorebirds. Eventually, the wide-running Thlewiaza became an even wider and deeper formality in the name of Ranger Seal Lake.

In accordance with its namesake, an entourage of ranger seals greeted us at the start of the lake. Thereafter, we followed an undulating margin of sandy shoreline where our presence panicked a gaggle of molting Canada geese. Unlike their urbanized brethren who challenge human access to parks and golf courses and pester humans for handouts, these arctic geese fled as though we were fire-breathing dragons.

We beached the canoes on a crescent of silken sand and walked around to un-kink our legs. Our boots made coarse imprints among the delicate etchings of shore birds and the paddings of arctic hare. To confirm our whereabouts, a curious siksik (arctic ground squirrel) popped its head up from peepholes along the turf-capped bank.

Soon, we said so long to the periscoping siksik and so long to the miles, too, as they passed quickly, allowing us to select a campsite early in the day. We chose a prominent high-centered polygon at the head of an island. A charred fire pit indicated that others had recently camped here. The surrogate mattress of spongy peat beneath our tent floors was a bonus, but the breeze blew faintly and the bugs gathered. Wishing to avoid their intimacies, we quickly erected the tundra tarp.

Immediately, grayling splashed in the pools of the narrow channel on the back side of the island. Mel and I decided that putting our fishing rods to use would be preferable to sitting around and waving off the flies. I rambled downstream and fixed my eyes on rising fish. Then, from the corner of my eye, I glanced into a cavernous hole in the cutaway bank. When I beheld the size of this den, my pace quickened and my adrenalin flowed.

The next morning, we paddled this same channel. Sedimentary rocks, layered like pages in a book, lined the riverbanks, and angular, charcoal-colored boulders, the size of garden sheds, lay diagonally across the river. We had a fun run, dodging these obstacles and darting down the chutes like skiers through a slalom course. At the bottom of the drop, on the sunny, south-facing bank, the lair of the bear awaited us.

Mel wanted to stop and check it out, up close and personal, as they say. I dropped him off but kept my distance and positioned the canoe for a quick exit. This den might have belonged to a formerly hibernating and now long-gone Barren Land grizzly, but it also could have been the currently-occupied summer retreat of a Hudson Bay polar bear. During the summer, polar bears, seeking relief from the heat, were known to occasionally stray inland where they dug dens to the depth of the permafrost.

Whether occupied or unoccupied, this cave wasn't my house. Common courtesy, in my estimation, suggested that we should keep a respectable distance, but Mel, contrary to his cautionary proclivities, approached it like a moth to light. Mel stuck his head through the opening, crouched down, entered the den, and then vanished from sight.

"Mel," I yelled, "Knock, knock, who's bear?" But there was no answer. I yelled again, "Is anybody home?" Still no answer. Mel was lost in the cave's darkness and could neither hear nor be heard.

Apparently, the bear, whether polar or grizzly, wasn't home. Mel exited, returned to the canoe, and reported that the den was about six feet deep, two-and-a-half feet high, and three feet wide. It seemed larger to me when I had passed it earlier.

"Mel," I asked, "did it stink?"

"No, but I don't think that I'd like to spend the winter there."

Chapter 12

The Tuktu

Free of traffic, the 24-hour news cycle, and digital umbilical cords, I began to realize how much of a stranger I was to this arctic land. Whether flora, fauna, or inorganic rock, I knew little about their origins or life cycles. Canoeing the Thlewiaza was like showing up at a neighborhood block party and meeting people whose names and backgrounds I should have known but didn't. I regretted weaseling out of my college geology courses. "Rocks" weren't "relevant" back then. I fussed about forgetting to take a field guide to birds with me. The meteorological mysteries of the atmosphere, the chemistry of photosynthesis, entomology—all of these things and more—were mostly voids, so I tried to console myself. Even if I didn't know all the names or much about their backgrounds, the least I could do was to enjoy the show.

Our topographic maps showed only one esker left between us and Hudson Bay. Farther downstream, the river would flow through a long, flat plain to the mouth of the Thlewiaza. To say farewell to these curious creases in the landscape, we decided to beach the canoes, ascend this last ridge, and look for caribou. We found plenty of trails, but no caribou, only a lone ptarmigan and some curious rocks.

One of these curiosities, near a rise of land, was a weathered stone standing on end and chinked at the bottom. Ah, I thought, maybe another tablet, but it held no inscriptions. The upturned stone's more likely purpose was a marker for the nearby ring of rocks, which stood several courses high and rose from an inside diameter of about five feet at the base. We theorized that this partial dome, too small for a dwelling, might have been the ruins of a food cache or even a burial cairn. A second, semicircular structure, a few feet away, indicated the possibility of another food cache or hunting blind.

Except for their distinct arrangements, these lichen-covered rocks were indistinguishable from all the others that dotted the hillside. The lichens here, I learned, were neither fungus nor algae, but the working partnerships of both living together. Scaly, flaky, and pale green to silvery gray, they were content to take root on seemingly bare stone and nurse their existence from microscopic sips of mineral nutrients while persevering at this hardscrabble life for millennia. Apparently, a living creature didn't have to be the size of a redwood to be equally old. I didn't have to wield a chain saw to bring them down, either. The casual scrape of a boot was enough to rub out a thousand years of algae–fungus teamwork. With neither radiocarbon equipment on-hand nor a desire to pack out samples, we used our amateur lichenometry skills and hypothesized that these lichen-covered archeological finds might have dated back to the Thule culture or earlier.

A few steps later, I came across an obelisk-shaped piece of milky white quartz. Thinking that this distinctive angular stone deserved a more prominent display, I tipped it on its end so that it looked like a knee-high Washington Monument. Mel, who did not appreciate my handiwork, said something under his breath and put the quartz obelisk back on its side. Mel should relax, I thought, but he was right. My violation of the landscape, in this context, wasn't endearing. I shrugged my shoulders to plead no contest and then impressed the sun-drenched view into my memory. On the way back to the canoes, I led my cohorts on a fast-paced shortcut through some marshy meadows and succeeded in twisting my ankle on a muskeg tussock—possible punishment for my boorishness.

Back in our canoes, the river's lazy mood soothed our dispositions, but the Thlewiaza was a symphony of alternating movements. Adagio would soon be followed by allegro. True to form, the river abruptly thrust us into one of its frenzied movements.

The indeterminate length of the next rapids dissuaded us from scouting them, so we shot them straightaway, which suited me just fine. Mel, on the other hand, often demonstrated a split personality in these circumstances. Although deliberate and hesitant by nature, once Mel consented to forego a portage, he often favored downstream runs of tricky zigzags, like a downhill skier on a slalom course. Every whitewater that we didn't portage or line became an opportunity for Mel to exhibit his skill set and thus required me to rise to the occasion.

At the head of a rapid, a piece of driftwood, dropped into the water, would have provided some guidance by allowing us to observe its downstream path. If we took the left-hand entry to the rapids, for example, could we still avoid the monstrous wave midway down? A piece of driftwood dropped into this left-hand entry would tell us that. My idea was to find a starting point that would minimize the required turning movements and to go with the rapid's currents instead of fighting them. Skydivers, according to Tom, used a parachute dummy to gauge the wind conditions prior to jumping. Similarly, the log or branch that I sought but couldn't find in the treeless tundra would have served us as a canoe dummy.

With neither scouting nor canoe dummies to aid us, off we went, zigging and zagging this next set of rapids. Immediately, Mel chose to ferry the canoe across the current and expose our broadsides to large, menacing waves. Then, pivoting in another direction, we paddled toward an immense tongue of water thrusting through a notch in a prominent ledge. Just as this tongue was about to give us a good licking, Mel dug in his paddle and slid the canoe into the protective calm of a backwater pocket. At this point, nudging back into the main channel would have been like steering a bicycle off the shoulder into a freeway full of speeding cars.

Instead, we aimed for quieter waters to the right, but the canoe hung up and teetered on another ledge, which fell farther and more steeply away than we expected. I jumped out, heaved the canoe like a battering ram to free it, and then leapt back into the stern. The canoe and its occupants, at this instant, performed something like a synchronized swan dive followed by a brief submarine experience in the pool below. We left a polish of red from the canoe's underside on the ledge and took on some water, but after a little bailing and air-drying of our clothing, all was well. The canoe had a new scrape but was really none the worse for wear.

Tiring of these wide swifts, we exited into the respite of a smaller channel, a fun, two-mile run of friendlier rapids and boulder dodging. A massive outcropping of fissured bedrock marked the eventual confluence of our minor channel's return to the main river. Below the ledge, the waters of noisy cataracts sought their many levels, flowing into a maze of pools of different sizes, shapes, and depths.

We wedged our canoes into the craggy bank, climbed to the top, and claimed the grassy plain above for our tent sites. On the other side of the island, whitewater tumbled down the river, from bank to bank, nearly a half-mile across. The river looked like a lake tilted up at one end and draining out the other. The pools below our camp served as our personal, cold water bathtubs while the riffles between them yielded a half-dozen grayling to our casts.

That evening, we watched harmless rains spritz the tundra. Then, just after a leisurely supper, a sucker punch of blustery cold wind hit us and abruptly flattened the tundra tarp. In panic mode, we piled rocks on the collapsed tarp to prevent it from flying away and then saw that our sleeping tents were also violently flapping. Fearing that they, too, would lift off and bounce across the tundra like tumbleweeds, we lunged inside the tents to anchor them with our bodies and then braced our backs against the poles so they wouldn't buckle. Eventually, the winds tired as did we, and sleep, which we welcomed, crept into our tents.

My slumber was deep and dear, but necessity eventually confronted me with the camper's age-old question: to pee or not to pee. This time I knew that this question had only one correct answer. I would have to shed the exquisite comfort and warmth of my sleeping bag and enter the chilly night. I emerged through a succession of zippers and tent flaps, cracked my eyes open, and then, guided by the sounds of the rushing river, I quietly tiptoed a courteous distance away from the tent.

This was the exact and only moment that I saw the Arctic's stars, stars that pierced the sky with brilliance greater than I had ever seen. Because the Barren Lands' summer sun delays dusk until it nearly merges with dawn, I beheld this brief night scene with privilege and awe. The now departed rain had washed away every spec of airborne dust and the cold front had wrung out every molecule of haze. The clarity of the night was flawless. By their size, rivaling that of the waning moon, the stars appeared to be three-dimensional and so close as to risk colliding with the earth.

Indeed, for my extant purpose, this bright, bejeweled dome provided little privacy of darkness. I stood out, plain as day, replete with shadow cast by celestial glow. Meanwhile, on the other side of the river, a narrow slice of solar-energized neon clung to the horizon, creating a parfait of oranges and indigos. Whether remnant of twilight, precursor of dawn, or some of both, I did not know.

The cold, however, truncated my stargazing. With the deftness of a cat, I slipped back into my sleeping bag. I wondered if I had been dreaming or if this interlude of night had been an apparition, but it was real. Then my eyes shut and I was gone from the world.

The next morning, sinister clouds blocked the sun and bruised the sky. Sliding over some and lining the others, we picked our way down a stairway of ledges. The river organized itself into a hierarchy of primary and secondary channels, winding through a treeless landscape that was now nearly shrubless, too.

At lunch, a weasel darted around our packs and sniffed out the possibilities of filching something while a falcon flew overhead. Everybody, it seemed, wanted something to eat. In the afternoon, a quartet of wary seals consented to entertain us.

The bouldery character of the Thlewiaza's banks also returned. Standing abruptly above the water line, these steeply inclined banks looked like castle walls made of stacked boulders replete with crenellated parapets. Sometimes, when we clambered about them to fish or camp, we ended up playing a treacherous version of boulder pickup sticks. The object of the game was not to "pick up" boulders per se but to get up or down without setting them into motion or risking an avalanche. Loosely deposited by the forces of ice and water, the boulders on the bottom acted as fulcrums and those on top as unstable levers, which if stepped on, sometimes caused them to tip like multi-ton teeter-totters.

The mile-thick glaciers that had once covered this continent, of course, were gone, but the Thlewiaza's banks bore testimony to the continuing power of water and ice in the seasonal reshaping of this land. During spring break-up, wind and waves pushed thick ice slabs around like giant bulldozer blades. These slabs would then pile up and clog the river's narrows. When they eventually loosened, the clogs would burst downstream and scour the riverbed like enormous Roto-Rooters, shoving huge boulders about like Ping-Pong balls and pushing them up along the river's banks.

On our last night on the river, Mel imposed his worries about camping too close to the shores of Hudson Bay where polar bears reportedly prowled. The Moores and I wanted a site closer to the bay, which would position us for a more leisurely pace and less distance to cover the following morning, but Mel was implacable. Preferring accommodation to conflict, we appeased our cautious comrade by camping ten miles upstream from the bay. We all wanted to see polar bears; we just didn't want to become their entrées, served up in sleeping bag wraps.

In addition to our concerns about polar bear run-ins, our pickup on the Hudson Bay, at least for me, was beginning to feel like an increasingly iffy proposition. We were putting a lot of trust in this man from Arviat, a Mr. Joe Savikataaq, to be at a precise time and place in the northern end of North America. A cloud of mild tension loomed over our team.

Our island campsite split the river like the bow of a ship. Wakes of current, peeling off the island's port and starboard sides, polished the bouldery broadsides with pearly sheens of salmon pink while the island's grassy deck above matched the surrounding landscape's horizontal plane. Were it not for the large glacial erratics deposited here and there, this land would have appeared as a perfectly flat, uninterrupted sea of tundra. The scattered placement of these boulders, some of them very large, suggested the aftermath of an inebriated Stonehenge-like gathering whose drunks, while wandering home, had passed out at random locations along the way.

We pitched our tents and then sat back to watch storm cells stampede across the tundra in a sky that otherwise remained cerulean blue. Each isolated cell lofted its own crown of bulging white cumulus, followed by a shadow of rain and a rainbow tail that trailed to the ground. Like seeds of weather systems thrust into the wind, they flew southward in a fury, seemingly intent on growing into disturbances of continental magnitude.

Tom suggested that we take pictures of Mel's collection of bear weapons: shotgun, ammunition, knife, and pepper spray. We laid them out all neat and tidy on the ground. The scene, brightly lit by the sun and framed by my camera lens, looked like an FBI evidentiary display of confiscated gangsters' weapons. I snapped a few pictures and then, sensing the creative presence of Tom's mind at work, I turned toward him.

"What do you think, Guy. Maybe we should submit these pictures to *Stab and Blast* magazine." Tom's *Stab and Blast* quip, which pierced the tension of the moment, convulsed me with laughter.

The humor of Tom's quip, however, was lost on Mel but perhaps understandably so. Of the several accounts that I subsequently read or heard involving canoe trips on the Thlewiaza, nearly all of them ended in hair-raising encounters with polar bears near the shores of the Hudson Bay. These carnivorous run-ins included discharges of weapons, emergency rescues, and sleepless nights. Mel's decision to camp upstream, in retrospect, was not overly cautious nor was his decision to bring a third party into our tent that night, his loaded shotgun. The three of us—Mel, me, and the twelve-gauge—all slept peacefully side-by-side. There were no white-furred midnight marauders. Mr. Contingency was indeed a wise man.

The next morning, Mel lifted the canoe's bow from the shore onto the water, placed his hands on the gunnels for balance, and then took his seat in the bow. I lifted and pushed the stern to dislodge us from our rocky berth and then jumped into the aft end of the now, freely floating canoe. With only the morning's first pale light to guide us, we had begun our final descent toward the Thlewiaza's delta with the bay. A short paddle later aided by gentle currents brought us to a steep set of rapids where we met a trio of seals playing peek-a-boo in the valleys of the large standing waves. These we slid through without incident. As for the seals, perhaps they were giving us a due send-off as this would be our last day on the Thlewiaza.

The river formed its delta by dividing into a multiplicity of intertwined channels. Originally, I expected a languid river meandering in oxbows through bug-infested bogs, maybe a treeless version of Louisiana's bayous, but this was no lazy river. While the landscape above remained tabletop flat, the river split apart and descended sharply. In its final dash to the sea, it was as though somebody had pulled a plug from the bay, which was now pulling us and the river into the accelerating vortex of a massive drain.

Since the end of the last ice age, the Arctic, free of its glacial overburden, had been gradually springing back or, which is to say, up. The coasts of the Hudson Bay, as such, were a series of raised beaches, the oldest nearest to the top. For archaeologists, this phenomenon of isostatic rebound meant a contrarian mode of excavation where the oldest artifacts were found at the higher elevations.

We continued to paddle under a sky of marbled gray. To our left and north, a low-lying finger of land edged with willow scrub separated the currents of the Thlewiaza from those of its sister river, the Tha-anne. The two sisters seemed to be in a spirited, side-by-side race to the bay, but this modest finger of land between them soon came to a point and the currents of the two melded as one. The Big River was now even bigger, much bigger. In front of us, a train of blackened, sooty clouds began to roll across the skies. It slicked the rivers in reflected darkness and occluded all but a hem of ashen light along the eastern horizon line.

As we joined the Tha-anne's choppy waters, moving silhouettes, back lit by this low-slung band of gray light, appeared on the distant bank. Finally—after paddling over two hundred miles—our route had brought us to one of the true wonders of the world. The silhouettes were those of the tuktu—thousands of them. We moved closer and, as far as we could see, caribou—bulls, cows, and calves—dotted the shoreline. Some walked lazily toward the bay while others stopped to graze. We looked at the expanse of these two side-by-side rivers of life, one flowing with water, the other with caribou. Clearly, what the Arctic lacked in diversity of species it made up for in numbers, whether in infinities of black flies or, in this case, countless caribou.

I regretted that we were upwind of this throng of ungulates. They could probably hear and smell our presence even if they couldn't clearly see us. Stiff winds, however, drove their noises—tendon clicking, snorting, and hoof pounds—away from us. For us, the effect was like watching a silent film—all image and no sound.

These caribou most likely were a post-calving aggregation from the roughly 500,000 strong Qamanirjuaq herd or the 290,000 strong Beverly herd whose calving grounds lay to the northwest of Arviat.[1] The caribou gathered in large herds to spread their individual risk from predators. As evidenced by their current position and direction, they also sought relief from the heat and bugs by heading to the seacoasts.

Unlike other deer species, all of the adult caribou, both the male and female, had antlers. In the winter, they used their antlers as tools to scrape the snow away from lichens and other forage plants. The bulls we saw, standing about four feet high at the shoulder, probably weighed 300–400 pounds.[2] They also had the larger racks, which nearly doubled their height. Surely, I thought, their necks must be sore from supporting such massive antler antennae.

We crouched below a line of shrubby willows and then crept closer. We got within about two hundred yards of the lead caribou, the apparent grandmasters of the parade, but our bobbing heads and cameras betrayed our cover. The caribou, associating bipedals with weaponized predation, warily moved another hundred yards away, just out of rifle range had we been hunting. In the winter, when caribou were accustomed to hearing loud, lone cracks from ice splitting up, a sharp-shooting hunter supposedly could avoid panicking the herd if his singular shot instantly dropped the target caribou. Two or three shots, on the other hand, might put them all on the run.

The only shots we took were with our cameras, but neither the experience of witnessing this migration nor the vastness of the herd could be conveyed in photographs. Even in person, the migration appeared as a veritable river of life that was hard to fathom. Although they were a rung or two down the food chain from humans, wolves, and other predators, this land belonged to the caribou. Here, by virtue of their numbers, they were the dominant species. We were just a tiny crew of visitors, four friends, who had strayed into the midst of their great journey.

The traditional Inuit used or ate every part of the tuktu, from the stomach linings that were used for canteens to the hooves that were used for spoons and children's rattles. The Caribou Inuit of western Hudson Bay could meet their entire nutritional requirements from this species alone.[3] Delicacies included the partially digested vitamin-C-rich contents of the stomach, the warble fly larvae lodged under the skin, and even the eyeballs, which were eaten like candy.[4] The Inuit shaped Caribou bones into ornaments, fishhooks, and arrow shafts and carved the antlers into arrow points, tools, utensils, and toys for their children. Separated sinews became threads. Tanned hides became ropes, tent coverings, and blankets.[5] For winter clothing, the Inuit wore two layers of lightweight caribou skin clothing, fur side in next to the body and fur side out on the outer layer.

Despite the dominance of numbers, the spectacle of this migration triggered another image: endless buffet line, which was true. In the winters, after they were done with their summer pup-raising duties, wolves were inclined to run down the stragglers of these herds. In the spring, wolverines rudely attacked calves and pregnant cows during calving as well as sick or weakened adults.[6] Eagles also joined the fray, killing the young calves with their talons while grizzly bears also took their share.[7]

The caribou's top predator species, of course, was the human being. Inuit subsistence hunting west of Hudson Bay sustainably harvested hundreds of tons of meat from these hundreds of thousands of animals each year.[8] Most Inuit ate caribou on a weekly or daily basis. The economic values of this resource were significant as were the cultural values of connecting the young with their hunting elders. Trophy hunting by nonresidents and limited commercial harvests also provided a modest flow of direly needed cash.

This procession of caribou could have mesmerized us for hours, but we had an appointment to make. My wristwatch, which I had ignored for days, became the object of worried glances. Its dial and hands seemed magnified in size, their crisp, clean lines surreal, like a Salvador Dali painting. Our pickup for the boat ride to Arviat was scheduled for 10:00 a.m. near an abandoned cabin on the north side of the Tha-anne River, about a mile upstream from the bay.

We reached the dilapidated little cabin, but we found no boat waiting for us in the waters nearby. On the other side of the river, stiff northerly winds flattened the willows in incessant waves as though they were bent-down fields of wheat. To the east, the combined currents of the Thlewiaza and the Tha-Anne rivers fanned out before us and extended into the distant, glittering waters of Hudson Bay.

Ten o'clock came and went. We waited. To duck the wind and pass the time, we moved to the leeward side of a low-lying island and chewed on some insipid leftovers from our food packs. Our eyes fixed on the bay's horizon line, but no boats rose above it. Tom tried to call Joe Savikataaq on the satellite phone, but no one answered.

On the more excitable waters of the wide-open bay, there was no telling where our skipper was or when he would arrive in his small craft. Even here, in the more protected estuary, the wind was in a punishing mood. I watched the gusts pummel the waves and shear off their crests. Then I began to sense the ghostly presence of the iron-willed seafarers of centuries ago who, in wooden ships, futilely and often fatefully sought their fortunes in these same waters.

One of these was Thomas Button who departed from England in 1612 with two ships. Ominously, one of these ships, the *Discovery*, was from Henry Hudson's earlier and ill-begotten voyage. When Button and his crews, which included several mutineers from the prior Hudson voyage, reached the latitude of the Thlewiaza, they appropriately called their position Hopes Checked and waited out the winter. Button then headed two hundred miles south to the mouth of the river that drained the second largest watershed in North America. He named this now dam-harnessed river for one of the ship's masters, Robert Nelson, who died there with an undetermined number of other men, most likely from exposure and scurvy.

Jens Munk, a Dane, followed in 1619 and wintered over near the mouth of the Churchill River, just to the south of the Thlewiaza. Munk's two ships became tombs of the dead. Only he and two other men survived to sail home in a single ship.

Luke Fox and Thomas James, who led competing expeditions, followed in 1631, but they had difficulty recruiting crewmembers once word spread about the gruesome results of the earlier voyages. To his credit, Fox, without a single casualty, made it out of the bay before winter set in. Although James and his crew were forced to winter over, most of them survived and successfully returned to England, where James published his *Strange and Dangerous Voyage*, the account of his harrowing experiences.

A century later, in 1719, the dreams of a metal river full of precious minerals and a magical strait to Asia persisted. These dreams enticed James Knight and his Hudson's Bay Company sponsors to undertake a voyage along the northwest coast of the bay. Fifty years later Samuel Hearn discovered the wreckage of Knight's two ships on the reefs of Marble Island, approximately one hundred miles north of Arviat. Knight's men had built a shelter from the flotsam of their shipwrecks. The Inuit offered them food from time to time, but one by one, the crew died from exposure and exhaustion until all were dead by about 1722. Hearne would later recount his discovery of the skeletons of the last two survivors, which he found on an island promontory. "At length, one of the two died, and the other's strength was so far exhausted, that he fell down and died also, attempting to dig a grave for his companion."

I didn't attribute any causal significance to being in the same vicinity where all these early explorers experienced their considerable difficulties, but the associative effect was sobering. Not that we would be stricken with scurvy or forced to winter over. No, nothing of that sort, but we now faced the prospect of camping on the coast—with the polar bears.

PHOTOS

"Landscape." Red River Valley near Whapeton, North Dakota.
Photo credit: Marsha Mueller.

Grand Forks, ND—East Grand Forks, MN bridge in Flood of 1997.
Photo credit: U.S. Geological Survey, http://nd.water.usgs.gov/photos/1997RedFlood/

Left: Satellite image of algae blooms spreading across Lake Winnipeg, August 2004. *Photo credit: Lake Winnipeg Research Blog (http://lakewinnipegresearch.org/blog) sourced from the Rapid Response imagery of the Land Atmosphere Near-real time Capability for EOS (LANCE) system operated by the NASA/GSFC/Earth Science Data and Information System (ESDIS).*

Below: Algae fouled shoreline on Lake Winnipeg. *Photo credit: Dr. Greg McCullough, University of Manitoba.*

Pisew Falls on the Grass River in the Boreal Forest of Manitoba.

Aftermath of a fire in the Boreal Forest near Lynn Lake, Manitoba.

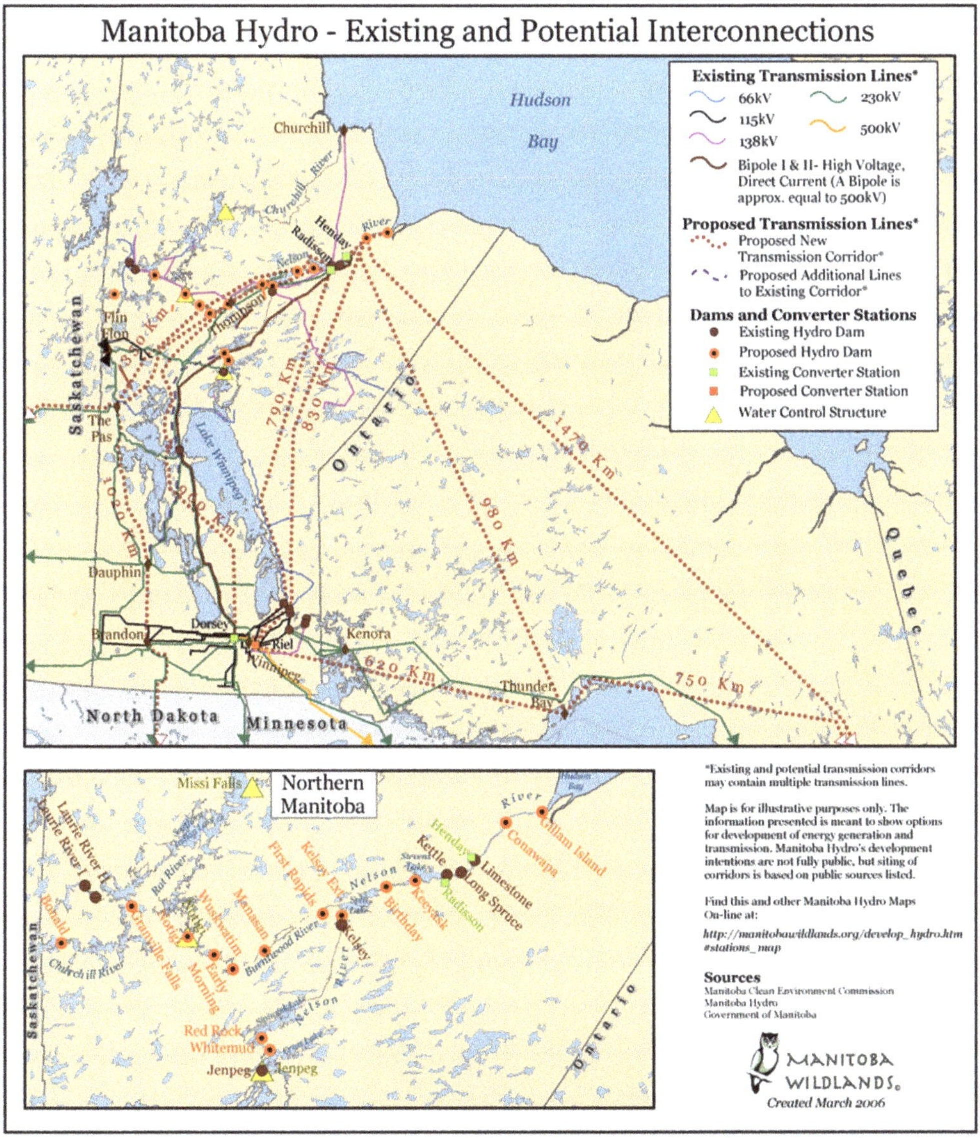

Above: Map of Manitoba Hydro's facilities. Inset more clearly shows the location of the Missi Falls Control Structure that diverts the Churchill River through the Rat and Burntwood rivers and then to the Nelson River. *Map credit: Manitoba Wildlands, http://manitobawildlands.org/maps/NorManExistPropDams_lg.jpg*

Right: Missi Falls Control Structure. *Photo credit: Manitoba Watershed Stewardship, http://www.gov.mb.ca/waterstewardship/licensing/churchill_river_diversion.html*

Orphaned mine and mine runoff near Lynn Lake, Manitoba.

A First Nation artist dabs on the finishing touches to a building mural in Lynn Lake, Manitoba.

The float plane departs as we start our trip down the Thlewiaza River. A propeller buzz cut? I duck to avoid the possibility.

Getting set to go.

The Moores navigating the start of the rapids at the outlet of Seal Hole Lake.

Finally, a big one that didn't get away! I released and returned this lunker lake trout to the river.

A picnic in July—on ice! Mel, Ruth, and Guy.

The Thlewiaza River, a.k.a. "the Big River."

In the Land of the Little Sticks.

Juvenile caribou, wandering alone, wonders who I am.

The hills are alive!

Tom and I lining a drop at Portage Rapids.

Ruth at Portage Rapids.

Ptarmigan in summer plumage.

Close-up of the tundra at foot level.

Caribou moss and flowers.

Shorebirds with plateau of ice in the background.

For Ruth Moore, on a warm summer day in the Arctic, the ice is nice.

The tundra holds billions of tons of carbon-sequestering peat—decayed vegetative matter—most of it locked in permafrost, but some is exposed, as shown in this river-eroded bank, and more is thawing each year.

Exposed peat in the foreground, our campsite in the distance.

Mel, just before he enters the bear den.

Wolf tracks left by our campsite overnight.

Our mess hall, the "Tundra Tarp."

The much-appreciated utility of mosquito netting.

Mel ponders the stone tablet, "Here Lies Wilderness , MMI."

Tom rides the Bison Boulder.

Left: Our campsite appears to be centered in a multi-lane freeway of caribou trails.

Below: An arctic tern nesting on the ground.

A seemingly endless herd of caribou near the confluence of the Tha-anne and Thlewiaza rivers. Neither this nor the other photos we took were adequate to convey the power and magnitude of this scene.

Tom on the satellite phone and Guy with a flare, trying to connect with Joe Savikataaq.

Joe's boat with our canoes lashed to the gunwales.

Jamie and Joe Savikataag, on the left, chat with the whalers.

Jamie with arctic tern chicks.

Whaler with harpoon.

Peter was a "Real Eskimo" and a good storyteller.

Arviat street.

The Arviat Northern Store.

Arviat waterfront scenes. Below: Resupply barge.

 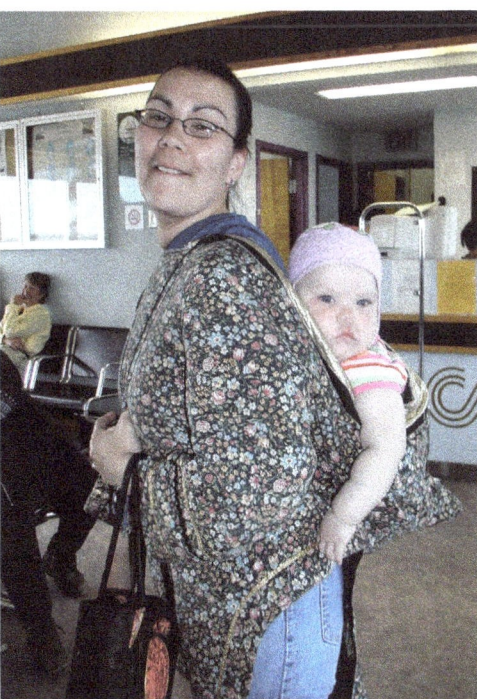

Faces of Arviat: Boy with puppy and mother with baby in amauti, a jacket with an integral pouch.

Evening sun on the Thlewiaza, a campsite view.

The Thlewiaza River crew, fellow paddlers—top row: Tom and Ruth Moore, Bottom row: Guy Mueller and Mel Baughman.

Part III
With the People

Chapter 13

The Whalers

"I think I see something moving."

Ruth pointed to a spec on the horizon line of the Bay. I thought through the possibilities. Either she had been deluded by Panglossian optimism, which would be doubly disappointing, or something *was* moving, which would mean a boat ride to Arviat and a testament to her hawk-like eyes. Mel passed his 8×40 binoculars around, giving each of us chance to verify the spec's identity. To me, the dot appeared to be moving, even levitating, but so were dozens of other dots on the horizon. Light refracting through the thermal gradients of the sun-warmed air above the Bay's icy waters was causing the entire horizon line to shimmer and bounce. Was Ruth's dot one of these bouncing mirages or a boat, preferably one headed our way?

With a surface area of 316,000 square miles and an average depth of only 300 feet, Hudson Bay had the geometry of a gigantic puddle. Its flat western shores were so gradual that ebb tides exposed more than a mile of shoreline. Glacial erratics—boulders and rocks lying above and below the water's surface— littered these tidal flats. They looked like a great line of defensive obstacles capable of deterring enemy landing craft should they ever approach. Threading a boat, even a canoe, through this geological clutter would be tricky, especially at night or in a fog.

We could have paddled the sixty miles from the Thlewiaza to the village of Arviat, but even under ideal conditions, it would take a day, a night, and possibly the better part of another day. Owing to the risks of harassment by polar bears, camping along the shoreline would be troublesome. Moreover, camping on dry land above sea level would entail either long portages over treacherously rocky and slippery tidal flats or waiting to both land and re-launch our canoes at high tides. The more likely prospect, that of sitting in our cramped canoes day and night, wasn't pretty either.

A few anxious minutes later, in fitting tribute to Ruth's vision, the distant dot revealed some bow spray and then a windshield above a cuddy cabin. Yes, it was a boat, but was it our taxi service or some random fishing boat? Whatever it was, if it was coming our way, it was fighting the river's current, the ebb tide, and nearly gale force winds, all head on. We could barely detect its zigzag progress toward us.

We faced a dilemma: Should we venture out and try to meet this boat or stay put? If we tried to meet the boat's skipper, it might not be Joe Savikataaq. It might be someone else unaware of our presence or disinclined to help. If it were Joe and his boat, what would happen if he didn't see us and took off in a different direction? The wind could easily sweep us into the Bay, a body of water whose nearest windward shore was five hundred miles away, a distance comparable to crossing the Mediterranean Sea.

If we paddled into the Bay, returning to the shore of origin against the wind and waves would be an impossible, Herculean feat. If we stayed put, we might have to wait for a day or more for calmer winds and higher tides. Then, we'd be camping on shore with the polar bears. Connecting with Joe and letting him know our whereabouts would relieve us of some of our anxieties, but that wasn't happening.

Lacking a phone connection, we decided to fire off our emergency flares. The flares' instructions claimed that their red plumes would be visible five miles away. This might have been true on a calm day, but this wasn't a calm day. The wind ripped the flares' plumes from their canisters and dispersed them no more visibly than a palm-full of dust. They were useless. We would have done better if we had waved Tom's red jacket overhead.

Instead of waving a jacket, we got into our canoes and started to paddle in the direction of the distant boat. This decision, to head out into the Bay, was one that, in an instant, transformed our wilderness trek from an experience to that which was to be avoided, namely, an adventure. Mature adults, who normally were painstakingly cautious, almost to a fault, accompanied me. Rather, I should say that I accompanied them. I wasn't sure what compelled them to take this risk. Was it the push of not wanting to camp with the bears or the pull of wanting to take a hot shower back in civilization sooner rather than later?

In the open sea, the risk of not connecting with this boat might be a permanent and fatally cold bath. Some people say that the only difference between a safe trip and a dangerous one is intelligence, which at this point was debatable. The only thing left was prayer: "Dear Lord, be good to me. The sea is so wide, and my boat is so small."

As usual, I took the stern and Mel took the bow. The wind, coming from our backsides, was pushing the river into a mean chop. Meanwhile the river's current and the tide's ebb were also moving in the same direction, thus compounding their effect, which was to forcefully rotate the canoe so that its bow pointed upstream and into the wind, opposite our intended direction. I needed all my strength to lever the paddle and maintain our downstream course. Lifting my paddle to take a stroke instantly put us off course while causing the canoe to twist broadside to the waves.

Over my left shoulder, I caught a glimpse of the Moores. They and their canoe were skimming over the waves like leaves across the pavement before a storm. If we had moved any faster, we might have been able to pull water skiers. Thankfully, all hands were still on deck and right side up. If one of our canoes had capsized here, only a miracle would have allowed the party still afloat to rescue the others.

The boat of our deliverance, now quartering portside into the wind and still tiny in the distance, struggled to close the gap between us. In our canoes, we were running with the wind. Eventually, our courses would intersect, but Mel wanted to cut the angle and aim directly for the boat, a shorter course, to be sure, but one that would have increased the risk if not the certainty of pivoting the canoe and broaching it into the white-capped chop.

It was clear that my paddling partner was not fully appreciative of the difficulties I was having in steering the canoe. Because I held the rudder, I made an executive decision to veto Mel and hold us to our original course. Regretfully, I wasn't entirely polite during this verbal exchange. The threatening jaws of disaster were starting to gnaw on our paddling karma.

The minutes that now separated our canoes from the distant boat passed like hours, each one with memorable intensity. Finally, with the wind speeding our trajectory, we came along sides, port-to-port with the Savikataaqs' boat. Mel, in the manner of a trapeze artist, kept his feet hooked to our canoe while he lunged up and grasped the gunnels of the larger, aluminum-hulled motorboat. A confident, smiling man stood above us on the deck and greeted us with dark and twinkling eyes. He wore a well-used Mustang Survival suit and an equally well-used so'wester hat. Clearly, this was a man of the sea.

"She's a bit windy, eh?" Yes, this was Joe Savikataaq. He was accompanied by his strapping first mate and 21-year-old son, Jamie. Were it not for my Upper Midwest cultural reserve, I would have hugged each of them.

History was repeating itself. A man whose last name was Savikataaq was pulling a bunch of tender Euro-Americans to safety, this time from the turbulent seas of Hudson Bay. We now shared a heritage with the early explorers who, in the words of historian, Keith Crowe, "sank and starved their way around the Arctic." Back then, it wasn't until aboriginal peoples fed, clothed, and sheltered their distraught visitors and then chauffeured them around on their dogsleds that these early agents of change were able to resume their missions of discovering their hosts' land and saving their souls.

A wave crashed into our canoe and jolted us up like a trampoline and then instantly slammed us down again, but we held fast and heaved the packs into the cockpit of Joe's boat. Next, we tethered the canoe to the aft of Joe's boat and let the canoe's empty hull swing downwind. The incessant gusts drew the slack out of the line faster than a mad dog straightening his chain. We repeated this sequence with Tom and Ruth's canoe. Soon, Joe and Jamie pulled in the canoes and somehow hoisted them onto the boat all the while fighting to prevent them from turning into kites. Then, with an amazing display of knot work, they lashed them to the deck above the fore cabin and along the gunnels of the cockpit. Joe's boat now looked like a chubby aluminum turtle with elongated dual shells—the upside-down hulls of two red canoes.

To our relief, Joe announced that we would wait in the mouth of the river until the wind died down and the tide returned, which, at the soonest, would be early evening. He and Jamie had already had a rough ride down here from Arviat. Under these conditions and with the additional bulk of us and our canoes on the boat, embarking on the return trip now would beg disaster. Joe recommended that we go to a pair of nearby islands. There we would spend the rest of the day with an encampment of Inuit whalers. Joe said that his friend, Peter, would be there and that Peter was a good storyteller.

Joe motored us over to the small side-by-side islands and nudged his boat onto the beach of the larger of the two. The ocean-rated deep "V" hull of Joe's boat was made of ¼" thick welded aluminum plate. Joe said that he paid more than C$40,000 for it a number of years ago and had it delivered to Arviat via barge from Churchill. Although only twenty-two feet long, it was an all-business, heavy-duty vessel, pushed by a 200-horsepower outboard motor.

We hopped off the boat onto the beach, and then Joe introduced us to Peter and the other four whalers. Three spoke English, including Peter. The other two, slightly older, were shy and not very conversant in English. Perhaps they just weren't comfortable around kabloona tourists.

The whalers were equipped with body-enveloping, multifunction survival suits. These marine versions of snowmobile suits served to shed the rain and break the wind. More importantly, if the wearer ever went overboard, the suit afforded eenough freedom of movement to allow the person to swim with the added benefits of both floatation and temporary insulation against the icy waters.

Jamie then introduced us to the birds and to himself in the process. Terns, gulls, eider ducks, and ptarmigans had colonized these island rookeries well before their temporary human occupants had arrived. The birds, especially the terns, were none too happy about the Inuit whalers or the newly arrived tourists. We learned, by the example of our hosts, to wave a paddle overhead to prevent the terns from pecking our heads. Then we waded through knee-deep water to the smaller adjoining island where the terns were nesting in greater numbers.

Jamie, who was home on vacation, had a new job as a Royal Canadian Mounted Police (RCMP) officer in Pelly Bay, about four hundred miles farther north and not too far from the magnetic north pole, close to Santa Claus Land, as Joe said. Jamie got his police training in the south after his pro-hockey career stalled while his former line mates advanced to the National Hockey League.

Once on the adjacent island, Jamie showed us the chicks and eggs of the aggressive terns as well as a completely docile eider duck—the ultimate pacifist—sitting on her nest despite our close approach. Then he held up two tern chicks in his palms to be photographed, but he must have seen worried expressions on our faces, because he couldn't resist a tease when he warned me not to touch the eggs. If I did, he said, "They would turn a bright purple and the mother would abandon them." Jamie was not just smart, he was proving to be a comic and joker. As a bilingual cop, hunter, and hockey player, he also had the makings of a twenty-first-century Renaissance man.

I asked Jamie about his toughest calls in Pelly Bay and about how it felt to be just one of two cops on continuous call in a hamlet of five hundred residents where everybody would soon know him by his first name. Jamie, mature beyond his years, said that his toughest call so far was a kidnapping. He explained that roving RCMP officers provide backup relief in the settlements so that the regular officers can take vacations, like the one he was now enjoying. He also said that the RCMP rotates assignments and that he would be moving to a new post in a couple of years, probably Prince Edward Island or one of the other Maritime Provinces of southeastern Canada.

"Sounds nice," I said. "Is that a place where you might like to live permanently?"

"No, after I get out of the RCMP, I think that I'll come back to Arviat."

"Really?"

"This is my home, where my family is. I like to hunt."

Interestingly, the Inuit generally have not been eager or successful as volunteers in the schemes intended to transplant them to the south. Convicted pirate Martin Frobisher, for example, who conned the queen to underwrite his wanderlust and thrice braved the waters of the Canadian Arctic, tried to uproot several Inuit in the 1570s. After declaring the dead-end bay in Baffin Island that bears his name to be the Northwest Passage and receiving an arrow in his buttocks from wary natives, Frobisher returned to England with three captured Inuit and two hundred tons of iron pyrite (fool's gold), amply proving that not all that glistens is gold. Upon reaching the shores of England, the transplanted Inuit soon became the objects of great curiosity, but all three, a woman, her baby, and an unrelated man, promptly died.

Robert Peary, in his quest for the North Pole, continued this tradition with the rendition of six Inuit whom he delivered to New York's Museum of Natural History in 1897. Of these six specimens, four quickly died and one was able to return to the Arctic. The remaining Inuk, the young orphaned son of one of the deceased men, lived a short and sorrowful life, but long enough to see his father's defleshed bones became part of the museum's collections. Later, in the mid-twentieth century, during the tuberculosis epidemics that sent hundreds of Inuit to southern sanatoriums, their homesickness was so insufferable that many of them tried to walk home.

Back at the larger of the two islands, the whaling party sheltered themselves in two canvas wall tents without mosquito netting. Although the windy, cooler bay curbed the bug population, just looking at these un-netted tents caused my skin to shiver. On the other hand, their sleeping pads and floor rugs, comprised of the thick hairy hides of muskox, were luxurious compared to our thin synthetics.

The whalers had been on the island for three days, pinned down by the wind and unable to hunt whales since their arrival from Arviat in two 16-foot open aluminum boats. Their extended confinement led them to thoughts of heading back as soon as the weather cleared. At the very least, our arrival on the island broke the routine of their encampment. We also learned a lot from our friendly island hosts.

"Can you tell us about whaling?"

Peter, a man of elder status with a ready smile and a taut but weathered face, complied. Having come of age before the settlements drew his people off the land, Peter happily referred to himself as an Eskimo. Among the elders, Eskimo was a self-selected badge of distinction, one that distinguished his generation from the modern Inuit who had only known settlement life. In this context, "Eskimo" defined a watershed in Inuit society and a personal experience that would never again be repeated. Peter was a phenomenon.

Peter said that he and his fellow hunters cruised along the coast and scanned the bay for migrating beluga whales. They could see the whales blow water only when they got closer to the whales. In the old days, hunters in kayaks would surround a pod of belugas, throw stones at them and then drive them into shallows where they could be trapped and harpooned.

Today, Peter said, once hunters spotted the whales, they would give chase in their motorboats until they could isolate one of the whales and get close enough to harpoon it. Aluminum boats and outboard motors, of course, are modern technology, but the harpoon, a technology perfected by the Inuit, is as old as antiquity.

Once imbedded, the harpoon's triangular pointed head, the igimak, dislodged from the steel shaft. The shaft itself was connected to a five-foot-long wooden throwing handle. The handle, including the metal foreshaft, would then float to the surface so that it could be retrieved. The point, stuck in the whale like a button, was attached to a coil of heavy cord with a float tied at the other end. The injured whale would then tow the float around and tire, allowing the hunters to approach. Once within range, Peter said, they would grab their rusty and perhaps less than trusty rifle, which looked like it had seen duty in one of the world wars, and "shoot the beluga in the head or the blowhole."

Instead of floats made from inflated seal bladders, these modern whalers used empty five-gallon plastic gasoline containers. Instead of a harpoon head made of bone, they used a triangular piece from an old hacksaw blade and pinned it to a discarded snowmobile part with a rivet made from a nail. It was an impressive hunting weapon made even more impressive by the resourcefulness required to fabricate it.

Peter said that they either butchered the whale at sea or towed it to land to complete the flensing. They only kept the outer layers of skin and attached blubber, the *muktuk or mattak*, for human food, which could be eaten raw or boiled to the texture of calamari. Raw *muktuk* was rich in vitamin C, virtually a nutritionally complete meal. To transport their harvest back to Arviat, the whalers put the layers of skin into large, rectangular, white plastic tubs fixed to the decks of their open boats. The rest of the meat and the carcass would be left to the bears, foxes, gulls, and other scavengers. The meat could also be used for dog food.

The belugas in Hudson Bay were the smallest of all beluga whales and, when it came to whales, belugas were on the small end of the spectrum. Peter said that they were white and looked like ghosts as they appeared and then disappeared beneath the bay's surface where they could hold their breath for twenty minutes. Adults, up to thirteen feet long and weighing a half ton, could swim at speeds over thirteen miles per hour.

Belugas, I would later find out, weren't the only whales that were hunted in the Hudson Bay. I would also learn, as I describe below, that it was the hunting of these larger whales in concert with European whalers that would forever tip the balance of Inuit lifeways.

Barely more than a century ago, huge bowhead whales swarmed the Arctic's waters. In the eighteenth century, the captain of a Hudson's Bay Company ship, sailing near Marble Island, just north of Arviat, observed "such sholes of whales and seals, as is nowhere to be met within the known world."[1] Whalebones still littered some of the shorelines near the mouth of the Tha-anne River and were evidence of past bowhead whaling activity just south of Arviat.[2]

By the mid-nineteenth century, the bowhead whale had become the obsession of American and Scottish whalers who followed them to Hudson Bay. Until that time, the Inuit of the Barren Lands largely kept to their ancient nomadic ways. But change was on the way, and the first winds of that change were those that filled the sails of the New England whaling schooners.

The oil and baleen revenues from a single bowhead whale, balena mysticetus, could more than cover the entire cost of a year's voyage for a nineteenth century industrial whaling ship and its crew.[3] Layered in fat up to two feet thick, a female whale could yield as much as twenty to thirty tons of oil.[4] A precursor to today's petrochemical industries, the oil rendered from whale fat lubricated the gears of industry and fueled the lamps of nineteenth-century houses. The baleen, a horny fingernail-like substance running the length of the bowhead's massive upper jaw, was converted into corset stays, buggy whips, umbrella ribs, window blinds, and fishing rods.[5]

Due to the Hudson Bay's remote, seasonally brief periods of open water, these nineteenth-century whalers provisioned their ships to "winter over," which gave them a head start and a chance to earn extra profit from a second season of whaling.[6] During the nine- or ten-month interval between the two open water seasons, the whalers moored their ships along the northwestern reaches of Hudson Bay at places like Marble Island.

These shore stations, in turn, attracted hundreds of people.[7] Inuit families built year-round settlements next to the ships, lived on the muktuk of the whale carcasses, and trapped the foxes that scavenged the remains.[8] The southern whalers hired the Inuit to operate their whaleboats, drive dogsleds, sew Arctic clothing, and deliver fresh caribou and muskox meat to the ships' crews. In return, these Inuit of the nineteenth century obtained a wealth of new material goods: ammunition, tools, matches, pots, needles, canvas, cotton and woolen cloth, beads, biscuits, sugar, and tobacco—even the whaleboats that were abandoned when the ship sailed away.⁹ On the ship, they learned to sing and dance to the white man's accordion and fiddle music, which they often adopted as their own.¹⁰ Cultures were shared and bloodlines became mixed.

In the blink of a generation, the Inuit who grew up around the nineteenth century whaling stations knew of little else. Diamond Jenness, Keith Crow, and others described the result: Lightweight canvas tents replaced those of cumbersome animal skin, imported metal pots ousted those carved from locally quarried stone, and woolen garments replaced animal skins. The Inuit discarded their sinew-backed, three-piece bows and stone-tipped arrows in favor of firearms that dramatically altered their hunting efficiency. They abandoned their driftwood-framed umiaks and kayaks and extended their hunting ranges with imported whaleboats that could be sailed against the wind. By a thin thread of contact, they tied their fates to the materials of the modern world.

During the latter half of the nineteenth century and into the early twentieth century, hundreds of whaling crews sailed into the Hudson Bay and wintered over, and each of these crews required thousands of pounds of fresh meat. To feed the whalers and maintain their access to trade merchandise, the Inuit, now armed with rifles, slaughtered the caribou and muskox at will. The tremendous lethality of rifles disrupted the old equilibrium between hunter and prey in which all parts of the slain animal were used. Some aboriginal hunters killed caribou and muskox only for their tongues and livers and other times only for their skins, leaving the meat to rot.¹¹

Like the myopic white men of their day, the early Inuit probably had little comprehension of the reality of finite population limits. The caribou herds were inexhaustible, were they not? From the traditional Inuit perspective that was true—the caribou would return as they always had. In their eyes, it was the spirit world, not wasteful exploitation that withheld or released the caribou to the hunters.

The southern whalers, in the meantime, did not limit themselves to baleen and whale oil. They put polar bear skins, animal pelts, mica, and anything else of value into the holds of their ships.¹² By the late nineteenth century, buffalo robes from the Great Plains, which kept the occupants of open carriages warm, had become rare finds. The whalers, eager to exploit a market, called for the hides of muskoxen, and the Inuit complied, hunting them to near extinction. By the end of commercial whaling in 1915, the whalers also started taking belugas, walruses, and even large seals, dramatically reducing their numbers.¹³

Although the nineteenth century Inuit of the Hudson Bay stood as witnesses to and participated in the decline of their own resources, what they could not see were the invisible invaders who accompanied the whalers. With neither natural immunities nor comprehension of the consequences, European diseases spread swiftly and indiscriminately. Syphilis, courtesy of the whalers, was among the first to ravage the Inuit. The first known cases of diphtheria among the Inuit occurred in 1883.[14] Most of these diseases—tuberculosis, dysentery, typhoid, smallpox, influenza, mumps, measles, and scarlet fever—attacked both young and old as well as hunter and homemaker, unraveling the vital interdependence among family members. Hardship begat hardship as there might be no one to hunt, no one to keep the fires going during the bitter cold, no one to control dangerously hungry dogs, or no one to carry wastes from crowded shelters growing with filth.[15] As late as 1944-45, a diphtheria epidemic hit Eskimo Point (Arviat) and took half the population.[16]

As for the bowhead whales, wherever they could be found, these great mammals were slaughtered. By about 1912, only a few remained alive in the Hudson Bay. Had electric lights as well as kerosene and lubricants from petroleum not replaced whale oil, and had spring steel and plastics not replaced baleen, the whalers most likely would have hunted down the last bowhead whale alive. In a befitting end, the last whaling ship to enter the bay, the Finback, struck a reef in 1919 and sank in Cape Fullerton north of Chesterfield Inlet, although the crew itself survived.

With an un-harpooned life span of one hundred years or more, bowhead whales were among the world's largest and longest-lived mammals. They and their mighty cetacean brothers—the blues, humpbacks, and sperm whales—were to the animal kingdom as the redwoods were to the continent's forests. Although commercial whaling activity in the Bay ceased, collisions with ships, harassment by military sonar, and entanglements in fishing gear continued to threaten whale populations, including the bowheads. Despite the devastation at the hands of the early whalers and the persistence of these modern-day threats, there was some positive evidence that, in Hudson Bay, this most endangered of all the great whale species, the bowhead, might be slowly recovering.[17]

Now, at the beginning of the twenty-first century, the Inuit of northwestern Hudson Bay were able to engage in highly regulated, sustainable harvests of bowheads for subsistence and cultural purposes. This they did at a rate of one bowhead whale every two to three years. In Nunavut, sustainability had become the guiding if not always agreed upon principle of wildlife management. It meant the harvesting of animals in ways and at levels that did not deplete their populations.

A real Eskimo, of course, whether of the nineteenth or the twenty-first century, was more than a hunter of whales. On our little island, we talked with Joe, Jamie, and Peter about other kinds of hunting and fishing they did. We told them about how we caught grayling and how we cooked it—boiled, fried, sautéed, and stewed in chowder. Next time, they suggested, we should place the whole fish, uncleaned, directly into the embers of a fire. After the skin blackens, they said, remove it from the fire, strip away the skin and guts, and it would be ready to eat. If the fish was gutted before it was thrown on the coals, they said it would dry out and lose its flavor.

For their part, Peter, Joe, and their friends netted Arctic char when they migrated from ocean to freshwater stream in late summer. They also took Arctic cod from the bay. They hunted caribou throughout the year, but their hides were best when taken in late August or September. They even went scuba diving in the spring and summer to harvest sea urchins!

They preferred to hunt seals in the fall and winter when the seal carcasses floated to the surface. If they shot them in the spring or summer, the carcasses would sink. In the fall, they shot the seals with rifles. In the winter, they shot or harpooned seals that surfaced for air through breathing holes in the ice. A hunter would slowly approach a breathing hole on his stomach with his upper arms tucked in and his forearms and hands flapping at his side to mimic a seal's flippers. When deep snows covered the seals' breathing holes, they used dogs to sniff them out.

According to Joe, who worked as the regional conservation officer (game warden) for the Nunavut Department of Sustainable Development, local Inuit could hunt polar bears on a regulated basis. Non-native people also could get licenses to hunt polar bears, but the non-refundable seasonal hunting fee was C$25,000, and the hunter also had to hire an Inuit guide. Guides took their clients to outpost cabins along the bay's shore during November. From there, they traveled by dog sled to concealed vantage points to wait for the bears to pass by as they followed the formation of the ice.

Joe told us of a hunter who paid C$25,000 and his guide's expenses, but refused to shoot a bear, because he felt that none of them were big enough. Another hunter paid C$25,000 for each of three licenses, one for himself and two for family members, but he personally didn't shoot a bear. He came back the next season with another family member and finally got a bear after paying C$125,000 in license fees during a two-year period. Two hunters from Mexico felt that their outpost cabin was too crude, so they snowmobiled back to Arviat every night. During the weekend, they flew back to Mexico in a private jet to warm up before returning to finish their hunt.

We declined the whalers' invitation to join them for tea in their wall tent;

we weren't sure how all of us could fit inside with seven others already seated. We also felt as though we might be crashing their party, but I regretted not joining them, especially when I returned to the States and learned more about Inuit culture, a culture deeply rooted in the values of hospitality and generosity, values that I, as our group's cultural attaché, should have known and welcomed more graciously. Regardless of our concerns about tent-overcrowding or our other hegemonic hang-ups, refusing their invitation was probably tantamount to pulling away from a friendly greeter's extended handshake. Despite our inadvertent boorishness, one of the whalers allowed me to take a picture of him proudly holding a harpoon in one hand and a coil of rope and float in the other, and I wished I could have seen him and his friends in action.

They did take their boats out to the bay later that day, but by then our routes diverged. I might have traded my prized fly rod to extend our trip another day and join them in spirited pursuit, racing over the high seas with a harpoon firmly raised, my eyes fixed in search, but the only harpoon I got to hold aloft was in my imagination, and none of the sleek white ghosts of the bay chose to show themselves during our brief visit. I also got to shake hands with authentic Arctic hunters, and if there were any endangered species in the world, it might be them. This was a place where hunters weren't "sportsmen." They were predators in the food chain and more part of the balance of nature than the cause of the whole thing going tilt.

For the Inuit whalers, their hunt was both a means and expression of their livelihood. If they filled their tubs with muktuk, they would earn a rousing welcome back in Arviat. Their bounty would be a gift of themselves, and their kin would partake of it in kind.

These whalers used the industrial culture's technology—aluminum boats, outboard motors, and imported fuel—but their role was more as equal players in the ecosystem rather than adversarial combatants. They exercised control over the cycle of production, from beginning to end, and they spent their time talking and loafing during this hunt as much as they labored. But there was nothing dishonest, alienated, or hypocritical about their endeavor.

They did not toil in abstraction or in the isolation of repetitive tasks in exchange for the replenishment of their checking accounts. They held harpoons, not debit cards. The object of their hunt wasn't a shrink-wrapped wad of chemically laced baloney scanned through the faceless electronic self-checkout counter at the supermarket. It wasn't made from the remnants of confinement-crazed hogs, factory-farmed and deprived of sunlight until the finality of their semi-trailer trip to the processing plant. These whalers did not detach themselves from the death of the animal that sustained them. Their environment and culture were bound as one, from the face-to-face intimacy with their dying prey to the art of living.

With time on my hands, I strolled along the rocky tidal flats and looked across the river to the tundra, a place that, for me, would soon exist only in memory. I pondered the culture and history of the people who once roamed here and wrested a living from this land before the arrival of the whalers and traders. I knew that traditional Inuit conditions had prevailed into the beginning of the twentieth century, but my knowledge, at this point, was sketchy. Eventually, by returning to the stacks and alcoves of the Wilson Library, I would learn more.

I would learn that the early Inuit relied on the examples of their elders and storytelling to impart generations of knowledge and skills. I would learn that, in this process, all the places, features, and living things about them acquired names and spiritual meanings. Without maps or global positioning devices, they imprinted the images of their environment in their memories—the subtle rise of land in a featureless expanse of tundra, the colorful lichens on a prominent boulder, the shapes of rivers and lakes.

Their travels in the wilderness did not include a little black box with a satellite telephone in case all else failed. If all else failed, they fell back on the only help they had, their own hands and wits. All of life's essentials, from the clothes on their backs to their tools, they made with their own hands. They did not take graphite paddles, Gore-Tex fabrics, freeze-dried foods, or canisters of petroleum distillates nor did they make use of porters or floatplanes. However, they did take their families with them, their children, their elders, even their pregnant wives.

With neither the hands of the clock nor the pages of the calendar to keep them on task, the migrations of animals and the passing of the seasons governed their lives. They measured their travel in sleeps instead of miles. Hunters needed to understand the complexities of the weather and the timing of the freeze-up and break-up of the ice. They needed to know when and where the caribou would rut, when the char would spawn, and when the geese would molt. In the words of Brian Goehring and John Stager, for the traditional Inuit, "time was mainly timing . . . when to stalk, shoot, strike, sleep, eat, travel, move camp, take shelter, and a host of other things. Otherwise, time was endless; children were born, people got old, died and for the rest, there was only the here and now."[18]

To an extent that can hardly be understood from today's perspective, the life of an Inuk—from birth to death—revolved around his extended family.[19] Although there were exceptions, families tended to consist of a father and mother, their married sons and wives, and groups of unmarried adult brothers.[20]

By focusing on a single set of hunting areas during their lives, fathers and sons increased their knowledge of the local environment and became more effective hunters.

Elders frequently chose marriage partners for their children as soon as a young man could hunt or a girl reached puberty. Extended relatives typically supplied the selection of spouses, resulting in complex kinship relationships where cousins, nieces, and nephews were also spouses and in-laws.[21] Marriages, however, were voluntary, and either spouse could end the relationship.

Families shared everything—skills, tools, and food—and, as a corollary, deplored stinginess, customs that continue to shape modern Inuit life. "Generosity," anthropologist Robert Spencer noted, "was a primary virtue, and no man could risk a miserly reputation. Thus anyone in the community, whether inland or coastal, could ask for help . . . and it was never refused."[22] The practice of giving, especially food, established a culture of continuous reconciliation that held animosities in check.

In addition to maintaining peace, this reciprocity reflected the practical side of living by the Golden Rule. It operated like a mutual insurance policy, pooling both risks and resources, blunting the consequences of individual failure while extending the rewards of success. Bad luck could befall even the best of hunters, and were it not for the help of companions, a single hunting failure at an inopportune time could be devastating. A large catch of seals, on the other hand, might overwhelm an individual family with unusable surplus. Communities that survived these irregularities most likely were those that shared their resources among families. To the extent that modern societies bear any attributes of fairness and generosity, we might thank the process of natural selection that favored these behaviors in our hunter-gatherer predecessors.

While each family depended on the contributions of both spouses, a rough hunt-home division of labor characterized the duties of husband and wife. According to archeologist David Morrison, marriage was a "matter of life and death, the union of a hunter and a seamstress."[23] To eat regularly, to be clothed adequately, to raise children, to approach old age with some security, and to survive day by day—all this required a spouse.[24] The taking of an additional wife (or husband), was not unheard of, especially if there was an imbalance of men and women, but the impracticalities of hunting or making clothing for an extra spouse favored monogamy.

Marriage did not impose strict boundaries on sexual relations. However, the exchange of spouses was generally neither indiscriminate nor shameful in practice. This custom reinforced community alliances and trading partnerships and affirmed that each man had a stake in the other man's family.

Inuit laws, although unwritten, drew from the basic expectation that everyone must live in harmony and contribute to the group's wellbeing.[25] Because its consequence could be hunger or starvation, the people condemned laziness in both children and adults. Families celebrated a coming of age of their daughters when a girl sewed her first mitts and mukluks and when a boy killed the first of each kind of animal that sustained his people.[26] In some groups, the young man was obliged to share his kill with others and take none of the food for himself.[27]

The remedies for breaking these rules emphasized the restoration of peace more than punishment.[28] The court of community approval served as the arbiter of justice, and those who failed to contribute risked the pain of its loss. When inattention failed to quiet discord, persistent antagonists could engage in a song duel, in which insults were exchanged, or a boxing match to settle grudges. If all else failed, chronic troublemakers would be exiled or killed.[29]

A well-respected patriarch often served as the chief or boss, but the real power of decision making rested in the consensus of the group. Inuit leadership also tended to be provisional and informal, drawing from whoever had the best skills and experience for a given situation. In a harsh environment, where survival to old age proved one's wisdom, young people logically sought the advice of their elders and held them in high esteem.

In many respects, the traditional Inuit and the world's other so-called primitive, nomadic societies enjoyed an inestimable aspect of freedom.[30] Vilhjalmur Stefansson, an explorer-anthropologist, who lived and worked among the Inuit of northern Canada from early 1908–12 wrote that the "Eskimo individually behaves like a sovereign state. The laws of others do not bind him. . . ."[31]

Samuel Hearne, who lived and worked among the eighteenth century Inuit, observed that the Inuit lived "in a state of perfect freedom, no one apparently claiming the superiority over, or acknowledging the least subordination to another, except what is due from children to their parents. . . . There is, however, reason to think that when grown to manhood they pay some attention to the advice of the old men, on account of their experience."[32]

Foraging societies may have endured a meager standard of living, but in many ways, they lived in a world of plenty. With neither yoke of mortgage nor burden of debt, their only obligations were to share in the work and to share the results with their kin. They had no employers, no employees, no taxes, and no unemployment. Among face-to-face friends, the most admired and influential were the most generous. Poverty, which required social stratification, was largely nonexistent; and while each band perceived a strong sense of territory, the land, unencumbered by fences and property deeds, belonged to all. The ability of families to detach themselves from the larger group and the vulnerability of coercive individuals to ambush, such as attacks while they slept, restrained the bullies and reinforced the egalitarian attributes of their society.[33]

The nomadic Inuit limited their possessions to those that could be carried on their backs, pulled on their sleds, and reasonably put to use. Other than tiny amulets to ward off evil spirits and a few other incidentals, material accumulations unrelated to subsistence were burdens to be shed rather than hoarded. Unessential possessions encumbered mobility, and mobility was essential to existence.

The vagaries of weather and animal migrations often put them in harm's way, but the traditional Inuit contented themselves with a dearth of wants and availed themselves to resources that generally satisfied them. This moderation of wants, as Marshall Sahlins explains in *Stone Age Economics*, put them within the reach of hunter-gatherers' means.[34] Like other early hunting societies, the principle of "want not, lack not" underpinned Inuit worldview. Affluence in this context, according to Sahlins, is gained not by abundance and producing much but by desiring little.[35]

Clearly, this outlook spurned the assumed imperatives of modern economics. Inuit wants, by the constraints of circumstances and culture,[36] were necessarily limited, not infinite. Beyond the level of the household, there was little reason to divide their labor into ever-greater specialization or to maximize productive capacity without end. Avarice over material objects had no real place in the Arctic. More than enough was too much.

Free of the burdens of accumulating, caring for, and transporting a surfeit of material objects, an Inuk achieved wealth from the artistry of nature and the leisure to enjoy it. Hunting, butchering, and moving about the Arctic required stamina and competence, but these activities engaged the Inuit intermittently more so than continuously. They balanced spurts of work, some long and grueling, with intervals of loafing and visiting other families, whether in the winter dance house or idling at a lakeside camp under the summer sun.[37] Rather than thinking of them as poor because they had so little, Sahlins suggests that we should think of hunter-gatherers as free . . . as members of the "original affluent society."[38]

Until airfields were built on their lands during World War II, the Inuit were neither a party to nor a witness of the apocalyptic impacts of the Holocaust's gas chambers, Stalin's forced famines, the enslavement of Africans on American plantations, or civilization's contributions of Hiroshima and two world wars. Diamond Jenness, who lived among the Copper Inuit of the central Arctic in 1912 and subsequent years, asked his Inuit friends why they chanted no songs about war or victory. "They asked me what war meant, for they knew of no enemies except the Indians far to the south, whom they seldom saw and carefully avoided."[39]

Of course, in industrialized America, where we now did most of our foraging by opening a refrigerator door, there was a temptation to romanticize primitive life as a sort of perpetual camping trip or endless succession of picnics. With the possible exception of the solitary aspect, Thomas Hobbes' classic pronouncement about life in a state of nature as "solitary, poore, nasty, brutish and short" had some applicability in the Arctic. The temporary villages of the Inuit were not Shangri-Las. For southerners like ourselves, the apparent charm and novelty of a skin tent or an igloo with an slab of ice for a window would probably be tempered by the realities of having to live in one, especially when it started to drip or leak.

Nor were these bands of imperfect human beings the epitome of peaceful tranquility. Kidnapping (usually another Inuk's wife when there was a shortage of women), murders, and blood feuds occurred on occasion, forcing some groups to split up.[40] Infanticide and parricide in traditional Inuit communities, although exaggerated, did occur. Finally, the Arctic was not exactly the world's best real estate or historically the most reliable hunting grounds. From time to time, these uncertainties shadowed the Inuit with hunger, occasionally famine, and, in the darkest of hours, reduced some to cannibalism.[41]

Modern institutions that allowed us to prevent, avoid, or moderate difficult life decisions did not exist until the mid-twentieth century in the Canadian Arctic. As historian Keith Crowe noted, the traditional Inuit had no nursing homes for the elderly or the disabled. They had no social welfare services; other than their families, they had no "safety nets" to catch them in times of peril. Nor did they have contraceptives or family planning devices.[42] For those who could not be carried or could no longer carry themselves, population control sometimes became draconian.

Mothers, already shouldering heavy packs and hard-pressed to breastfeed one infant, could seldom nurse another and carry both over the tundra. Prospects for a newborn following too soon after the birth of an older sibling became dire when no adoptive mother could be found. With special care not to give the baby an *atiq*, meaning a spirit name, parents sometimes suffocated untimely offspring or abandoned them to freeze in the snow—gruesome practices made more bearable by the Inuit belief that an unnamed infant had no human soul.[43] Baby boys, who would become hunters and support their parents in old age, were spared more often than girls. The parents who dealt with these dilemmas presumably did not become mired in today's ethical issues about whether life began with procreational intent, the formation of a zygote, the quickening of the fetus, or a baby's first breath.

Life's end also could be harrowing. When hunger haunted their camps, the frail and gravely wounded typically accepted their fate with equanimity.

Sometimes they voluntarily stripped to the skin, hobbled into the night, and pleaded for the cold to take them with merciful quickness. Where relatives assisted, not as heinous acts but as solemn duties, they might quickly stab or strangle suffering loved ones or block them up in a snowhouse.[44] Intravenous feeding tubes, oxygen tanks, dialysis machines, and other measures to extend the lives of the barely living did not present moral dilemmas. They did not exist.

 Their numbers rose and fell with the benevolence of the weather and the availability of prey. Nature could be fearsome, but her cruelties, as Jenness noted, did not stir the emotions of revenge like the cruelties wrought by man, to whom the Inuit were neither subservient nor dependent. Nor was Inuit life without its pleasures and honors. None was greater than the rewards of sharing success with neighbors and accumulating the wealth of their companionship. Judged among themselves by who they were rather than what they owned, they found identity in a common culture and dignity in the shared pursuit of survival. Sparse and scattered, upon their environment they left little more than a trace.

Chapter 14
The Road to Arviat

The day wore on, the wind eased, and the tide rose. The tiny island where we were parked became tinier, but our prospects for navigation improved. We said farewell to our whaler friends, climbed aboard Joe's boat, and slowly motored into the river's widening mouth. Immediately, the boat wedged itself against the rocky bottom. Ah, yes, a little more time and little more tide would have served us better.

Joe cut the motor and tilted it up to protect the propeller and then let the Thlewiaza's current bump us over the rocky bottom toward the Bay. By polling and prying the boat with an oar, inch-by-inch we gained enough distance and depth to lower the motor's propeller. The whalers in their lighter open boats trailed behind us. Soon, we sped northward paralleling the shore while the whalers split off eastward into the bay. They yelled to us in parting, saying that they had spotted beluga whales.

Cruising at around twenty-five knots, we bucked the wind and crashed over swells that rose, from trough to crest, to the height of a man. The sticky turquoise waters, filled with clouds of plankton, and the brackish bow spray clearly told our senses that this was an ocean, not a freshwater lake. We all stood upright and flexed our knees to absorb the pounding of the waves. Unless one was willing to risk a crushed vertebra or dislodged kidney, sitting was not an option.

I asked Joe about the new territory of Nunavut. Did he support the creation of the new territory? Was the support for it widespread? Did the new territory promise a better future?

In 1993, the Inuit, Canada, and the Northwest Territories signed the

Nunavut Land Claims Agreement, which led to the creation of the Nunavut Territory government in 1999. The intent was to create a groundbreaking model of "aboriginal self-government." Under the agreement, the Inuit received title to a sixth of the territory's land, mineral rights to a tenth of that area, and hunting and fishing rights in the vicinities of the settlements. Canada retained the balance of the mineral rights while preserving for Nunavut a share of any mining royalties. In return, Canada agreed to pay the Inuit C$1.148 billion over fourteen years. The payout yielded about C$45,000 for each Inuit man, woman, and child, but spread over fourteen years and thinned by population growth, it was not exactly like winning the lottery.[1]

Joe felt that the creation of Nunavut doubled the number of capitals and administrative expenses, leaving less money for government programs and services. The territory-wide vote to divide the Northwest Territory and create Nunavut passed by a 56 percent majority in 1982. Joe questioned whether the pride and identity of an essentially Inuit territory was worth the expense. From Joe's perspective, the benefit was more symbolic than substantive.

Joe also felt that the government should use either the syllabic- or the Roman-lettered form of written Inuktituk, but not both. Mastering two alphabets and written forms of the language was difficult. Joe preferred the Roman-lettered version to make translations between Inuktituk and English easier and to improve the actual prospects for bilingualism in Nunavut.

Schoolchildren, he said, were taught in Inuktituk through the early grades, only. Due to a lack of books and teaching materials published in Inuktituk and a shortage of Inuktituk-speaking teachers, students switched to English in the middle and higher grades.

English use occurred at the expense of declining proficiency in Inuktitut, especially among the young who favored English among themselves. Popular media from the south added momentum to this preference. In some Inuit families, other than body language and a few simple words, English-speaking grandchildren and Inuktituk-speaking grandparents were unable to communicate.

Was he or Jamie born in Arviat? No one, Joe said, is born in Arviat or anywhere in Nunavut anymore. Mothers are flown south to deliver their babies in hospitals in places like Winnipeg. In the early days of the settlements, pregnant, non–English-speaking mothers flew south alone, which must have been a lonely and frightening, if not an occasionally calamitous, experience. Nowadays, nurse escorts accompanied expectant mothers. Whether escorted or unescorted, delivering in the south meant separation from family members. It also meant that traditional Inuit midwifery had disappeared.

I wanted to gain some insight about local religious practices, so I asked

Jamie about weddings. He recited a typical sequence: a wedding service at one of three churches (Alliance, Anglican, or Roman Catholic) followed by a reception and a dance. Maybe he was only telling me what he thought I wanted to hear or was appeasing me with a watered-down reply. It all seemed a bit humdrum and "southern" to me. He didn't offer insights about ancestral spiritual practices nor did I press him on the topic. I surmised that I was becoming an awkward, irritating *kabloona*, a white guy from the south, bearing down with too many questions. Once again, better pre-trip preparation as our group's cultural representative might have helped me with a little more finesse in these exchanges.

Clearly, my overall knowledge of the Far North required some remedial attention. I promised myself that when I returned to the US I would pick up where I had left off and that, among other topics, I would learn about the evolution of Inuit religion. What were the traditional religious beliefs of the Inuit, and how did it happen? How did a people who once knew nothing of the Holy Trinity, the virginity of Mary, the resurrection of the body, and life everlasting, come to embrace these precepts? How did a people who once knew nothing of all this become believers, believers, in one manner or another, of God's creation of the earth in six days, His smiting of oppressors with plagues of flies and frogs, the parting of the Red Sea, and the drowning of the entire human race save for a single family thanks to the patriarch's divinely inspired ark-building skills? I would keep this promise and find the answers to these questions.

Traditional Inuit belief systems held that everything on Earth contained a spirit worthy of respect. People, both dead and alive, had spirits, as did animals, rocks, the sea, the forces of nature—all objects, both animate and inanimate had spirits. Inexplicable events and phenomena, from injuries to foul weather, found their explanation in this spirit world. Storms, for example, were the work of the wicked spirits escaping from vents in the earth.[2] Sila, the spirit who lived in the sky, made the sun rise and set and could carry off a man and hide him, but Sila could also be gracious and cure the sick.[3]

Angakut (shamans) served as counselors, medical advisors, and liaisons with the spiritual world. By invoking and assuming the identities of other spirits, such as polar bears or wolves, shamans claimed fantastic feats: seeing objects beyond normal sight, foretelling the future, and spiritually traveling to distant places in the universe. They also appealed to the spirits to cure the sick and entice the seals and caribou to return.

Rather than seeking salvation of life after death, traditional Inuit spirituality focused on living in harmony with these powerful forces and complying with their taboos. Taboos, too numerous to remember, governed every aspect of life, from birth to death and everything between. In addition to keeping objects from the sea and the land separate, hunters were required to slake the thirst of a slain seal with a cupful of water. This kindness, according to taboo, would dissuade the slain animal's spirit from alarming the living seals and scaring them away. In matters of illness, it was the *angakok's* job to diagnose the cause, usually a breach of some taboo, and to prescribe the cure, reliably still another taboo.

The Caribou Inuit west of Hudson Bay believed in Hila, the universe's supreme force that determined which acts were good and which were bad. A female counterpart to this force, known as Pinga, dwelt somewhere in space, where she monitored human behavior and sometimes intervened in people's affairs. The souls of those who had lived in accordance with Hila's taboos would ascend to Pinga after death and then return to Earth in the body of another animal, human, or other life form. Those who did not comply were condemned to eternal misery.[4]

It was into this milieu of myths and magic that Europe's Christian soldiers marched, competed for converts, and seldom hesitated in their disdain for native spirituality. At the same time, the authority and influence of the shamans foundered. They were powerless against the foreign diseases that decimated their people. The *qallunaat* (white people), however, who were largely immune, provided the sources for their cures and promised the stricken, if they believed, the comfort of eternal rest.[5]

Soon, the people of the Arctic found themselves in a cauldron of cultural turmoil. Missionaries coaxed the Inuit away from their ancient beliefs, but they also chipped away at their identity. Some missionaries forbade drum dancing and body ornamentation, and most baptized the children not with their parentally given names but with Christian names.[6]

Remnants of traditional Inuit spirituality survived on a parallel basis with Christianity well into the 1950s, but soon thereafter and coinciding with the people's movement to the settlements, such practices became increasingly rare or well concealed.[7] By this mid twentieth century mark, the missionaries had effectively suppressed the animistic traditions of Jamie's recent ancestors, and, in the span of a generation or two, the last of the practicing shamans who professed abilities to communicate with the spirit world had passed away. Jamie's description of Arviat weddings served to confirm this historically recent and widespread absorption of Christianity into settlement life.

We continued on our northward course to Arviat. It was a course that required us to head directly into the wind and the punishment of the steepening waves. To cushion the climbs and crashes, we fixed our feet in surfboard position. Then the engine droned, gasped for fuel, and surrendered to silence. Without its internally combusted propulsion, the boat became a piece of bobbing flotage and we its hapless passengers. Free of the overburden of motor noise, the sounds of breaking waves and wind pleasantly returned, but worried glances were shared all around. While we idled and drifted, flotillas of tall-masted white clouds, trailed by bronzy shadows, sailed across the western sky.

Jamie asked me if I wanted to see a mermaid. Without waiting for my answer, he walked to the aft and delivered the punch line by relieving himself over the transom. I didn't choose to look at his mermaid, but I did reflect on how a little rough humor had a way of leveling the social hierarchy and perhaps issue a form of commentary on my pattern of direct questioning. Then he methodically removed the fuel filter and discarded a shot glass of scummy filtrate. The motor, free of its phlegmy intake, gulped in gas and, once again, asserted its dominance over nature. The culprit was bad gas, an apparently common frustration in the North. Before we got to Arviat, our guides had to stop and purge the fuel filter twice more.

Just south of Arviat, the wind, now fully exhausted, gave up the day, as did the sun. Slicing through the now listless waves, we cruised by a lone ocean freighter anchored several miles offshore. Joe explained that Arviat's harbor was too shallow for the larger ships, so a smaller barge-like vessel ferried the supplies from ship to shore. The ship, based in Montreal, made several rounds of stops to Hudson Bay's various communities throughout the shipping season, which typically lasted from mid-July to the end of September. Supplies also arrived from the railhead at Churchill, Manitoba, where they were transferred to a Hudson Bay barge that towed them the last 160 miles north to Arviat. With no highways or railroads to the outside world, pricey airfreight was the only year-round option to get emergency supplies and perishables like produce into the grocery stores.

Nunavut's inaccessibility explained the high cost of living, roughly twice that of the rest of Canada. Everything, from soda pop to fuel oil, came by boat or plane. Except as a metaphor, the "*Road* to Arviat" (or any other Nunavut settlement) did not exist.

As day faded to dusk, a flickering of village lights appeared on the horizon and guided us toward the shores of Arviat, which, in Inuktituk, means "the place of the bowhead whale." Houses and buildings, first seen as tiny silhouettes against a backdrop of twilight, hugged the shoreline like lichens to a rock.

A couple of hundred people, mostly youngsters on bicycles and ATVs, gathered on the wharf to scrutinize our arrival, but our drawing power as celebrities quickly faded and the crowd dispersed. We loaded the packs and gear into Joe's pickup truck and carried the canoes to the yard of a small government office building just up the hill from the wharf.

Joe invited us to stay overnight at his place a couple of blocks away. We stored our packs on the deck of his modern wood-frame house where his preteen daughter and her friend had pitched a tent for a sleepover. While we middle-aged southerners had been tenting on the land, the local children were safely tenting on their parents' deck in town.

We entered the house through a coat-and-boot vestibule and then climbed the stairs to the loft and spread our sleeping bags on the loft's floor. A sewing machine workstation occupied a corner of the large, open room. On the table, portions of an insulated quilted parka awaited final assembly and stitching. Back downstairs, we entered the main part of the house through the kitchen, which included a dining area and the standard complement of modern appliances.

Earlier, Mrs. Savikataaq had prepared a supper of caribou roast, carrots, potatoes, pasta, cake, fruit punch, and tea. The tea was hot, and the pasta dish was freshly cooked, right out of the box. She served the previously cooked caribou roast and vegetables at room temperature. While the four of us took our shift at the table, Joe and his family watched television on a widescreen TV in the living room. Jamie worked the telephone, arranging to meet with friends.

Wishing to acquaint myself with the flavor of caribou, I helped myself to a sampling of the cuts. The beefy taste was distinctive and palatable, not unlike the sandwich meat that Calm Air would serve us on our flight out of Arviat the next day. Ruth and Tom favored the pasta dish but politely avoided the caribou. I prodded the Moores to join Mel and me in partaking of the local "country" foods.

Apparently, I was upstairs or not listening carefully when Mrs. Savikataaq had said that the somewhat picked-over roast had been on the table for a "few days." I don't know; maybe something was lost in translation. The cultural differences in food preservation expectations created a slightly awkward moment, but whether cold and old or hot and fresh, it was a generous spread. I left nothing but clean bones on my plate and suffered no ill effects. When in Arviat, do as the Arviatmiut do, and I did.

The mechanical systems of Joe's house as well as others in Arviat had three tanks: one for fresh potable water, one for wastewater and sewage, and another one for heating fuel. Tanker trucks drove through the neighborhoods on a daily basis to replenish the water and fuel tanks while honey wagons followed in the afternoons to drain the wastes. We talked to one of the drivers the next day. He said that the morning job was better, that it was truly better to give than to receive! Buried water and sewer pipelines for these purposes were impractical in Arviat due to the permafrost.

Joe's house reminded me of the Field Museum of natural history. The outer wall of the living room extended the full one and one half stories of the house. The Savikataaqs had adorned nearly every part of this wall with wildlife trophies, enough of them to provide extended job security for a taxidermist. There were mounted fish, a muskox head, walrus and narwhale tusks, and the skins of wolves, foxes, seals, and wolverines. Expertly presented and supplemented with photographs, these mounts were prized family keepsakes.

While I waited for my turn in the shower, Joe explained the wildlife trophies to me. Those most prominently displayed were the first significant catches or hunting successes of his children. The huge lake trout on display belonged to his daughter who caught it while ice fishing, the silvery white wolf skin was from the first wolf shot by his oldest son, Joe Jr., and so on.

Joe and his sons hunted wolves for their furs. The previous year, they bagged about thirty wolves whose tanned pelts earned him close to C$300 each—a decent source of secondary income for the family. Bushy wolf fur was favored for rimming the hoods of parkas. For an entire wolf coat, the fur colors had to be matched, and several pelts were needed to make up a single coat. Surmising that their purchase might require a serious personal investment, I tried to inquire about prices when I got home, but the salesperson at Marshall Fields claimed that wolf furs were illegal in the United States. I wasn't sure about that, but in any event, none were for sale at her store.

I could have chatted with Joe for hours, but the day had grown long. The hot shower was exquisite. The thinly carpeted floor of the loft, despite the addition of my sleeping pad, however, was hard. I tossed and turned and then got up early. Maybe I missed the spongy peat of the tundra. Maybe I was just anxious about making our connections and completing the last four steps of Tom's master plan that would return us to the Midwest.

Chapter 15
The Northern Store and the Bay

The next morning, Joe and his wife left for their jobs while we stayed at the house to repack our gear for the flight home later that day. With everything set to go, except for the canoes, which we would deal with later, we walked down the town's gravel roads in search of the Padlei Inn where dining services and breakfast meals were reputedly offered. Along the way, we passed the Northern Store.

Clad in glossy, cream-colored vertical panels, Arviat's Northern Store, more so than retail shop, had the outward persona of an industrial warehouse. To the left of the front door, a line of four, porthole-like rectangular windows horizontally divided the single-story wall. To the right, the panels, in deference to the Arctic's winds, stood windowless. Overhead, the red-lettered line trailing the large green "Northern" sign read "Your everyday value store." Inside, cash or credit cards were the preferred means for acquiring groceries, fast food, guns, ammunition, CDs, ATVs, skidoos—everything and anything. The Northern Store was the Arctic's version of a Wal-Mart or a Fleet Farm, smaller in square footage but more diversified in inventory.

Later in the day, we would return to the Northern Store for lunch at the Colonel Sanders' Kentucky Fried Chicken franchise located inside. There, surrounded by white interior walls, we would replenish our bodily reserves of trans fats while seated on molded plastic chairs and dining on a white Formica-topped table. Clearly, neither this furniture nor the chickens who gave up their lives and breast meat for our sandwiches were locally sourced. We would also watch Tom entertain us with his dessert. It was the kind of treat he had been dreaming of during his days of "deprivation" on the trail. The long-awaited materialization of Tom's fantasizing would be a chocolate éclair, replete with ultra-white swirls of synthetic-looking whipped cream topped with an incandescent maraschino cherry. In the land of caribou and seals, it was a surreal object to behold.

As we ate, I expressed my amazement about the Colonel's geographic reach. I also sensed that this building had a richness of meaning beyond its austere substance. More so than just the tangible outcome of an architect's design, a work crew's assemblage of imported construction materials, or a corporation's inventories of products, the Northern Store here suggested a sort of three-dimensional snapshot in the timeline of Barren Lands history. It was the precedent part of this timeline that got me to wondering.

How and when did the Hudson Bay Company, whose trading posts once extended across the Far North, switch from a bartering, fur-trading empire into a retail chain now known as the Northern Store? From a business standpoint, I guessed that this event must have taken place more as a dramatic metamorphism than incremental evolution. I knew that the HBC played a leading role in the European settlement of Canada, and I had also heard the joke, which asks what the letters H-B-C stand for and delivers the punchline "Here Before Christ," but beyond this, I knew little.

My image of the historical trading post, no doubt distorted by popular culture, was that of a homey log cabin with a wisp of smoke curling from the chimney and neat piles of beaver pelts and sundry trade goods stacked up inside. Among these sundries were those sturdy HBC blankets appealingly striped in bands of black, yellow, red, and green. As for the early HBC trader, my image was that of an evenhanded gentleman and rugged frontiersman all rolled into one, a jack-of-all-trades fatherly person who could mediate disputes and help keep the peace in places beyond the reach of Canadian officialdom. The trader, in these early days, I imagined, was the kind of fellow who could pull his own teeth if he had to as well as the aching molars of any willing native people, and it is true that the HBC did hire physicians as mangers for some of their posts.[1]

And when Canadian law enforcement arrived on the scene, was it not always, as it was in my mind's eye, a black-booted, red-shirted, diagonally-strapped, square-jawed Mountie? My image was that of a brave man of few words and perfect posture verified by his iconic circumferential hat brim, the plane of which seldom deviated from perfectly level. Reliably, was he not also a man who, through patient restraint and chivalrous conduct, set himself apart from his pugnacious, trigger-happy cross-border counterparts whose attempts to tame the American West invariably involved liberal exchanges of gunfire? I was dubious of these folklore-tainted images and mused that I might be channeling Mountie

Dudley Do-Right of the Rocky and Bullwinkle cartoon series of my youth, but these were the only and thus the best notions I had.

When I returned to Minnesota and reentered the stacks and alcoves of the Wilson Library, I would learn, as they say, the rest of story. To be sure, these prior images held some measure of truth. It also proved true that, from the very beginning of post-contact history, no other institution was more intertwined with the culture and economy of the Canadian Arctic than the venerable HBC or the "Bay." The Bay's traders, in fact, had arrived well before the missionaries and well before the Mounties.

It all started in 1670 when King Charles II issued a charter granting the Hudson Bay Company all the land, waters, and rights to commercial trade within the watershed of Hudson Bay. That this charter did not include any compensation for the land's current occupants meant that it was more edict than a real estate transaction underpinned by a purchase agreement, but it was geographically huge just the same. As for the pelts collected at the Arctic's trading posts, these were not the black furs of beavers as they were in the more southerly, treed parts of the continent. The furs in demand in the Far North, in fact, were white.

Looking back at the turn of the 20th Century, when the bowhead whales had nearly vanished, one might logically guess that the Inuit would have faced an abrupt and harsh retreat to their nomadic lifestyles on a land bereft of resources. It was fortuitous for the Inuit—as I would learn from my post-trip research—that this dire outcome did not prevail. Instead, a new economic boom followed in the wake of the collapse of the whaling industry. It was the "white" gold rush, and it took place, not on the high seas of Hudson Bay, but on the tundra of the Barren Lands. Moreover, the HBC, the precursor to the Northern Store in which we sat, made it all possible—that and the little, white-furred arctic fox.

At the time, prolific and bushy-tailed arctic foxes lived everywhere above the tree line as they still do today. Not much larger than a common house cat, they are the little white shadows trailing behind and scavenging the carcasses left by polar bears and other larger predators. Unlike their wary, red-haired southern cousins, white-furred arctic foxes are curious and trusting, eager to sniff out and fall victim to freshly set traps.

For the Inuit, arctic foxes traditionally held little value, food or otherwise. Just after the turn of the twentieth century, however, the outside world of fashion promoted arctic fox fur for women's coats and stoles, and the trend was set. Trading companies rushed into the Arctic to build new posts and garner their share of the white gold, and the Inuit, eager for trade goods, set their traps and delivered the pelts. In 1921, an HBC post sprung up on the shores of Eskimo Point (present day Arviat).

While the prices for furs remained high, times were good. Inuit trappers fed their families and their dogs, and some gained modest affluence. The woolens from the posts didn't provide the warmth of caribou skins nor did imported foods match the nutritional value of raw seal and caribou, but the trader's goods, from tools to tea, were welcome additions beyond what hunting alone could provide.[2]

The HBC trader, meanwhile, held a position of nearly unchecked power. Although the HBC's officially sanctioned monopoly ended in 1870, the Bay maintained control of the market through predatory pricing, reprisals against disloyal trappers, acquisition of competing traders, and saturation of competitors' trading areas with mobile HBC trading posts until the competitors were driven off. HBC merchants decided what supplies would be extended on credit to grubstake their trappers, what goods would be sold in trade, and the prices, in tokens or "sticks," that would be paid for the pelts. Unlike cash, tokens could be used to buy supplies only at the HBC post. Until the late 1950s, money, for all practical purposes, did not exist in the Far North.

The traders' interests lay in encouraging the people to use and depend on trade goods. Productive trappers enjoyed easy credit and supplies from the trading posts.[3] Those who were not or who preferred a more subsistence lifestyle were denied.[4] With the HBC's control over debt and credit established, the traders also held sway in the selection of Inuit campsites whose locations favored proximity to the trading posts and good fox habitats over good hunting grounds.[5] Deficiencies in the wildlife around these camps, by necessity, were offset by greater reliance on imported goods.

Eventually, trade supplies and food—steel traps, guns, hatchets, knives, saws, needles, matches, rubber boots, woolen clothing, flour, and lard—became essentials. The small luxuries of tea and tobacco became addictive. The use of the rifle, motorboat, and the primus stove required imported ammunition, gas, and kerosene.

As the focus shifted from hunting to trapping over the course of a generation, the traditional hunting methods fell out of practice. Indigenous weapons and tools were discarded. Ancient skills disappeared. Diamond Jenness gives the account:

> Fewer Eskimos now could track down the breathing holes of the seals in the ice that mantles the winter sea; few could harpoon a seal from a kayak, or approach it within harpoon range as it drowsed on the surface of the ice. With the introduction of rifles, they had forgotten the

art—no longer needed—of driving whole herds of caribou into snares or ambushes, or into lakes and rivers where hunters could pursue the swimming animals in their kayaks and spear them with lances. The kayak itself had almost disappeared, for now they were demanding boats with outboard motors, and schooners with diesel engines. The inherited lore of centuries was fading, and the younger generation of natives neither valued the knowledge and skills of their forefathers nor cherished any desire to cling to the ancient ways.[6]

Unable to survive without tools, weapons, and other imported goods—literally the trappings of civilization—the fate of the Inuit fell into the hands of the traders.

The emphasis on collective relationships and the sharing of food, skills, and property shifted toward individual work and material accumulations. Instead of families joining together to hunt or fish, the trap line was a solitary pursuit. Instead of wandering about with his family in tow, the trapper left them at the base camp where they awaited his return. Once apprehensive about possessions that would hinder their movement, Inuit families now equipped their semi-permanent base camps with Victor gramophones and paid for them with fox skins. Exposure to the white man's goods brought desire, desire brought discontent, and the trade that ensued brought dependence. Rather than a reciprocal trade among equals, the new economy of the Far North was essentially feudal, one of trapper serfs and trader lords.

The missionaries and the Royal Canadian Mounted Police (RCMP) followed behind the trail blazed by the traders—the clergy to save Inuit souls, the Mounties to overlay Inuit customs with Canadian law. Although usually collaborative, the members of this triumvirate occasionally clashed. Idle post loungers, vulnerable to the next ship-borne disease, were the scorn of the HBC and the Mounties. They preferred their trappers scattered about the land, able-bodied and working their trap lines. The missionaries, on the other hand, needed a flock to shepherd. They coaxed the people into the settlements with emergency food rations, medical care, occasional schooling, holiday festivities, and the use of the mission's motor boat for fishing and hunting.[7]

Ultimately, the reliance on a single, luxury commodity ran its economic course. In the end, neither fox furs nor the fatherly HBC proved infallible. The Arctic's sentinels of cold and distance, which had kept the masses from her shores, were powerless against the rippling effects from the Great Depression and the dictates of fashion from New York and Paris. Arctic fox furs, once the height of style, became objects of derision. European prostitutes suddenly decided that they couldn't walk the streets without a telltale arctic fox stole.[8] Respectable society began to revile the signature hooker look and the demand for fox apparel plummeted. The fur-clad occupants of open carriages and early motor cars also began to travel in enclosed vehicles and thus shed their heavy furs.

Fox pelt prices crashed from C$70 each in 1920s, to $9 in 1939, and then to less than $4 each in the late 1940s. The HBC closed its inland posts and withdrew them to the coasts where they were further consolidated. While Inuit incomes fell, the prices of the commodities on which they depended, from flour to ammunition, continued to rise.[9] The Inuit, caught in the jaws of this economic vice, saw their new way of life crushed before their eyes.

The score of years beginning in the mid-1930s were times of hardship in the Barren Lands. The Indians from the south, white trappers, and independent traders, who had chased the white gold rush into the Barrens, added to the depletion of the caribou herds that had begun with the whalers.[10] Weakened by hunger, the Inuit were worn down by white man's diseases. Even their poorly fed dogs took ill and died by the hundreds.[11] A mixed system of relief rations, administered by the traders and Mounties and augmented by the clergy, carried many Inuit families through these hard times, but in the Barren Lands' remoter regions, hunger turned to famine.

While the lives of the Inuit fell into disarray, the government's attention was diverted to the Great Depression, the Second World War, and then to the Cold War. The United States and Canada built the Crimson Air Route network of airfields and communications facilities in the Far North for evacuating casualties from Europe and defending against possible Nazi invasions. Canada also saw this infrastructure as a means for developing her northern resources, such as the nickel ore discovered on the Rankin Inlet peninsula, just north of Arviat. Later, these arctic footholds were linked with the Cold War-inspired DEW (Defense Early Warning) Line radar installations.[12]

Lured by day-labor jobs, the Inuit moved their camps next to these military and communication facilities and appropriated scraps from the dumpsites to build shacks that mimicked the residential style of the invading culture. Unlike their snow huts that annually melted away, the scarcity of wash water in this frozen land and the relative permanency of these "new" shelters added to their sordidness.

However, when World War II ended and the Cold War ebbed, so did the jobs. The poverty of the Inuit returned, this time accentuated by their loss in stature. In the past they knew no other world and accepted theirs as the best available, but the new abundance around them—movies, laundries, pool tables, and all manner of industrial technology—shattered these assumptions. Feeling adrift, if not apathetic, many saw little future in returning to the land.

For the Inuit who had made their camps next to the bases, most were no longer equipped or able to make such a transition. Donald Marsh, the second Anglican Bishop to serve the Arctic, described their prospects:

> Soon shovels and crowbars took the place of rifles. Fur clothing was useless for the work [at the military bases] and after a year or two, dirty and discarded white men's clothing took its place. Tents were discarded in favor of scrap materials, which became dirty shacks. Dogs were a nuisance—they were only rarely used—and they had to be fed without a return. The dog teams were therefore disposed of. Traps were discarded or given away as they too were useless to a man employed daily. . .
>
> Years went by. Young men grew up in the camp [camps near the military bases]; they reached maturity without ever having hunted a seal or set a trap. Girls never learned to prepare and sew skins or make sealskin boots. Then the blow fell. In three days, the camp [base] was to be closed. Here were the Eskimos with no more work, no tents, no rifles, no traps. They had no canvas, canoes, kayaks or fishnets. . . . They had no food, and many didn't know how to go back to the traditional way of life. Promises that they would be taught trades hadn't been fulfilled. The Eskimos were rendered destitute by the white man and his empty promises.[13]

Soon, the popular image of cheerful Eskimos living carefree lives in the land of the midnight sun was eclipsed in stories like Farley Mowat's *People of the Deer* and *Desperate People*. U.S. service members stationed in Canadian Arctic, in their reports and letters home, confirmed these wretched conditions.

Canada, in the late 1950s, could not ignore the starvations of the Inuit in the Barren Lands. Fear of famine, to use Peter Jull's phrase, and its stinging international publicity caused the pendulum of Canadian policy to swing from austerity, bordering on neglect, to the ascendancy of the Canadian welfare state.[14] Freed of the burdens of the Depression and the Second World War, Canada's policymakers moved forward to relocate, resettle, house, and heal the Inuit.

In their new status as Canadian citizens, initiated by the 1939 Supreme Court decision, *Re: Eskimos*, the Inuit finally became eligible to vote in the 1960s. They also became eligible for family allowances, old age pensions and assistance, and other forms of government relief. The most significant of these, the Family Allowance program, started in 1944.

Because the Arctic was a cashless economy, the government initially held Inuit family allowances in "trust" and paid them "in kind." The RCMP created lists of eligible items for each family—food, clothing, sewing equipment, rifles, ammunition, and other approved items—and the HBC disbursed them. Under this arrangement, the HBC served as the source for supplies still earned in trade from trapping, which required work, and for supplies provided by the Family Allowance program, which required no work at all.

Control over family allowance supplies gave southern administrators a fulcrum for levering Inuit behavior in the image of mainstream Canada. Instead of traditional foods for infants, administrators advanced the use of powdered milk, pabulum, and infant bottle-feeding, which was later proven to increase the risk of infant ear infections.[15] Faced with the difficulties of administering the program in a society where extended family members shared the responsibilities of child rearing and where adoption by non-parental relatives was common, officials imposed southern Canada's standards of motherhood and family structure.

To ensure the wise use of family allowances, the government published a pamphlet, the *Book of Wisdom for Eskimo*, which explained that the "King is helping all the children of his lands . . . but he does not wish you to become lazy." The pamphlet's wisdom urged the Inuit to aim their rifles carefully, to get to a doctor quickly if they became frozen, and not to spit in their igloos.[16] The *Book of Wisdom* was a sequel to the *Book of Knowledge*, published earlier by the HBC, which advised the Inuit that "our father," the king, was looking after them and that they should remain loyal to the HBC. After portions of the Bible were translated, these two books were the first nonreligious works printed in Inuktituk.

For the Mounties and the HBC, administering family allowances was an accounting nightmare. It placed the HBC traders in a conflict of interest that required them to produce bottom line results while benevolently supporting their customers.[17] Concerned that regular disbursements would curb trappers' work ethic, traders paid the allowances in the form of occasional destitute relief.

By the late 1950s, the same direct cash entitlement program applicable to other Canadian families replaced the traders' convoluted system. Inuit cooperatives took over the dwindling business of marketing of furs and pelts through auction houses in the south. The federal government took over relief duties from the HBC as well as the responsibilities for schooling from the churches. Meanwhile, the regular issuance of monthly family allowance checks brought more people into the settlements.

In 1957, after ruling the fur trade since the seventeenth century, the

HBC closed its trading headquarters at York Factory. This preserved, white-washed wooden edifice, perched on a wedge of land between the Nelson and Hayes rivers near the southwestern shores of Hudson Bay, became Canada's most remote National Historic Site and museum, and the once-powerful trader, the Bay, became a retail merchant.[18] Operating in the Arctic under the name of the Northern Store, it sold everything, from pins to anchors, and, of course, a cornucopia of junk foods, from nacho-cheesy Doritos to cherry-topped chocolate éclairs.

As we sat in the Northern Store's KFC dining area, I did not then know or fully appreciate that we were sitting in a branch of this museum, the part that was still living and evolving. In effect, we were players as well as audience in the museum's ongoing performance art. These dual roles, of course, extended beyond the doors of the Northern Store and defined the entirety of our being here and walking around the settlement now known as Arviat. In a final rite of passage before we headed to the exit doors, Tom lifted the chocolate éclair to his smiling mouth, and I said *bon appétit*.

Chapter 16
The Walk around Town

Still in search of the Padlei Inn, we continued our morning walk past the Northern Store. Despite the absence of street signs and no map to guide us, we quickly found our destination at the south end of town. Arviat, after all, was an isolated little hamlet of only about 2000 year-round residents. If you walked too far in any one direction, you would soon find yourself in the boggy tundra or the briny waters of Hudson Bay.

The town seemed a little slow in waking up, but later in the morning it was bustling. All-terrain vehicles (ATVs), a.k.a. 4-wheelers or the "Honda," buzzed around and everyone drove them, from teenagers to grandmothers. Flat cargo racks, one over the front wheels and the other over the back, doubled as passenger seats. In this fashion, an entire family of four or more, including the family dog, could perch themselves on a single ATV and motor around town. The first time I saw this spectacle of family togetherness, I said aloud, "Watch out, one family on wheels coming through!" During the long winters, I assumed that this spectacle would be repeated except with snowmobiles.

A few recently built row houses and apartment buildings lined the streets, but most residential structures were stand-alone single-family houses of modular or partially prefabricated construction. The crouching, curving lines of igloos and the cones of animal-skin tents had long given way to the boldly colored and abruptly vertical walls of industrial housing imported from the south. Tucked in the shadows of these newer buildings, a few smaller and older shacks also held their ground. I guessed that some of these might have been the remnants of the first government-supplied, wooden, 250-square-foot "matchbox" houses constructed of plywood panels back in the 1960s. To prevent the heat from Arviat's buildings from melting their permafrost foundations, the typical house in Arviat was perched above the ground, elevated by posts or layers of pallets, three to five feet high.

Upon reaching our breakfast destination, the Padlei Inn, we found that it had been shifted about by the tundra's poorly drained soils and notorious frost heaves. Like many of the buildings in Arviat, it was not unique in this regard. The Inn's east wing had cracked apart and was tilting away from the main structure in an apparent search for its own unique planar identity.

More disconcerting were the Inn's doors. They were all locked and thus required us to keep walking, which we did until we found a new two-story blue-paneled office building about a city block away. It turned out to be the national headquarters for Nunavut's Housing and Education departments. We explained our predicament to the receptionist who enlisted the help of a supervisor, who in turn called the Padlei Inn and confirmed that our dining needs would be met. We also learned that these two departments were located in Arviat as a part of a master plan to decentralize the government rather than concentrate public facilities in the capital city of Iqaluit on faraway Baffin Island.

We thanked the Housing and Education people, who were doing fine job doubling as an ad hoc tourist information and service bureau, and then retraced our steps to the Inn whose doors were now open and whose innkeeper was present and eager to serve. In contrast to the Inn's structurally challenged exterior, the modestly furnished interior décor was clean, orderly, and pleasant. The menu featured southern fare—no seal meat or muktuk—but the omelets and toast were satisfying just the same.

In all our encounters with the Inuit of Arviat, including the whalers at the mouth of the Thlewiaza, their hospitality and courtesy were faultless. We were qallunaat (white people) from the south, but there was never any animosity. The server at the Padlei Inn, as a case in point, was so delighted with our ordinary tip that she ran to us and gave Ruth a pair of earrings, which she had personally crafted in the shape of tiny Inuit drums.

Indeed, this Far North-of-the-border land was a wonderful place—a place of liberation from the petty extortionists and chill of anti-American sentiments that sometimes fester in other parts world. Forget the polar bears and the northern lights, I thought, just come here to be with the people. Of course, it may have been brevity of our stay or pure luck that kept us away from the glares of sullen souls. There was also the possibility that these smiles hid more conflicted feelings, but I didn't see any need to let a post-modernist funk cast a pall of gloom over their sunny dispositions or mine. I took them at face value.

We continued to roam the streets and to mentally inventory Arviat's notable structures. In addition to the territorial office building, Padlei Inn, Co-op, Eskimo Point Lumber, and the Northern Store, there was the Arviat Nursing Station, the Nunavut Arctic College, Qitiqliq secondary school, and the Levi Angmak elementary school. We also passed a couple of churches, the John Ollie ice arena and community center, a small indoor swimming pool building, the Donald Suluk Library, and the Margaret Aniksak Visitor Center. Later, we stopped at a community arts and crafts shop where Mel and I each bought some jewelry for our wives.

Throbbing in the heart of the hamlet were the Nunavut Power Corporation's diesel engine generators, which fed the town's electric power lines. Their noise was a constant reminder that, throughout Nunavut, a people who once lit and warmed their homes and cooked their food with sea mammal oil or willow twigs now depended on imported oil. And Arviat, like all the other Nunavut settlements, was a place where heating systems operated nearly every month of the year.

The population in Arviat and the rest of Nunavut was booming as was the waiting list for housing.[1] All the houses that we saw, both old and new and even the smallest and oldest shacks appeared to have someone living in them, tangible evidence of a zero vacancy rate. I didn't see any "For Sale" or "For Rent" signs, either. The territory's Housing Minister reported that over half of the households in Nunavut lived in overcrowded conditions, some families sharing apartments and sleeping in shifts.[2]

Although the housing and fuel costs were twice that of southern Canada, landscaping was one area where economy and uniformity prevailed. No lawns, trees, or shrubs complicated the village scene. Gravel, and just gravel, covered the land. The streets were gravel as were the yards, the airport runway, and even the "golf course" on the outskirts of town. At the time, I didn't have my wits about me to ask the local golfer we bumped into what the sand traps were made of. For that matter, who would have thought to bring golf clubs?

Despite the austerity of the landscaping, a boundless sky accented the town's montage of colorful buildings with cerulean cheer. One homeowner had decorated his front yard with a balustrade of interlocked, sun-bleached caribou racks. Aside from these kinds of creative possibilities, as an Arviat homeowner, life would be simplified: no lawn mowing or irrigating and freedom from the twin torments of crabgrass and dandelions.

It wasn't universal, but clutter was a highly favored yard ornamentation. Perhaps it was my qallunaat obsession with tidiness, but I was impressed with its prevalence—a rusting bicycle flung up on a roof, skeletal remnants of snowmobiles, chewed over caribou carcasses here and there, and empty fifty-five-gallon fuel drums, affectionately referred to as Arctic daisies, a truly perennial and invasive variety. While snow would help with a bit of cover during most of the year, not having any grass or shrubs to hide these items accentuated their summertime visibility. Litter might have also been an understandable if not acceptable trait given the difficulty of "getting rid" of things in the Arctic.

Nowhere was the closed loop of our environment more evident than in the Arctic. The cold preserved everything—whether household trash or oil spills—for years. The permafrost limited the use of covered landfills and, in these little communities, modern incinerators were unaffordable. Faced with few practical options, two time-honored traditions, the town dump and open burning, were employed to convert trash and garbage into their slightly less objectionable forms—that and just letting stuff randomly accumulate.

Arviat's nursing station anchored the north side of town. It was smartly housed in a light blue building that stood on steel stilts and was obliquely kinked to follow the curving ridge of land beneath it. The station humbly started in 1962 and by the time of our visit it had grown to provide clinic space for five nurses plus support staff.

Both medical services and medical needs had evolved over the years. While the earlier epidemics of European origin—influenza, mumps, scarlet fever, diphtheria, smallpox, polio, and syphilis—no longer ravaged the Inuit, modern living's maladies had replaced them—diabetes, obesity, and heart disease, to name a few—all of which were correlated with shifts by the from country to imported foods and from active to more sedentary lifestyles in the settlements. The shadow of one of those earlier diseases, however, still lingered: *tuberculosis*. It was a topic, like others, that I would learn more about when I returned to the States to continue my travels, not on land or water, but through the pages of journal articles, books, and websites.

No other European disease has caused greater despair in the Far North than tuberculosis. This disease, also known as "consumption" for the way it wastes away or consumes the body, attacks the bones and joints, skin, intestines, lymph glands, and brain, but it has a special affinity for the lungs. Once a person is infected with TB, the infection remains dormant or can become active, but the victim can never be free of it. TB was and still is a life sentence.

For the Inuit of the twentieth century who were carriers, the infection might lie dormant for years before stress or fatigue triggered the "tubercles" that pocked their lungs. The slow-motion course of this disease was to weaken the body and then to cripple it, stealing life away breath by breath. Undeterred by the Arctic's cold, this scourge dwelt in overcrowded housing and flourished in the exhaustion and poverty of its occupants—conditions that were prevalent among the Inuit in their new coastal settlements in the 1950s and 1960s.

It was a time when tuberculosis actively infected more than a third of the Inuit population. By 1956, one in every seven eastern Arctic Inuit resided in southern sanatoriums. At one time, Mountain Sanatorium in Hamilton, Ontario, with 332 Inuit patients, was the largest year-round Inuit community in all of Canada.[3] The family members who stayed behind in the Arctic and waited for the return of loved ones often congregated around the posts and thus added momentum to permanent residency in the settlements.

In 1950, the Canadian Coast Guard ship, the *C. D. Howe*, made its first voyage to the eastern Arctic to wage medical war against the "white plague." Authorities ushered Inuit men, women, and children onto the ship, which was outfitted with a small hospital and x-ray equipment. With open-water navigation limited to a few months and tuberculosis at epidemic levels, warlike urgency governed the ship's operations. White "medicine men" decided who would return to shore and who would be held on the ship headed to southern Canada.

Few tubercular Inuit went willingly. Some who knew they were infected bolted when the hospital ship arrived. Some had to be escorted by the Mounties. The great majority went in silence, offering no resistance as their relatives stood by and quietly watched them depart.[4]

Medical personnel took the actively infected to Inuit quarters below where men, women, and lone children from different regions slept in triple-tiered bunks, children two per bed.[5] Many had no chance to collect their belongings, say farewells, or make arrangements. Infected mothers were separated from their un-weaned babies who were returned to shore with other women.[6] For the Inuit, the ocean voyage to a distant land where they could not communicate was like a death sentence.[7] Indeed, many never came back.

A TB-infected Inuk typically stayed in a southern sanatorium for two-and-a-half years; many stayed for five or six.[8] Once recovered, the released patient might take the slow train to Churchill and then wait for the next outbound ship or plane for which there were no regularly scheduled departures. Sometimes they were left at the wrong settlements with only light southern clothing. When children finally reunited with their parents and when husbands and wives embraced after years of separation, unbounded joy contrasted with the apparent lack of emotion during their original separations.[9]

However, many found their reunions bittersweet. After years away, children and family members sometimes could not recognize one another. Children who grew up in the south forgot how to speak their native language and could not communicate with their own parents. "Some patients," historian Keith Crowe noted, "came home with lungs or bones missing and could no longer hunt or trap."[10] Others, having spent years in heated hospitals with little exercise, constant cleanliness, and prepared foods, found it difficult to fit back into northern life.

In the south, the keeping of patients' records fell short of perfection. When loved ones passed away, information about the burial place or other details of the death were often nowhere to be found.[11] For those who died from TB, most died alone. Many were buried in unmarked, paupers' graves, their souls given to the grace of God, but the whereabouts of their remains unknown to their next-of-kin.

Modern antibiotics, vaccinations, and fly-out hospitalizations finally put TB in relative check, but this disease still persisted and, in the Arctic, the infection rate at the time of our trip was ten times the Canadian national average. Moreover, new antibiotic-resistant strains of TB were emerging. For Arviat's Inuit population over the age of 45 or 50 who were not actively infected, most were dormant carriers. Only death would purge the disease from their bodies.

Although our time in Arviat passed quickly, with twenty hours of sunlight, our single day in Arviat, in some respects, seemed like a short week. We made full use of that bonus of light, too. Other than the curiosity of the gravel golf course, I don't think we missed much of anything. One of the more prominent structures that we saw was the new multistory school being built in the center of town.

Judging by the size of the exposed steel skeleton, it was clear that this new school would soon be the largest and the tallest building in Arviat. The steel posts and I-beams, so raw and large, seemed out of scale and out of place in this little village. In traditional times, bits of copper and iron from the flotsam of shipwrecks and scattered natural deposits were so precious that they became the objects of complex trade networks. But today, despite their immensity and long, midafternoon shadows, no one seemed impressed with these steel girders. Passersby just passed them by, but here again was another story, one that I wished to learn and, if not the rest of the story, more of than I knew at the time. My post-trip readings took me on another Wilson Library journey where I began to understand and appreciate just how much had changed from the days, not so very long ago, when Inuit children played with toy tools and weapons and learned from their elders' storytelling.

The written word first entered the Arctic in 1876 when Anglican Reverend

E. J. Peck adapted Cree syllabics for use with the Inuktitut language, thus making it possible to translate portions of the Bible into Inuktituk. Thereafter, missionaries occasionally instructed a smattering of Inuit in the manner of the "four R's"—reading, writing, 'rithmetic, and religion—but it wasn't until the 1950s and the 1960s that compulsory education moved north.

Bringing teachers to the widely-scattered camps proved impossible. Instead, Mounties took children beginning at age six and escorted them to centralized day schools and to church-run residential schools, like the one in Chesterfield Inlet, around two hundred miles north of Arviat. Here, children lived in spartan dormitories and were separated from their parents for nine months of the year.

In their new schools, a regimented existence replaced children's lenient home environments. Traditionally, Inuit parents viewed their children's capacity for adult rationality as something that would develop in due time. Inuit families, both past and present, treated their children with fondness more than firmness and cherished them, some might say, to a fault.[12] In a land where hunger was common, anger wasted physical energy and emotional strength. Fits of temper could neither improve the weather nor cause the caribou or seals to return any sooner.

Angry outbursts, too many questions, obtrusiveness, or interference with other people were all considered bad form. This calmness and patience carried over to the parenting of children, who were seldom struck, scolded, or refused food when they asked.[13] The new teachers from the south, in contrast, prodded Inuit children to ask questions, speak up, compete among each other, follow a strict schedule, and engage in other behaviors to which they were culturally averse.

The contrasts between their home environments and the discipline and corporal punishment of their new schools were abrupt. For some parents, the assurance that their children would have something to eat eased the heartache of separation. Authorities also withheld government family allowances unless children attended school. Many families abandoned their outlying camps and took up residence around the settlement schools to be near their children.

Isolated from parents and elders as role models, children were taught skills for jobs that did not exist. They learned little about the land or making a living from it. Teachers, as Keith Crow observed, taught Inuit children how to read with southern primary readers—*Fun with Dick and Jane*, *Our New Friends*, and *Streets and Roads*—in a land without streets and roads. The teachers, who only stayed for only a year or two, formed a steady stream of strangers in the lives of the people.[14]

The church-run residential schools in Canada (and the United States) focused on removing native children from the "deleterious influences of the family environment."[15] Parents were seen as impediments to the proper assimilation of aboriginal children. Although the schools focused on Christianizing their students, when it came to involving Inuit parents, the Lord's fourth commandment, to honor parents, wasn't much of a priority.

Calling these early schools "institutions of cultural cannibalism" might be tempting, but the record was more complex. Most educators were well intentioned and the challenges they faced did not offer any easy solutions. Some former students of the Chesterfield Inlet School, just north of Arviat, felt that their rigorous education was superior to the diluted pedagogy in the government-run schools that followed. Many of Chesterfield's early graduates also rose to rank among Nunavut's leaders later in life.

There was, however, a price to be paid. Students learned little about their heritage, spirituality, or strengths as a people. Residential schoolteachers prohibited older or younger siblings attending the same school from talking with one another. Teachers strapped students who spoke Inuktituk. Officials forbade drum dances, traditional clothing, long hair, and the use of Inuit facial expressions for communicating, such as blinking for saying "yes" and squinting for "no."

Because students were separated from their families, their observation and inculcation of parenting skills suffered as did relationships between generations. Parents felt insecure about their children's ability to support them in old age and could not understand their children when they spoke English. Kept apart from each other, parents had difficulty teaching their children about the traditional ways. Children were ashamed that they could not hunt or sew skins as their parents did but also considered their parents somewhat ignorant and old fashioned.[16] Many students felt apart of neither native nor southern cultures and, as adults, fell into self-destructive, addictive behaviors.

In 1970, the residential school at Chesterfield Inlet on the western coast of Hudson Bay closed in disgrace. A quarter century after the school closed, the Royal Canadian Mounted Police completed a twenty-one-month investigation of 236 allegations of child abuse, but did not issue any criminal charges. Some of the accused had died, and some of the claimants, after so many years, could no longer name their abusers.

Three decades after the government assumed responsibility for the control of these formerly church-run schools, the churches and the government issued apologies. The Statement of Reconciliation was Canada's official apology to the former students of these schools, which operated in every province. In 1998, the government also launched the Aboriginal Healing Foundation and followed in 2005 with an offer of compensation to former students, starting at a minimum of C$10,000.

Among the former students still alive, some saw the Statement of Reconciliation as political contrivance and the compensation as too little, too late—a painful reminder of a painful past. In mainstream Canada, some could not see the logic or justice of atoning for the conduct of a former, largely passed-away generation. Yet, delaying that apology most likely would have only shifted the wounds of the aggrieved from one generation to the next while diminishing the redemptive values for those offering remorse.

By issuing the Statement of Reconciliation and acknowledging their faults, regardless of their generational source, mainstream Canada could begin to carry on its affairs with self-respect. As for the aggrieved, they would eventually realize that persistent resentment indentured them to their abusers. Endless anger and futility were one and the same, and unending grief was debilitating, both physically and emotionally. The purpose of forgiving in this context was not for the Inuit to forget. It was to remember and then to forgive—to forgive, to heal, to renew hope, and ultimately to reclaim the power over their lives.

An excerpt of Canada's Statement of Reconciliation follows. It was remarkable if for no other reason than its last four words, which are rarely heard in public discourse, perhaps in any kind of discourse.

> Sadly, our history with respect to the treatment of Aboriginal people is not something in which we can take pride. Attitudes of racial and cultural superiority led to a suppression of Aboriginal culture and values. As a country, we are burdened by past actions that resulted in weakening the identity of Aboriginal peoples, suppressing their languages and cultures, and outlawing spiritual practices. We must recognize the impact of these actions on the once self-sustaining nations that were disaggregated, disrupted, limited or even destroyed by the dispossession of traditional territory, by the relocation of Aboriginal people, and by some provisions of the Indian Act. We must acknowledge that the result of these actions was the erosion of the political, economic and social systems of Aboriginal people and nations.
>
> Against the backdrop of these historical legacies, it is a remarkable tribute to the strength and endurance of Aboriginal people that they have maintained their historic diversity and identity. The Government of Canada today formally expresses to all Aboriginal people in Canada our profound regret for past actions of the federal government,

which have contributed to these difficult pages in the history of our relationship together.

One aspect of our relationship with Aboriginal people over this period that requires particular attention is the Residential School system. This system separated many children from their families and communities and prevented them from speaking their own languages and from learning about their heritage and cultures. In the worst cases, it left legacies of personal pain and distress that continue to reverberate in Aboriginal communities to this day. Tragically, some children were the victims of physical and sexual abuse.

The Government of Canada acknowledges the role it played in the development and administration of these schools. Particularly to those individuals who experienced the tragedy of sexual and physical abuse at Residential schools, and who have carried this burden believing that in some way they must be responsible, we wish to emphasize that what you experienced was not your fault and should never have happened. To those of you who suffered this tragedy at Residential schools, we are deeply sorry.

Although it was high summer in Arviat, parked snowmobiles, locally referred to as "skidoos," were ubiquitous. There was also a scattering of komatiks, transport trailer sleds, which looked like oversized, prostrate wooden ladders—often hitched to the back of the skidoos. Beneath the intense summer sun, these wintery transport devices stood out like seasonal anomalies. In addition to the horsepower of skidoos, the town's ample canine population suggested that dog power still had a role in the pulling of komatiks.

Many houses had one or two dogs tied to them, pets we presumed. On the outskirts of town, where roads and houses yielded to tundra, teams of forlorn sled dogs sat idly, tied to pickets, each dog well separated from the other. These dogs were beasts of burden, maybe working partners, but not cuddlesome pets. On this midsummer's day, they looked perfectly annoyed. Grumpy about the lack of snow and cold, they looked as inclined to take chunks out of our hands as to let us pet them. We hoped that their chains had no weak links.

Separating the dogs prevented them from fighting, and that alone was a good enough reason to keep them picketed. The early Mounties quickly encouraged the practice of tethering dogs by shooting those that ran loose. Operating in virtual isolation, the Mounties of the early twentieth century were the embodiment of Canadian justice. Their word was law, and they exercised it without the kinds of checks and balances that were customary in southern Canada's society of equals. While often helpful, some Mounties built reputations as bullies as they shot dogs, took Inuit children away to schools, and abruptly introduced Native people to the principles of southern justice and morals.

The canine populations reminded me that, unlike skidoos, dogs had to be fed even when they're not in use. The recovery of local caribou herds undoubtedly had benefited from the substitution of skidoos for meat-eating sled dogs. Snow machines, despite these very positive attributes, however, were not always the perfect solution. Dogs had personalities and that probably made them a little more interesting, and, compared to skidoos, dogs probably "started" more reliably, even in extreme cold. They also spread out more safely on fragile ice floes and tended not to abruptly stop in their tracks due to parts failures or empty fuel tanks. "Refueling" a dog team, with luck, was obtainable on the trail, just the nearest caribou haunch or seal carcass away. On the distant tundra, the driver of a stalled skidoo might quickly discover the inedible qualities of his snow machine's metal and plastic parts. A dog team musher, in contrast, was never without an emergency supply of warmth or fresh, albeit gruesome protein—a la canine.

Except for the absence of trains, Arviat residents enjoyed a truly multimodal transportation system: dogsleds, bicycles, boats, airplanes, helicopters, skidoos, innumerable ATVs, a taxi or two (one was immobilized on blocks), a few cars, and a lot of pickup trucks. I was puzzled by the practicality of owning a vehicle in a town where the distance to nearly every destination never exceeded a short walk. Other than construction work or local hauling, maybe residents owned cars and pickup trucks to show off Nunavut's winsome nonrectangular license plates, which favored the profile of a polar bear.

Many households also had canoes or small boats stored in their yards. Less than a hand-count were moored in the local harbor. Other boats, mostly their battered remnants, dotted the shoreline, which functioned as a sort of marine junkyard. On the gravelly beach, an older Inuk and an attentive young boy quietly worked on the hull of an overturned canvas-covered freighter canoe, a vintage forest green vessel about twenty-five feet long.

The wharf at the opposite end of town, in contrast, shuddered with the roars of large front-end loaders. Their determined drivers raced back and forth, using the forklift front-ends to unload shipping crates from the barge docked at the wharf. The operators held these rubber-tired behemoths to the straightest possible lines between starts and stops, and only the suicidal would consider jaywalking across their routes. To replenish the emptied barge, a red tugboat pushed the barge out to the cargo ship anchored offshore, the same one we had passed the night before.

In the 1940s when there were no front-end loaders or mammoth shipping crates, Inuit stevedores and Kablunaat worked side-by-side, hauling the supplies on their backs and sharing breaks of tea and biscuits. It was tough work but also a festive event. When the stevedores finished, the ship departed giving a long whistle, and the Inuit, for their payment, could buy on fixed credit at the trading post.

A common refrain in Nunavut was that working to survive had now been traded for working for a wage—if a job could be found. But wage-paying jobs were scarce, and it was telling that the largest employer was the government. Just by walking around Arviat, it was plain to see that there weren't enough places for the town's adults to work. Nothing resembling a manufacturing plant existed.

When I returned to the States, I learned that when the definition of unemployment included people who didn't seek work because there wasn't any, the jobless rate in Nunavut was probably closer to fifty percent or more. Of those unemployed, virtually all were Inuit. Abysmal high school graduation rates frustrated efforts to employ Inuit workers in government jobs. Only about a third of all Inuit students finished high school, and many were socially instead of academically promoted.

Since its 1950 nadir, Nunavut's population had doubled with each new generation. Due to high birth rates, especially among teenage girls, the proportion of people under twenty was twice that of Canada as a whole. A local newspaper headline read: "Babies having babies: an explosion of infants born to teenage mothers . . . exploding numbers of new immature teenage mothers are putting a strain on Nunavut's health and social service system." Nunavut historian Kenn Harper noted that services, housing, and job creation stood little chance of keeping up with population growth.[17]

For the most part, Inuit livelihoods had evolved into what Harper called a "tenuous mix" of wage labor and subsistence harvesting. Hunting allowed Inuit men to remain engaged in supporting their communities, which still depended on country foods as economic and dietary necessities. But hunting and trapping had declined and, in doing so, had diminished the role of Inuit men. Hunting was now a part-time activity that focused on out-and-back trips, sometimes taken in the manner of family vacations.

Money, ironically, had become the necessary means for engaging in subsistence hunting. Long trips were required to get beyond the heavy hunting pressure around the settlements. Modern equipment—motor boats, ATVs, skidoos, fuel, and ammunition—made these longer trips practical and more productive, but it also required large outlays of wages. Fortunately, sharing networks among extended family members helped hunters get much of the cash they needed and allowed wage earners to receive a share of the country foods in return.[18]

In the 1960s, an emerging market for sealskins held the possibility of an economic lifeboat for some of these communities, but those hopes foundered under the weight of the animal rights movement. Media images of Newfoundland hunters clubbing baby seals mobilized public sentiment, and pictures of actor Bridgette Bardot cuddling an equally photogenic white-coated pup made the seal a mantra.

The Newfoundland hunters killed the baby harp seals for the profit of their pelts and, for the most part, didn't eat the meat.[19] The Inuit, using rifles and harpoons, hunted a completely different species, the ringed seal, to feed their families, just as their ancestors had done for generations. For the Inuit, who now wore boots made of rubber instead of sealskin, selling the pelts was a bonus.

Failing to see these distinctions or the plight of native peoples, the United States responded with the 1972 Marine Mammal Protection Act, which banned the importation of *all* sealskin and other marine mammal products. Europeans followed suit. As the market prices for sealskins crashed, the co-ops stopped buying sealskins and Inuit suicides increased, but the number of seals harvested hardly changed.[20]

In other Nunavut settlements, small-scale facilities for processing caribou and musk ox meat, leather, and qiviut (muskox wool) provided a handful of wage-paying jobs and promised to add a few more. A small number of Nunavummiut, including some in Arviat, also made a living as sculptors, weavers, print makers, and jewelry designers. Mining, with good reason, promised economic hope, but the benefits often fell short of expectations.

Mining, in addition to its vulnerability to boom-and-bust cycles and environmental impacts, often employed "air commuters" who worked twenty days on and ten days off, or some equivalent cycle. Rather than building a full-fledged town to support a mine and hiring locally, mining companies cut costs by flying in equipment and skilled workers from other parts of Canada and housing them in temporary buildings onsite. Facing a worldwide glut of zinc, Nunavut's most recent working mine, the Nanisivik zinc mine, located near the community of Arctic Bay, ceased operations in 2002.

Of all the extractive industries, diamonds might be Nunavut's best friend.

The new Jericho diamond mine near Bathurst Inlet promised to employ as many as 175 people during its life expectancy of eight years. Diamond mining was already underway across the border in the Northwest Territories (NWT). Yellowknife, the NWT's capital city, served as a center for cutting and polishing. High in price and low in bulk, diamonds seemed to be the perfect antidotes to the high transport costs in these remote regions.

Next to mining, tourism and commercial fishing represented Nunavut's strongest economic prospects. If successful in increasing Nunavut's share of nearby government-regulated turbot and shrimp fisheries, the territory conceivably could acquire new fishing vessels and invest in local processing plants. As for tourism, eco-tourists like us, "sports" hunters, and everyday tourists, in fact, did come to Nunavut. They came to ride in dogsleds, gaze at the northern lights, experience days without nights, observe exotic animals, and see unforgettable scenery, but their numbers were few. Hideously high airfares and meager tourist facilities hampered this tiny industry.

Regrettably, all the cheery talk about development was probably just that—talk. Even if the outputs from all these industries—fishing, harvesting, food processing, mining, tourism, and art—doubled, Nunavut's economy undoubtedly would continue to be dwarfed by massive infusions of cash from Ottawa. The Canadian federal government funded close to ninety percent of Nunavut's budget. In 2005–06, Ottawa's subsidies to Nunavut amounted to C$29,400 per person per year.[21] But some progress toward economic self-sufficiency, in any form, was better than none.

The evidence that idleness held no joy was widespread. Substance abuse, domestic violence, and suicides were significantly higher in Nunavut than in the rest of Canada. Violent crime rates, led by domestic violence and assaults, were eight times higher.[22] Heavy drinking and drug abuse were three to four times greater. A quarter of the Inuit population had sniffed aerosols or solvents, a swift and debilitating form of abuse, often with permanent effects.[23] Suicides haunted Inuit families at rates six to ten times greater than other Canadians.[24] Sometimes the feelings of hopelessness, especially among young Inuit men, were overpowering.

As we neared the south edge of the town, the buildings grew sparse and the streets, like vignettes, faded away. Tuffs of tundra reemerged and a cemetery, straddling a modest ridge of land, came into view. A gently curving pathway followed the spine of the ridge and linked two, large, life-sized Christian crosses, one at each end of the cemetery. Two rows of burial cairns crowded this pathway, one row on each side of the path, and each cairn was marked by a small, whitewashed wooden cross. These smaller crosses stood more or less erect, about knee high and side-by-side, in the manner of a military muster at attention. Beneath the piles of stones, occasional gaps revealed the presence of weathered wooden coffins resting on the permafrost below.

The cemetery ridge, just slightly above the surrounding tundra, fell away to the shoreline that framed the bay, about a half mile to the east. The bay's horizon line divided the water's steely hues from the lighter blue sky above. This boundary between ocean and sky appeared to be the locus of infinity, but the earth's curve put it only a few miles distant. That was the reality of it. It was the same kind of the illusion that allowed me, as a young man, to equate age seventy with eternity.

Peter Freuchen, who lived among the Inuit in the eastern Arctic during the early 1900s and married an Inuit woman, reported that he saw men and women meditate at the site where "the dead ones were set in stone." Dressed in their finest clothes, they would sit and look out over the land and sea for hours. During this meditative stillness they hoped to receive the wisdom of their ancestors. No form of devotion, in Freuchen's eyes, was ever so beautiful.[25]

The graves in Arviat's cemetery were decorated with plastic garlands and assorted mementoes, some protected under small panels of clear plastic. The remembrances and amulets included children's shoes, a hockey stick or puck, poems, and letters from a sister or a lover. The vital dates, at least those that were still legible on the crosses, corroborated Nunavut's lower life expectancies. For the parents who came here to meditate about the sons or daughters who preceded them in death, I wondered what kind of wisdom would come to them.

Back in town, we met two construction workers who told us about the multimillion-dollar school building. The work crews, we learned, were imported from the south, lived in special workers' housing, and ate in a company mess hall. These same workers were the ones who advised us about the depth of the permafrost: "like kilometers" and "all the way to China." They also said that coils of liquefied nitrogen kept the new school's foundation posts permanently frozen. This refrigeration system ensured that the building's foundation would stay level and anchored to the permafrost, even if the seasonally thawed depth of the active layer above the permafrost varied, whether due to global warming or transfer of building heat.

Although friendly, one of the workers spoke about the "welfare leeches" whose children would attend the new school. Native artists and sculptors, according to the worker, abused the programs intended to help them. Instead of using the tools and supplies provided for artistic work, they supposedly sold them on the black market to visiting construction workers in exchange for cash.

The worker claimed that, regardless of the tool's worth, the typical price equaled the amount required to close a drug deal. He said that his fellow tradesmen had updated their toolboxes with new cordless drills and other items at "hot" prices. He finished by railing about Inuit parents' indulgence toward their children's candy addictions, their rotten teeth, and, in general, the corrosive effects of welfare.

There we stood, the six of us—four tourists and two construction workers—in the middle of a gravel road under a sun so hot sun that it had no business this far north. To mask my unease, I decided that a polite, mute manner was most apropos for the circumstances, but I am afraid that the involuntary furrows in my brow may have belied the civility I was seeking to portray. If this construction worker was not talking about the Inuit who pulled us from the choppy waters of Hudson Bay, who told us stories about whaling, who kindly invited us into their tents and houses, who offered us tea and fed us, who served us breakfast, and gave Ruth earrings, just who was he talking about? What gave him license to condemn all in single breath?

As we parted and went our separate ways, I grumbled to myself about this familiar and sanctimonious sport, that of ranting about welfare and blustering about self-reliance. Clearly, a life on handouts was no good, not to mention undeserved in the case of the purely indolent, but this kind of noise echoed hard in my ears, especially when it came from those who hadn't looked in a mirror lately. Maybe we did look in our mirrors, but the mirrors we favored seemed to be those that possessed some kind of amazing photoshopping capabilities, the kind that magically removed any traces of the warts of hypocrisy and complicity.

If Inuit artist and hunter-support programs were welfare, I had to ask myself: What were the rangeland subsidies to western ranchers, the price supports for Midwestern farmers, and the cotton and sugar tariffs to their southern counterparts in my home country? What about the market distortions and subsidies in a medical industry that now threatened to financially drown American families in a pervasive tide of unaffordable procedures, questionable tests, and overpriced pharmaceuticals, the very same pharmaceuticals we could purchase in Canada for a fraction of the price? What about the cocoon of tax shelters—royalty relief, depletion allowances, and expensing of capital assets, to name a few—spun by our politicians on behalf of the oil and gas industry? What about the boondoggle stadiums for millionaire players and their billionaire bosses? What about the dueling subsidies between states and cities to lure favored businesses to locations where rational economic and environmental considerations alone might never have placed them? What about the captains of industry who, with the acquiescence of their lapdog boards-of-directors, haul in unconscionable compensation packages and then proudly proclaim the virtues of rugged individualism, personal accountability, and the invisible hand of free enterprise while the other, supported by legions of lobbyists, begs for bailouts, regulatory impediments for competitors, and immunity from moral hazard and legal recourse, typically through the offloading of their companies' health and environmental burdens to the general public? Good Lord, it was enough to give hypocrisy a bad name!

Ranchers and farmers, of course, were a hardworking lot, not exactly an idle people, and so were doctors and nurses, most of them compassionate as well. Nor was there anything less to admire when an independent oil wildcatter, after risking everything he owns, finally hits a gusher. These things made a difference, but who among us hadn't leaned on economic props, a little welfare now and then, even me, the former son of a boss, or my friends, who stemmed from comfortably middle-class, Caucasian roots and supportive parents? Other than fate's random hand, what entitled us to the privilege of our upbringing? And what about my hardhat friend in Arviat whose job was created by the new school's construction?

It was uncanny, a short time later, when an Inuk approached us on the street and asked, "Do you have anything to sell?" His nervous body language made it clear: he wanted drugs. I suppose I shouldn't have been surprised that the worst of civilization's tentacles were inescapable, even in this remote arctic hamlet. Then my unease compounded when it dawned on me that the construction worker we met on the street had spoken with a measure of truth. To be sure, it was the kind of shallow truth comes from snippets of evidence—from observations in a single point in time—but it was enough of the truth to be disturbing.

Of course, it was one thing to observe, and it was quite another thing to understand. Also, if there was ignorance here, it was shared ignorance, because, at the time, I had neither the knowledge nor the confidence to say anything that might have brought a kinder balance to this exchange. To crawl out of my ignorance, I would once again have to wait until I returned to the US, and, in due course, I would learn about the history of welfare in the Canadian Arctic.

By the turn of the twenty-first century, it was true. Canada had built up a welfare state that followed in the European tradition of income support, healthcare, housing assistance, and the like, and it was also true that lessening the dependency on this assistance in the Far North had no quick-and-easy, silver-bullet solutions.

To look forward with clarity and secure a better future, whatever that might be, my belief was that we had to learn how and with what attitudes to approach the present and that, in turn, meant that we had to understand ourselves, to comprehend the events and factors that influenced who we were and how we came to be, which is to say our history. Lest we put our future in peril, we could ill afford to detach ourselves from our past or to stumble in the shadows of our ignorance of it. In the Canadian Arctic, the recent history of the Inuit was the history of culture shock, and in the early- to mid-twentieth century, as in the case of the residential schools, the official policies intended to help the people often hurt them by aggravating rather than mitigating this shock.

When Canadian authorities first began extending aspects of this modern welfare tradition to the Far North, they decided that the best way to rescue many of the struggling Inuit would be to relocate them. Fundamentally, these relocations would prove that welfare policies and benevolent charity were not always one and the same. The official rationale was that by moving the Inuit to new unhunted and untrapped locations, sometimes to the Arctic's most distant reaches, they would be better off. While their intentions may have been charitably noble, officials often selected these new settlement sites with little regard for their ecological attributes or the preferences of the Inuit. From the Inuit perspective, the southerners who relocated them to far-off lands did little to end their hardships. They often began them anew.

The first relocation was undertaken in 1937 when the Hudson Bay Company, under authority of the Canadian government, moved some fifty "volunteers" from three Baffin Island Inuit communities north to Devon Island, just east of the magnetic North Pole. Authorities promoted Devon Island as a pristine land of abundant game and promised that, if the venture failed, the Inuit would be returned to their homes. That promise was never honored. Conveniently, the occupation of these High Arctic locations also served to bolster Canada's claims of sovereignty over northern mineral resources and aerial routes. If welfare is a charitable act that draws from a nation's heart, clearly, something else was at play here, too.

Devon Island proved pristine, but it was no "promised land." The island's ice-packed seas were so heavy and the weather so severe that hunting was impossible. Instead of bringing the Inuit families home, the Hudson's Bay Company (HBC) successively relocated them, first to the village of Arctic Bay at the northern end of Baffin Island where their presence strained the local community's resources. A year later, the HBC relocated them again, this time to Somerset Island where heavy ice floes prevented the establishment of a permanent trading post. The HBC finally abandoned this post, known as Fort Ross, in 1947, and then left the Inuit to fend for themselves. Most of the Inuit families eventually wandered south along the coasts of the Boothia Peninsula and started trading at Spence Bay (Taloyoak) where they were considered "outsiders" and, for many years, struggled to integrate with the local Inuit and learn the local dialect.[26]

Similarly, we might ask whether charitable welfare was the true intent when the Canadian government relocated Inuit families from the southern Arctic to Grise Fiord and Resolute Bay, two of the most northern and coldest places of human habitation on the planet. The Inuit name for Grise Fiord was Aujuittuk, meaning "the place that never thaws," while that of Resolute Bay was Qausuittuq, "the place with no dawn." On the frozen deserts of Devon Island, just south of Ellesmere Island's Grise Fiord, where the average yearly temperature is 2.3 degrees Fahrenheit, NASA conducted tests under Mars-like conditions, including chronically fierce winds. In 1953, Canadian officials selected these sites as the lands of new opportunity for the Inuit.

The preservation of Inuit self-sufficiency held sway as the official justification for the 1953 High Arctic relocations, but, again, it was Canada's concerns about sovereignty—against the perceived incursions of the United States and other countries—that steered public policy. "Flag detachments" of the Royal Canadian Mounted Police (RCMP) accompanied by Eskimos, the only people considered capable of living at these latitudes, became the surest way to occupy these lands and assert *de facto* ownership. The transplanted Eskimos, in essence, were to serve as Canada's human flagpoles and no-trespassing signs. Authorities promised relocatees that they could return to their homelands after two years. In fact, this promise was not honored until forty-five years later.[27]

Of the ten families headed for Resolute and Grise Fiord, seven came from northern Quebec and had traveled over a thousand nautical miles in a ship's cramped native quarters. Here they were fed hardtack biscuits and shown movies in which pioneer railroad builders shot up villainous Indians.[28] Mid-voyage, the Inuit from Quebec learned that they would be split into two groups; some families would be left at Grise Fiord, the others at Resolute Bay, 250 miles away by dog sled over sea ice to the southwest. As mothers cried and dogs howled, fathers huddled on deck to try to make sense of their fate as a divided group.[29]

By the time that the Inuit were dropped off, it was September and it was snowing—with little time left to obtain and stich together winter caribou skin clothing. Besides, no caribou migrated through the vicinity of Resolute Bay. Making matters worse, the Resolute camp on Cornwallis Island had no nearby source of drinking water, the fish from the local lake were wormy and couldn't be eaten, and the wind scoured environs held insufficient snow for building igloos. Instead, canvas tents and seal-oil lamps provided the only protection against average daily Fahrenheit temperatures in the minus thirties and the only drinking water came from the melting of grounded freshwater icebergs.[30] To augment these limited resources, the Resolute Bay Inuit scavenged the dump of the nearby military airfield for discarded food, shipping crate debris, and other salvageable items. These, it was said, had become the unofficial relief rations of the Canadian government.[31]

The relocatees at Grise Fiord on Ellesmere Island found better wildlife resources, but hunting regulations forbade the taking of muskox. Owing to concerns about sustainability, the local constable also restricted the annual caribou harvest to one animal per person.

While confined to cold tents, the Inuit complained of hunger and shortages at the posts, including food and soapstone for carvers. Resupply shipments to the trading posts were often skipped or delayed. The Inuit accumulated trade credits, but there was no accounting for them, and they often had nothing to spend them on in the sparsely stocked government posts.[32] To appease the HBC, the government posts at Grise Fiord and Resolute Bay charged the Inuit higher prices for trade goods and paid them less than market rates for furs.[33]

In a few years, the conditions of the Inuit of Resolute Bay and Grise Fiord stabilized and then dramatically improved with the construction of new housing and the provision of electricity and running water, but the isolation of the high Arctic took an emotional toll. The residents longed to reunite with friends and family members who had stayed south and even to visit with those who now lived at the other High Arctic island, but authorities discouraged travel between Resolute Bay and Grise Fiord. These hamlets were so small that young people had difficulty finding marriage partners.

Greater Canada, including the churches and the Hudson's Bay Company, touted the virtues of these High Arctic relocations.[34] Grise Fiord, in particular, achieved some success in preserving a subsistence culture supplemented by trapping and the reduction of relief outlays.[35] At the time of our trip, both Resolute Bay and Grise Fiord were surviving as small but growing Inuit communities in difficult environmental settings.

Among the Inuit, however, a more poignant perspective prevailed. In 1998, the Canadian government finally delivered on its promise to return the Inuit to their eastern Arctic homes. Twenty-two individuals, some having lived in the High Arctic for more than four decades, accepted the government's belated offer.

More so than a chance to return home, the families of the High Arctic relocations wanted an apology. Instead, in 1996, forty-three years after the Inuit of northern Quebec and Baffin Island first landed at Resolute Bay and Grise Fiord, the government of Canada offered C$10,000,000 in total compensation.

Wishing to see the matter settled before their surviving elders died, the Inuit accepted the unapologetic offer and carried on with their lives.[36]

Finally, we might ask whether the relocations of Inuit from the interior of the Keewatin (Kivalliq) region of the Barren Lands' during the 1950s constituted charitable welfare. These relocations began when Canadian officials determined that the Ennadai Lake Inuit, known as the *Ahiarmiut*, would be better off in new surroundings. What followed was a succession of harrowing moves that began just to the west of the our canoe trip's starting point and eventually found most of the Ahiarmiut at Eskimo Point, the coastal village now known as Arviat.

For the Ahiarmiut, in the aftermath of the Arctic fox market collapse, the distance to the nearest remaining trading post lengthened to more than two hundred miles.[37] Ammunition shortages developed, dogs grew hungry and starved, and the Inuit had no means of transport, other than on foot. Spearing caribou at water crossings in the manner of their ancestors had become a lost or, at the very least, an impractical skill.[38] During the 1940s, the Ennadai people "missed" the caribou migration on several occasions and they could no longer depend on the decimated muskox herds. By the late 1940s, Ahiarmiut numbers through disease and starvation had fallen to a few dozen survivors.[39]

In 1949, the government built a new radio station and airstrip at Ennadai Lake, about 250 air miles inland from Arviat. The RC Signals Corps operating the Ennadai Station shared their rations, medicine, and generally helped their newly found Inuit friends who, while "looking like they had emerged from the Stone Age," reciprocated by outfitting the soldiers in caribou skin clothing and doing occasional work around the base.[40] Troubled and distracted by these sick and hungry people, the soldiers asked for help.

In the spring of 1950, police and soldiers loaded the Inuit families on an airplane and flew them to the south end of Nueltin Lake, into the forests of northern Manitoba where their ancient Indian rivals lived. Although they had neither boats nor shelter and little more than the clothes on their backs, they were expected to become fishermen and supply the workforce of an illusory commercial fishery, an operation that never materialized. Feeling unwelcome, cold, and hungry, the Ahiarmiut—men, women, and children—walked roughly one hundred miles over the land, across rivers, and around lakes before they made it back to Lake Ennadai in early winter. When the Ahiarmiut reached their homelands, they had nothing. The police had earlier destroyed their shelters and tools.[41]

Again, the neighborly "Sigs" responded, sharing their food and medicine, even flying out sick people to southern hospitals, equipping their newly returned neighbors with rifles, traps, and ammunition and then transporting the furs to

Churchill in exchange for trade goods for the Ahiarmiut. The radiomen, in effect, ran an unofficial trading post, and the people survived several following winters.

In September of 1954, Canadian Department of Transportation (DOT) took over the station's operation. The RCMP, working from their Churchill, Manitoba, office, and the DOT personnel continued these arrangements on behalf of the Ahiarmiut, but the DOT administrators complained about the "burden of the Eskimos."[42] Poor caribou hunting followed, and, by the spring of 1957, the people had little to eat other than pieces of boiled caribou skin and the leftovers from the radio workers.[43]

The solution to the Ennadai Inuit "problem" rested in the hands of the RCMP, the Northern Service Officer, and the manager of the nearest inland HBC post, which was in Pedlei, to the north. These officials decided to remove the Ennadai Inuit to the Pedlei area. Here, the RCMP and the HBC post manager reasoned that they could watch over their charges while they "recovered their ability to live off the land." The HBC also preferred this option as a means to eliminate the Ennadai Station's competitive trading operations.

The RCMP herded up the fifty-nine surviving Inuit and, in a succession of flights, transported them to Henik Lake, some fifty miles west of the Pedlei HBC post and 150 air miles west of Arviat. Just prior to the first flight, DOT personnel bulldozed the rest of the Inuit's worldly possessions, including tents and kayaks, as the Inuit stood by in bewilderment.[44]

The Inuit knew that caribou were scarce in their new place of exile, but their southern bosses apparently did not.[45] Fishing prospects were better, but with just one government-supplied canoe, the transplanted Inuit families had trouble finding and subsisting on the lean caloric content of fish. Matters deteriorated when several of the Inuit men, in search of food for their families, broke into the storeroom of a nearby prospector's camp. Wishing to set an example, the long arm of the law quickly put the men in jail where they could no longer steal but also where they could no longer hunt or fish for their families.[46]

That fall, the caribou failed to return. Facing the prospect of the "long sleep," some of the people split up and started the three-day hike through snow and wind toward the Pedlei post in search of help. Some didn't make it. Officials then moved most of the survivors to Eskimo Point (Arviat) where they pitched their tents next to the RCMP station. There they had no dogs, sleds, kayaks or other tools for living off the land, only the certainty that they were now "dependent on the white man."[47]

Confronted with the tragedies of Henik Lake, Canada's Department of Northern Affairs (DNA) relocated the refugees *again*, this time from their temporary camp at Eskimo Point, to the new settlement of Wale Cove, one hundred miles to the north. This fourth relocation occurred in the summer of 1958, but Wale Cove's shallow harbor forced the cargo ship carrying the construction materials for the new village to anchor offshore. Pilots, facing stormy seas, tried to ferry in the supplies using smaller craft, but these were scuttled on the reefs, and the cargo ship then retreated to Churchill. With Whale Cove's construction postponed, the Inuit would be moved, yes, again.

The DNA moved some of the Inuit to the Keewatin Re-establishment Project on the outskirts of Rankin Inlet, the town that had sprung up by the new mine. Crowded in a cluster of tiny, twelve-foot-by-twenty-foot matchbox houses, the families waited in idleness and confusion, many of them sick. Another group split off and camped along the Wilson River to the west where they lived in "traditional" tents and snow houses.

The next summer, in 1959, the DNA persevered and succeeded in building ten houses in Whale Cove and reported that hunting for seals and beluga whales had been successful.[48] While some of the Ennadai diasporas found refuge at Whale Cove, these inland caribou hunters were unaccustomed to garnering sustenance from the sea. Most eventually walked back to Eskimo Point.[49] Here, in the hamlet where our footsteps undoubtedly crossed their mid-century paths, the journeys of the *Ahiarmiut* finally ended.

We might also ask ourselves about many other aspects of this era. Was it charitable or even useful when administrators gave each Inuk a metal disc engraved with an E or W (East or West) prefixed number and required the Inuit to wear these discs as neck tags? Was it charitable when regulations forbade whites from "fraternization" with Inuit for fear of "improper relations"? Was it charitable when whites attended church services separate from the Inuit or when whites and Inuit workers at the Rankin Mine ate in separate mess halls and saw movies on alternate nights?[50] Was it charitable when transient southerners kept to their own kind and isolated themselves in insulated, suburban-style houses, while they drew extra pay for their biennial tours of duty in the Arctic? Was it welfare?

A few blocks beyond our encounter with the construction workers, we found the light-gray and somewhat whale-shaped Margaret Aniksak Visitor Center. The young docent patiently showed us samples of traditional clothing, hunting weapons, tools, musical instruments, and games. She summarized Arviat's history, talked about early Inuit dwellings, and then enthusiastically discussed the importance of storytelling and elders' recorded verbal histories.

Interestingly, our young tour guide's knowledge of traditional activities seemed to draw from studied effort more than direct experience, but this was understandable. After all, neither I nor my own daughters would be able to explain how their pioneering ancestors churned butter, made their own soap, wove fabric on a loom, or even how their own grandfather butchered chickens in the barnyard for Sunday dinner.

With the day nearly spent, our plane would be departing in a few hours, and, with nine large packs to carry, a ride to the airport would be more than mere convenience. We needed to find a ride. Tom also had to meet with the airfreight company to wrap up the details about transporting our canoes to Thompson, Manitoba. However, before we left the Visitor Center, I wanted to get an Inuit perspective on the question that I started this trip with: What caused the Inuit living on the land to move to the settlements along the coasts?

"In the 1940s and 1950s," the docent said, "poor caribou hunting caused great hardship, and the Canadian government created the settlements to help the people." It was the official line and, although brief, sufficiently honest. Given the impromptu nature of our visit and the price of admission, which was free, I'm not sure what I wanted to hear or what I could have reasonably expected. Maybe an acknowledgement that my question had no easy answers, certainly no quick ones. We smiled, thanked her, and then left the museum.

A couple of years later my mind drifted back to Arviat and the Aniksak museum, and I wondered what the docent there *could* have said to someone like myself or even the construction worker if either of us had casually wondered in and asked this same question again. Then I wondered, if I were the docent, what I might have said.

I would, of course, want to talk about the collapse of the Arctic fox market and the slaughter of the caribou and muskox brought about by the introduction of rifles and the arrival of the whalers and the traders. I would describe how compulsory schooling and the exhortations of the police pushed the people from their once scattered camps into the settlements, how family allowances, medical care, government-supplied wooden houses, and electricity eventually pulled them in, and how the bonds of kinship finally drew in the last who held to the old ways. I wouldn't sugarcoat it, either. I would point out that it was the government, not the Inuit, who selected these settlement sites, primarily for their proximity to anchorages and runways so that shiploads and planeloads of civil servants could conveniently come and go.

I would test the attention spans of my museum visitors and press on with the details, the details of how, in the winter of 1957–8, famine spread through the snow houses of the Barrens and how the people, in order to survive, ate the skeletal survivors of their dog teams, pieces from their caribou skin clothing and kayaks, and fish bones picked out of the garbage and how mothers, unable to nurse, watched their babies weaken. I would recount how nineteen people—men, women, and children—starved to death in the Back River–Gary Lake area, how six more died at Chantry Lake, how five died of starvation and exposure at Henik Lake, and how an additional two died in violence when one Inuk, delusional with hunger, attacked another.

I would tell the stories, the stories of how the people were broken in body and in spirit by waves of white man's diseases, how they were ensnared in a global fur trade that used them and then chucked them out like obsolete machinery, how they were separated from their familial tutoring and schooled in ways that explained nothing about their traditional livelihoods, and how some of them were picked up like chattel and moved from one place in the Arctic to another. I would explain how the Inuit at the time could neither return to their old ways nor foresee their uncertain future and how, to paraphrase historian Keith Crowe's words, the people, who once pitied the clumsy foreigner or at least saw themselves as equals, had become bewildered bystanders without a voice in the economy, laws, or religion that took control of their lives.

I would ask my patrons' indulgence to consider the Hobbesian choice the people of the Far North faced: to accept the settlement's promise of material security where the physiological needs of food, shelter, and basic survival could be met while allowing others to intervene in the control of their lives, or to retain freedom, self-expression, and dignity but face the prospects of living on a land where life and environment rested in an increasingly tenuous balance. Gain the rudiments of physical comfort but forego independence. In the extremes, one option risked the impoverishment of the spirit, the other, death.

Could I, in a short visit, really explain how the inconceivable had finally become the inevitable, how the people had become cultural refugees in their own homelands? Could I answer the question, the question of how and why, in the vast interior regions of Canada's tundra, where small bands of people once roamed, these lands were now as barren of people as they were of trees?

I hoped that I could, that I could gain some understanding and share it with others, too, but I was not the docent nor would it ever be my place to become that docent. Even if I were to somehow assume that role, compressing all this information into a single presentation would be daunting. So, instead, I wrote this book. I wrote it so that I could continue to ask the same question posed by Diamond Jenness nearly a century ago: Were we the harbingers of a brighter dawn? It was, of course, a reflective question, one suggestive of an episode tied to the past. Yet the reality was that this question had never gone away; it was still with us and it would always be us. Jenness, who died in 1969, could not comment, but I wondered what he might have said about my desire to rephrase it, to bring this question into the present: *Are we* the harbingers of a brighter dawn?

Chapter 17
The Trip Home

Our excursion into the Barren Lands in the summer of 2004 was coming to a close. For the native people here, roughly two generations had now separated them from the tumultuous decades of the mid-twentieth century. Many of the wounds from their collision with the industrialized world were on the mend, but some of them had morphed into western civilization's various forms of malaise, the worst of these being having no job and too much of nothing to do. Although a modest trapping industry still survived along with the perennial concerns about the market prices for pelts, new worries joined the mix. Many of these focused on Ottawa's shifting fiscal capacities and Canada's political will to underwrite Nunavut's settlements.

Nunavut's prospects for economic development remained as challenging as ever. The blizzards that grounded airplanes and the nearly year-round ice that obstructed shipping hadn't gone away. No transcontinental highways had been built across the frozen tundra to truck supplies in or out to markets that remained as far away as ever. Large reserves of oil and gas waited to be tapped in the basins of the High Arctic, but—global warming notwithstanding—most were still locked in seasonal if not year-round ice.

Yet, unlike other First Nation peoples of the continent who were overrun and scattered about until only traces were of them left, the Inuit had survived, from around 5,000 in all of Nunavut in the early 1950s, to around 25,000 at the time of our trip. They had confronted the juggernaut of the global economy and, while having adapted, they had not wholly abandoned their traditional ways. The embers of their cultural identity were still alive.

Nunavut's leaders had steeled themselves to contend with the political and economic challenges that faced them at every turn more as equals and less as compliant trappers acquiescing to the trader. Starting with informal settlement councils, their political sophistication had grown, from the Inuit Tapirisit Kanatami, an Inuit umbrella organization that promoted the creation of Nunavut, to the Inuit Circumpolar Conference, an organization that advocated on behalf of Arctic peoples from three continents.

While the Inuit took pride in their sweep of elected political positions in their new territory, the pace of progress was frustratingly slow. Expectations were high, perhaps too high, back in 1999 when Nunavut became a territory. A little more patience by everyone, outside observers included, might have put matters into a more realistic perspective. After all, the Inuit were trying to make sense of a mess that was more than a century in the making.

During the twentieth century, the Inuit of the eastern Arctic had seen a steady procession of people intent on rescuing them. The rescuers brought the cures, but they also introduced the diseases, and the souls that they intended to save were often driven to despair. As Inuit policy advisor Derek Rasmussen observed, the people of the Far North may not need any more "experts" or "rescuers" to show up on their shores.[1]

To start, we who live in the more southerly regions might do well enough to take care of our own problems instead of exporting them to our northern neighbors. Owing to the Arctic's unenviable role as a planetary sinkhole for toxins, this would mean putting a tighter lid on the pollutants exhaled from our incinerators, smelters, and power plants. This toxic cocktail consisted of mercury, radioactive compounds, PBDEs (brominated flame-retardants), and a dozen POPs (persistent organic pollutants) known as the "dirty dozen": PCBs, dioxins, DDT, chlordane, toxaphene, heptachlor, HCH (hexachlorocyclohexane), and a half-dozen other cryptically named insecticides and fungicides.

Originating from our chemically pampered farms and belching from factories far removed from the Arctic, this poisonous brew drifted in the northerly currents of both air and sea. Over the frozen Arctic, the airborne compounds condensed and precipitated. The wind-driven snow, hardly pure anymore, melted into the tundra and open seas. Similarly, the Arctic Archipelago acted like an oceanic seine, stalling the ocean's currents and trapping its contaminants.

As these pollutants worked their way up the food chain, they bioaccumulated and biomagnified, concentrating in exponentially greater densities in parts per billion. In the water, they moved from algae and plankton to fish and then to the birds, seals, and walruses, and eventually to the polar bears. Because marine mammals are long lived and the marine food chain has many intermediate links, these animals, the seals and especially the polar bears, carried the highest contaminant loads.

On land, this toxic fallout was absorbed by the lichens and mosses, which were eaten by arctic hare and caribou. These, in turn, became the prey of the wolves and other predators. At the top of these aquatic and terrestrial pyramids were the Inuit who still depended on hunting as an economic and dietary necessity.

Once they entered an animal's body, these toxins lodged in the fatty tissues. When spawning or giving birth, females transferred the contaminant burdens to their young. Mammals in their mothers' wombs or nursing were especially vulnerable because of the rapidity of their development.[2] High concentrations and chronic exposures were correlated with cancer, birth defects, vulnerability to infections, reproductive abnormalities, and neurological disorders in both animals and humans.[3]

In hindsight, the link between Inuit consumption of arctic mammals and toxicity in their own bodies should have seemed obvious, but no one made that connection until 1987. That's when Dr. Eric Dewailly discovered elevated PCB levels in the breast milk of Inuit mothers. Originally, he was looking for a pristine, pollution-free control group among the Inuit for his cancer research. Unexpectedly, he found the opposite. Subsequent research by Dewailly and others determined that Nunavik's mothers' elevated exposures to PCBs, mercury, and lead suppressed their babies' immune systems. Their babies had higher incidences of low birth weights, ear infections, and developmental problems. Throughout Nunavut, large portions of the population, both male and female, carried unsafe levels of mercury and other chemicals.[4, 5, 6]

As the ice floes melted away and we fouled our planet to the point of poisoning Inuit mothers' breast milk, just what were we doing to ourselves in the names of progress and civilization? The United States, with only a twentieth of the world's population, accounted more than a fifth of the world's energy use and greenhouse gas emissions.[7] Were we confused about our proper role and responsibilities? A possible answer, in the words of the Prophet Isaiah 1:16–17, came to mind: "Wash yourselves; make yourselves clean; remove the evil of your doings from before my eyes; cease to do evil, learn to do good; seek justice, correct oppression. . . ."

In 1999, the *Nunatsiaq News* reported that U.S. wildlife officials in Buffalo, New York, confiscated six sealskin and whalebone marionettes. Their entry into the country had violated the U.S. Marine Mammal Protection Act.[8] Made by Pelly Bay (Kugaarut) elders, the marionettes were bound for Rhode Island for specialized repairs. The elders had taken more than a year to make the puppets from the hair of ringed seal, muskox, and caribou and from driftwood and whalebones washed up on the Pelly Bay shores.

The elders used the puppets to teach their children about the adventures of Kiviuq, an Inuit folk hero. Happily, Kiviuq and his fellow puppets were eventually repatriated without further international incident. But not for real Canadian Inuit who, upon crossing into the United States, claim that U.S. customs officials impound their personal sealskin clothing.[9]

The Inuit now inhabited our globalized economy. Like flies on flypaper, they were stuck here like the rest of us. They could not give up their skidoos, their rifles, their wooden houses, or—just yet, for the too many people with too little work—their dependency on Canadian social support, any more than we southerners in the United States could survive with our Canadian electricity unplugged or our imported oil cut off. The question was whether the march of globalism would grind the world's cultures into a monotonous uniformity. All hearts beat beneath the same sun, but must the passions that drive them be struck from the same mold? Would our compulsion to conform others in our own image lead to a dull, if not dangerous result? If distinctions were to blur and differences ceased, what could anyone claim for a point of reference, and, without reference, who could claim an identity? Did the greater light and hope lie in the culture of one or a constellation of many? Would the reality of a world of one culture be a world without culture?

More to the point, where would the Inuit, these arctic hunters, fit into this interconnected world, a world that no longer conformed to their historical ethos? Granted, the passing of each new day wedged distance between them and their ancestral past, but it was a past that would never leave them, either.

The timelines of families revealed unique and varied stories, but much of the Arctic's history was and would continue to be shared in common. To adapt some of playwright August Wilson's words, it is the mutuality of experience that forever colors and shapes a people's culture, from the language their children acquire and use, to their eating habits and gestures, to their attitudes toward work, to their thoughts and feelings about sex, to their beliefs about beauty and justice, and to their sense of grace and passion.

It was from these mutual roots that the spirit of the Inuit people would continue to grow and evolve. Its traces would course in their blood from one generation to the next. Already, it could be seen in their attempts to embrace Qaujimajatuqangit (Inuit Traditional Knowledge) in Nunavut's new government, in their hunter support programs, in their distinction between store-bought food and niqituinnaq—genuine food that is hunted, in their patterns of community sharing, in their consensus approaches to decision making, and in their respect for elders.[10] Exactly how the rest of this story would unfold, however, remained to be seen.

As the world shrunk about them, I wondered: Would these Arctic hunters find a place where they could feel at home? Would they find a way of life that suited their sensibilities? Would their future find them grounded in purpose and renewed identity or would they risk being swept away like random bits of swirling, windblown dust? Would they be something or nothing? It was a story whose pages would turn with time, and, no matter what the outcome, there was some hope that it would now be written more by them than others.

As for me, I, too, had a story to write, and the questions I faced were no different. They were the same.

Mel, Ruth, and I sat in the afternoon shade of a metal-sided building and watched the ATVs and their riders swarm in front of Arviat's Northern Store across like buzzing bees entering and exiting a hive. Jamie pulled up beside us in his dad's pickup truck and offered to drive us to the airport. Tom, at the time, was settling the details with the airfreight company to fly our canoes back to Thompson, Manitoba.

In a few hours we would be piling five adults, eight overstuffed packs, and a large bag filled with canoe paddles, fishing gear, and life jackets into the Savikataaq's pickup truck in the manner of Okies on their way to California. Fortunately, our ride would be only a couple of miles to the Arviat airstrip.

Less than an hour later, Tom found us and then started grumbling about his encounter with the freight forwarders.

"You'd think that they'd be happier chewing on glass than processing our paperwork. They said our canoes didn't exist. 'Couldn't find 'em!' But guess what? The canoes are red, seventeen feet long, and there are two of them. There aren't any bushes around here to hide them, either. I had to go over to Joe's office building with one of the 'helpers' and show him."

"But you got everything taken care, right?" asked Ruth.

"Yes, but a feel a headache coming on."

"It couldn't have been that bad, was it?" asked Ruth, sympathetically.

"No. Anyway, it's over and the canoes are set to go. What's up?"

"We're just sitting here in the shade, watching the hustle and bustle at the Northern Store," I said. "In a few hours it will be, 'Arrivederci, Arviat.'"

"It's not what you'd call a 'destination' city," Mel said, "but it's been interesting."

"No kidding," said Tom. "There are probably grandmothers and grandfathers around here who were born in igloos. Now they're hot-rodding around town on ATVs, sleeping in, and watching reruns of *Buffy, the Vampire Slayer* on satellite TV."

"You know," I said, "the old-timers in my family talk about the streetcars back in the '40s and '50s. I can hear them now: 'They were yellow and had woven cane seats, and you could get anywhere you wanted to go. By golly, it was a different world back then!'

"But I wonder what kind of reaction we'd get around the Thanksgiving table if they told us, in a dialect we could barely understand, that they were their own doctors, pharmacists, policemen, butchers, tailors, and teachers. What if the old-timers told us not about the streetcars, but about how they survived off a frozen land without money, cars, electricity, telephones, television, computers, newspapers, schools, or hospitals, and then lived to tell about it, too?"

"I know what some of my relatives would say," said Tom.

"What?" I asked.

"Well, like duh, we got all that stuff now, so what's the big deal?"

"Ouch," said Ruth.

"Yeah," I said, "but don't you think those stories would be pretty interesting? I suppose it won't be long before all the old storytellers around here are gone. Most likely, the next generations of Inuit will be joining our version of the rat race if they haven't already."

"I don't know, Guy," said Mel. "They've got medical care, new schools, even a new government."

"I suppose, but what are they aiming for? More to the point, what are we aiming for?"

"And your point, Guy?"

"I mean we've got everything, don't we? Cars, bigger houses, and you-name-it, but I'm not sure that this bigger business is better. Not sure this hedonistic treadmill makes us any happier. Where's the 'liberation' from all this . . . all this stuff?

"After World War II, my family, four of us to be exact—Mom, Dad, my sister, and me—lived in a four-hundred-square-foot Quonset hut. Mind you, I wasn't much older or larger than a freshly baked loaf of bread. We were cramped, I suppose, but my parents always had a pretty good outlook on life."

"Guy," Tom quipped, "maybe your family had a good outlook because they knew they were going to move out of that closet-sized house. Are we supposed to cram everybody back into 400-square-foot domed huts?"

"No, but turning back the clock in some ways might be okay. At least when it comes to crime, depression, alcoholism, and the like, because, no matter how you measure them, these rates are up, not down over the last fifty years."

"You sure about that?" asked Mel.

"Yes. Not only that, half of today's teenagers don't live with their biological fathers, single-parent families have tripled, and hardly anyone takes a family meal together. The culture of 'self' prevails.

"We clock more work hours, skip vacations, forego exercise, and starve ourselves for sleep. Nobody has a minute of time or an ounce of trust for anybody, so we slip away . . . into the bowels of our obese houses."

"Speak for yourself, Guy. If the shoe fits. . . ."

"Okay, you got me, but these 'affirmations' are never quite enough, are they? When the Joneses lap us with a place twice the size or strut their portfolio of palatial stuff with a second or third home—maybe a place down by the coast, if there's any of it left—we have to keep up, don't we? You know, add another address to our real estate holdings and, for good measure, throw in a couple of billboard-sized flat-screen TVs.

"So what if we devour the planet and smother it with our trash? It's bigger, more, nothing down, and worry about the costs tomorrow. But all this abundance, what is it?"

"Okay, okay, Guy. Take a breath," said Tom. "Enough of this angry old man stuff. You're gonna have a stroke. Besides, it isn't all that bad, is it?"

"No. Maybe I'm having a hard time expressing myself. Maybe I'm just homesick."

"On that note," Mel said, "We need to get going in that direction—home."

We plodded back to the Savikataaq house where Joe's pickup truck was parked and our gear was stashed. Along the way, we met a couple passing in the opposite direction and exchanged hellos. They asked us where we were from and what brought us to Arviat.

I paused and thought of saying something like, "We are southerners. We canoed the ancient waters of the Thlewiaza, down the big Big River with the fishes and the seals and the birds and the bugs. We rambled over rocky shores, through the Land of the Little Sticks, and left our footprints high upon sand hills. We saw the tundra reach out to meet the sky and every day we heard it in the wind," but I thought better of it. One solo performance a day was enough.

Instead, my greeting was, "Howdy. We're from Minnesota, U.S.A. Just got back from a canoe trip. Down the Thlewiaza, you know, the Big River."

"Gee," the man said, "maybe you want a shower, huh? Come to our house. Use our shower."

Now, where I come from, an offer from a stranger on the street to use his shower would be most unusual. I didn't know whether to be wary or overwhelmed by this Good Samaritan.

"Ah . . . thank you. That's kind of you, but we have a plane to catch."

Maybe, despite having taken showers the night before, we looked in need of some general hygiene. We, in fact, had accumulated a patina of dust from walking Arviat's gravel streets. Self-consciously, I looked down at my hands, leathered from sun and wind, nicked here and there, and filmed over with road dust. They were toughened, swarthy hands, like those of a working man. I liked the look of them, the dust, too, which was a sort of keepsake from Arviat, but washing them would soon be the end of that.

Back at the Savikataaq's house, we jammed our packs into the bed of Joe's pickup truck for the short drive to the airport. The assortment of fishing tackle, map cases, hiking boots, and other items that we had previously either worn or carried in the canoes but outside the packs, was now stuffed inside of them. Without a scale, we couldn't tell, but some of these bulging packs, now the size of small chests of drawers, must have exceeded fifty pounds, worrying us whether they might be too heavy to check at the airport.

Mel and I climbed onto the bed of the pickup truck and wedged ourselves between the piles of gear while Tom and Ruth crowded into the cab with Jamie. Ten minutes later, we were there. The little terminal building had the look and feel of a small-town bus depot.

Jamie helped us carry the packs inside. When I tried to pay him a fare for his taxi services, he refused. He shook his head from side to side, saying "no, no," but I prevailed and also embarrassed both of us. After I pressed the bill into his hand, it dawned on me that my money was patronizing. In matters involving favors among equals, in a land where generosity and hospitality were the norms, money had no place. Putting aside this awkwardness, we shook hands and then walked out of each other's lives. It also struck me that I was re-enacting a time-honored *kabloona* tradition of coming to the Arctic but always leaving it, never staying.

The quiet woman behind the counter, who doubled as the baggage handler, dutifully went about her work. To our relief, our swollen luggage posed no problems. Dwarfed by our packs, the diminutive agent hoisted them onto the baggage carts with little effort and no hesitation. With bags checked and tickets in hand, we were set to go, by turboprop, to Thompson, Manitoba.

Soon, the chairs in the waiting room filled up with other passengers and well-wishers, mostly young Inuit women, many with happy, chubby babies in tow. Several aboriginal men, carrying harpoon shafts and other whaling gear also arrived. Where might they be going and why? I wanted to ask but didn't. Seated across from us, one of the hunters looked askance in my direction.

Maybe we impressed him with our oddity as tourists or maybe he pegged us as members of some kind of save-the-whales group. From my perspective, the presence of ancient hunting technology and the airplane taxing on the gravel runway created a fascinating juxtaposition. People-watching, I reflected, was a two-way street.

The sun, which had shone so brilliantly throughout the day, now began to burnish the landscape with a hazy softness. The motley gathering of humanity in the terminal then walked out, onto the runway, and climbed the steps into the plane. In a few minutes, we lifted off and out of the Arctic.

A short hop of about 180 miles put us just south of the tree line in Churchill, Manitoba, where we had a brief layover but enough time to deplane and stretch our legs. Surprisingly, the terminal in this remote and tiny town bustled with travelers infused with schedule-driven energy. The greenery of scrubby trees beyond the runway confirmed our re-entry into the subarctic part of the continent. I felt like a deep-sea diver pausing at an intermediate location to decompress and avoid the bends prior to emerging into the atmosphere of the fully industrialized world.

It was here, in Churchill, the Polar Bear Capital of the World, that we finally encountered our first and only polar bear. It was a magnificent specimen, locked in pose and standing erect, but only the white furry pelt and head of this trophy remained. Lacking its breathing, fleshy body parts and protected in a glassed-in case that stood in the middle of the airport terminal, no threat issued from the taxidermic remains of this once great animal. It was a good thing, too, because the pepper spray, shotgun, and shells, which we had lugged all over the continent, were now stowed away in the plane's cargo hold. After taking a minute to marvel at the bearskin's size and contemplating that these may soon be the only kinds of polar bears left in this part of the world, we were back on the plane.

The next hop put us into the airspace over Thompson where we landed in amid acrid smoke from upwind forest fires. We claimed our packs, hauled them outside, and then became reacquainted with the novelties of sidewalks, curbs, paved streets, and—marvel upon marvel—even functional taxicabs. While the rest of us waited at the airport, the cab driver took Tom to his van. The van and trailer had been successfully shuttled from Lynn Lake and left in the parking lot of the local fire station, all according to plan. Tom drove the van back to the airport to get his fellow paddlers and take them to a nearby circa 1970 hotel. Inside our rooms, we found vintage 1970s dark oak paneling and yet another novelty—beds with white sheets.

The next day we got an early start, just after sunup. Tom drove the entire way, all seventeen hours of it. With only a sliver of twilight to spare, we arrived in the northern Minneapolis suburb of Andover where we unloaded and sorted our gear in the Moores' driveway. Marsha arrived a few minutes later to greet the returned wayfarers, reclaim her husband, and then drove him home.

As we turned into the driveway, the car's headlight beams revealed that our house was still standing, that it hadn't burned down or been blown away. The college kid from down the block had dutifully mowed the lawn in my absence, which reminded me of the economic advantages of Arviat's gravelly yards. Just the same, the place seemed a little alien, a little different somehow. Clearly, it had not changed. Maybe it was me.

Epilogue
Summer 2006

Two years had passed since I said good-bye to Jamie at the Arviat airport in Nunavut, Canada. Since then, I'd dirtied my fingers in a variety of pots but not chosen to transplant myself in any of them. Owing to an inability to say no, I'd found myself volunteered for or casually elected to several community service positions. Acknowledging that we get what we deserve in a democracy, I'd even done a little politicking.

Sitting on my hands and carping from the sidelines, I told myself, was just one annoying and hypocritical step above the lameness of outright apathy. If the ship is listing, by God, we needed to get involved, didn't we? Close the bulkheads, crank the bilge pumps, get the lifeboats ready, do something, but don't sit there! I still believed that, but I also found that I was not entirely well suited for the political arena.

As for Marsha and me, changes still swirled about us, but our lives together had become more settled. We backpacked across the Grand Canyon together, from one rim to the other and back again, forty-six miles in total, not to mention the mile down and up done twice over. Our sunset embrace on the canyon's rim provided a nice spark to our romance. Tenderly, she said that she loved me in rapid succession, "I love you, I love you, I love . . ." and this gray-feathered cob answered back in kind.

While I dabbled in polity and community during these two years, former business associates called and occasionally treated me to lunch. I couldn't say that I minded these solicitous interruptions, but my suitors seemed to have mistaken my good luck for talent. Just the same, the prospect of working together with a group of people in productive enterprise held appeal—more so than two years ago. Delivering the goods, keeping the customers happy, meeting the payroll, running an honest business, and paying taxes—all of these were reasonably ennobling if not compelling virtues. Maybe it was nothing more than the siren of industrial culture that continued to call, not to entice me, but to remind me that I had never left her iron embrace.

As for activities and things, someday I might find comfort or worthy challenge in them, but none of them seemed to strike a chord. I was as vexed as ever. Without the foil of work, even fly-fishing had diminished appeal.

My father would be pleased if I became a third-generation philatelist, but I was the weak link in this family legacy. The stamp collection that began with my grandfather and continued with my father, I knew, should not have been interrupted. My father expressed no hesitation about the sale of the family business, but the stamp collection was different. Clearly, I was not to sell or discard these books of stamps.

Duty tugged at me, but I could find no motivation for this activity, so the stamp albums lay dormant. The requisite passion to become their curator eluded me, and my father said that he was too old to tend them. Thus, they sat stored away—idle sheaves of paper with little bits of postage history affixed to them—awaiting the possible interest of my children or my children's children.

Despite its somewhat diminished appeal, I still did some fly fishing. Mostly, I went with my octogenarian uncle so that I could be with him and ride in his faded aluminum rowboat. Uncle Pete's pre-owned boat, purchased for the princely sum of $50, caught fish as well as any overpowered bass boat costing tens of thousands more. Sometimes he allowed me the honor of helping him lift the outboard motor on and off the transom. I also went with him to be with someone who understood the simple rhythm of an overhand cast and displayed it well, despite his crooked hands, crippled by years of working in the trades.

Sharing a kindred spirit, my uncle and I fished together with intensity, and why not? We sat between water and sky and celebrated the answer in the communion of his little boat. A crown of green trees rimmed the lake and their leaves, tiny in the distance, fluttered applauses in the wind. Life, Uncle Pete said, is like the ephemeral plume from a lit cigar; I told him about my soap bubble analogy. "Yup, you never know when you'll make your last cast." Then we smiled, reached back, and let our fly lines shoot into the gaps between the lily pads and all the while I could not evade this sense, a sense that a Comprehending Being was among us.

If anything had captured my creative energies, it had been the pages of this book. I couldn't seem to leave them alone. I whittled away at the sentences and paragraphs, trying to carve them into something coherent, something that might be worthy of my effort.

My little journey—whether through the Boreal Forest, out on the Barrens, or in pages of books and journals—allowed me meet new people and to see the beauty of the Earth, in particular, my home continent of North America. I stood in awe before these holy shrines, renewed in spirit, but staggered by their vulnerability. I was staggered by the environmental and economic shock waves buffeting the peoples and cultures of the world and which now had reverberated in its most distant reaches, the Arctic perhaps most of all. I learned how the people of the Far North, the Inuit, had come to live in their modern coastal settlements. I learned that the land we shared on our continent, inseparably and irreplaceably, was the one infrastructure that underpinned all others. I learned that the progress of our industrialized world was a term most appropriately colored in shades of gray, for it was from arrogance that the stark and useless hues of black and white found their prominence.

Pride, according to medieval theologian Thomas Aquinas, was the deadliest of the Seven Deadly Sins, the root cause of all other sins, the sin that brought us farthest from God. For their sins, the prideful, we are told, will be delivered to hell where their bones will be broken on the wheel, a device of exceptional torture. Personally, I'd rather be crucified than put to the wheel, and I may deserve that for stating something so obvious, namely that pride can be sinfully deplorable.

Granted, perseverance in any decent endeavor required us to believe in and, thus, have some pride in our capacity, but, just like seasoning, a little pride went a long way. The trouble started when that belief became immoderate, when it became self-congratulatory, because excess pride kept some bad, sanctimonious company—arrogance, contempt, and hubris—the kind of company that obstructed our decency as human beings, the decency we needed to esteem our neighbors and revere our universe.

It did not please me that many of my countrymen had taken to swaggering about and polishing their self-attached badges of American "exceptionalism." Among our global neighbors, I sensed this attitude was irritating if not insufferable. If we were winning any friends or influencing enemies, it couldn't be because we were running around touting our exceptionalism and exhibiting a pure strain of narcissism as one of our most distinctive, national personality traits. Perhaps I shouldn't have been so hard in my judgments and instead allowed for the considerable difficulties my fellow exceptionalists faced. I'm sure it was hard to be humble let alone overcome our obliviousness toward other cultures when we were so damn exceptional in every way.

Of the various permutations of the Deadly Sins, pride was not only the deadliest. It seemed that it was the most insidious, too, because, from the perspective of the perpetrator, this sin was invisible or nearly so. The glutton may see that he has become fat, and the slothful may find himself mired in disarray, but among the arrogant, a sort of blindness prevailed. Our sin was the hardest to see or admit.

In one manner or another and despite the tumult of the world, the Inuit would move forward to shape their destiny, and so would I. There was a time for every matter under heaven, and, for me, the time for becoming was now. I could not pause indefinitely. Aimlessness haunted me. I had to flee it. I could not rest; the hunger for identity was too strong. Whatever that might be was not entirely clear, but the question moved me forward, affirming—if nothing else—that I was still alive and embracing life, despite its ambiguity. Maybe even because of it.

Sages from Socrates to Shakespeare had told us "to thine own self be true," so I complied in earnest effort. I asked, who am I, just as the Inuit must have asked, who are we, and then I was struck that these questions could not be considered apart from one another. Like vines on a trellis, the searches for self and cultural identity were inseparably intertwined. We were, after all, social animals who lived in context, and, except for the psychotically self-absorbed, the more meaningful of these two questions was the latter: *Who are we?*

I reckoned that from time to time peaks of clarity might emerge from the clouds. Indeed, they might beckon me forward, but I knew. I knew that despite my reach they would always lie beyond my grasp. Yet, of this, I was certain: We were not deterministic robots programmed to endlessly optimize our material intakes. Our minds were more than algorithms, our behavior more than microeconomic assumptions. Something more than selfishness governed our lives. Despite our terrifying capacity to harm or, even worse, to ignore each other, moments of grace, from the serendipitous to the purposeful, were possible. Life, I sensed, was a longing, a search that never ended, but one we could renew by looking into the hearts of others. If we did, we might find our own.

Afterword

2019

An Update on Energy, the Environment, and the Inuit

The story in these pages took a slice of time that began with a canoe trip in 2004 and ended with the roughhewing of a manuscript some two years later. At that point, I decided to step back from writing and take a full-time job. The rewards from this reentry into workplace, while welcome, unavoidably triaged the manuscript to secondary status. Without compelling deadlines, the writing and rewriting, done in dribs and drabs, also became a tribute to procrastination—an explanation, but not a justification, for the long lapse between the first rough draft and final publication.

Along the way there were weddings of children, funerals for parents, and births of grandchildren, so the years, well, they just ticked by. Sometimes it was only during rainy weekends or bouts of insomnia that I revisited the manuscript— to tweak and polish, to write, and rewrite. Finally, in 2017, with the inevitable abandonment of the editing work past due, it was time to put "The End" on it and to begin the publication process, but there was yet another interruption: a change in residency from Minnesota to the other side of the Mississippi River, to Madison, Wisconsin. Here, in the capitol city of the nation's Dairyland, my wife and I would start the process of building a new house and reestablishing ourselves where we would be closer to our daughters and their families. The move and the new house stalled the book's launch, so I decided to add some updates, including this Afterword, and restart the publication process in the form of a second edition, this time in earnest. Despite this halting approach and regardless of the year,

2017 or 2019, an unavoidable question remained. It was the proverbial elephant in the room. After more than a decade, was there anything in this book that was still relevant? What has changed since 2004-2006?

In terms of fundamental trends, the short but not fully correct answer is not much. The trends that defined the beginning of the millennium, in substance, are still with us. Beyond the McDonaldization and Disneyization of society, our blue, cloud-marbled planet is now an evermore "globalized" place. We've been Googled and Amazoned. Likewise, our human intelligence continues to be augmented and sometimes supplanted by the digital, artificial kind whose underlying logic is concealed by the opacity of technology and whose eerie controlling effects are altogether too real. While these world-shrinking phenomena may occasionally pause or slow, they continue to homogenize our cultures and spread their material rewards unevenly in both developed and developing countries. The unevenness of globalization's rewards is especially true among the peoples of indigenous cultures whose livelihoods, languages, and lands are under constant threat.

The irreversibility of globalization seals our fate. Cries of protest are futile and most likely folly, too, because the only thing portending more hardship and chaos are the ham-fisted attempts of nations to elevate their sovereignty above others and turn inward. We share this world together, and somehow, we must learn to manage together, not only to coexist more gracefully among ourselves but also with our planet of current residence because—and with apologies to those who are offended by the obvious—no feasible exit strategy exists.

Here on earth, we are online, plugged in, and mesmerized by our screens. Held within their hypnotic glow are limitless choices that, while expanding our interconnectedness, have also allowed us to retreat into divergent, personalized versions of reality, realities that are often walled off from our neighbors. My sense is that these walls, while affirming, also enclose places of anonymity and isolation—dark places where anger and paranoia sometimes smolder and common decency drifts away. Never mind whatever the truth might be because the truth has become a matter of refracted perspective, all of it mired in a palpable distrust. I wonder what will become of us when nobody can believe anything anymore, when every message is discredited with doubt, when the absence of truth and honesty cause neither alarm nor embarrassment, let alone shame.

By selecting our own personalized versions of reality, have we become, at least in some respects, a meaner, more vulgar, more bullying, more uncivil civilization? Maybe I'm just getting old, but it seems to me that the boorish flaws, which we've traditionally tried to reign in, have been cut loose to freely roam about in our daily lives. Will we remember the turn of the twenty-first century as the beginning of the era when our filters began to fail us? Along this road to dot-com modernity, am I correct in saying that, among the roadkill splatters I glimpse at in my rearview mirror, there appear to be the remains of our basic values, namely those of grace and courtesy?

As technology-stoked globalization makes our world smaller and possibly ruder and cruder as well, it has also become an increasingly crowded place. Over these several years, the wondrous web of life sharing our biosphere has had to make room for another wave of human inhabitants, an additional billion to be exact and all of them hungry—hungry for land, hungry for forests, and hungry for energy. All the while, our wildlife neighbors are finding themselves pushed into ever-smaller pockets of marginalized habitat.

In Western Europe and North America, incremental increases in renewables such as wind and solar energy as well as efficiency improvements and the offshoring of manufacturing have served to level off greenhouse gas emissions from the burning of fossil fuels, but the rest of world wants to play catch-up. Its craving for carbon-based energy persists, including China, the world's manufacturer, which now consumes 30 percent of the global total.[1] Despite our improvements, the United States and Canada on a per-person basis still remain the all-time fossil fuel hogs, together accounting for 18 percent of the world's greenhouse gas emissions but only 5 percent of the global population.[2]

The upshot is that in the spring of 2019 the earth's atmospheric carbon dioxide content marched past the milestone of 400 parts per million to 410 ppm even as my country's anti-science, albeit elected leaders have persisted in denying the certainty of climate change and its causes, dismissing it as a hoax—nothing more than a bogus conspiracy theory.

History doesn't always repeat itself, but as philosopher Will Durant noted, it tends to go around in dreary circles and, from time to time, seems to give us a feeling of déjà vu. Copernicus, Darwin, and all the others—the memories of them come eerily alive today as we consider how important theories, from heliocentrism to global warming, have been slowed by the speed bumps of fundamentalism, ideologues, and the reptilian souls who bask in the sun of the status quo. Back in the sixteenth century, Galileo ran into some of these bumps when he lived his last years under house arrest for advancing the idea that the earth revolved around the sun and thus did not occupy the center of the universe. At least he was not burned at the stake like others of his time.

Science, of course, is a human endeavor. Fettered by our biases and surfeit of limitations, it sometimes hobbles about, but it also enables us to keep searching and verifying, and by steps both large but mostly small, we are eventually returned to a path that leads us to a better understanding of our universe. Nor is science some kind of god. We may do well to approach it with reverence, but with the kind of reverence anchored in humility—an understanding that our understanding will never be complete, that we will never know everything we need to know. Not everything we learn from science is put to good use, either, but that is another matter, a matter regarding our choices and our moral compass. However, if our aim is not to welcome science in the first place but to shut the door on it, then our reach will extend no further than the walls of a darkened room, and no moral compass, no matter how strong, will be able to open that door.

The impetus for scientific inquiry—the hungry, curious mind—is perhaps best fed with heavy doses of wariness but also steady courage. In 1894, University of Wisconsin President Charles Kendall Adams spoke the words inscribed on a plaque that still sits atop the University's Bascom Hill. He claimed these words for his own academy, but they are as broadly relevant today as they were well over a hundred years ago: *Whatever may be the limitations which trammel inquiry . . . we . . . should ever encourage that continual and fearless sifting and winnowing by which alone the truth can be found.*

As my country's leadership moves to muzzle scientists and starve their research, our carbon-insulated atmosphere continues to cook the planet. There has been no letup nor, as we back away from clean air and water standards and shrug off international commitments, are the prospects very encouraging. The polar ice caps melt, sea levels keep rising, and storm events cycle with greater intensity. The vast carbon sinks of the tundra and permafrost are not only thawing and releasing methane, they are now burning on an unprecedented scale. These persistent wildfires, like cancerous tumors on the skin of the arctic, penetrate deep into formerly frozen peaty soils and tap into carbon layers sequestered thousands of years ago. In the summer of 2019, I rafted down the Kisaralik River in Alaska and saw the effects of these smokey fires firsthand—vast swaths of open, treeless tundra being slowly but incessantly devoured, acre after acre, their sooty remains left to starve the caribou and then intensify the sun's heat with their blackness. This once seemingly eternal sink for carbon has now become a smoldering source for its release.

Interestingly, oil and natural gas, which at the onset of the millennium were scarce and pricey, have now become plentiful and cheap. Any influence that prices might have held to temper consumer behavior has been crushed. We are awash with oil and owe this outcome to our amazing ingenuity in developing unconventional ways to squeeze more of it from the earth's crust. These technologies include hydraulic fracturing or "fracking"—a process that pumps sand, chemicals, and copious amounts of water into deep rock formations—and also the extraction of oil from Canada's oil sands. The disruptions of fracked natural gas and oil to the energy markets has dashed any realistic hopes for reviving "clean" coal, and given that "clean" coal, as the bumper sticker reads, is a dirty joke, its displacement is not entirely unwelcome. Fracked gas has even extended its challenge to Big Hydro.

Indeed, in the case of the hydroelectricity produced by provincially-owned Manitoba Hydro, a perfect storm of trends has threatened to put this builder of dams underwater. In addition to the abundance of fracked natural gas, there is the nascency of competitive wind and solar. Finally, there is the self-inflicted threat of inertia, namely the utility's unwavering fondness for multibillion-dollar, budget-busting megaprojects.

Project contracts and jobs for engineering firms, construction companies, and labor unions, of course, are difficult to resist. They are compelling plums and talking points for government ministers. For the Manitoba government, new dams also yield an immediate inflow of new money: water rental fees, debt guarantee payments, and other non-tax revenues. Without ornery taxpayers to deal with, it's almost like "free" money, except that it isn't; ratepayers eventually pick up the tab. And, at a certain point, the always-more-and-bigger paradigm becomes unsustainable, even in Manitoba where utility rates are still among North America's lowest. But not for long.

In 2014, the Manitoba government started the construction of the Keeyask dam based on an investment decision that the Boston Consulting Group would later call "imprudent."[3] Another understated term might be "premature." On the domestic side, the forecasted needs for Manitoba's residents and businesses were already more than fully met; the Keeyask dam's construction would only add to the province's internal surplus. On the export side, which was and still is needed to soak up this excess, Manitoba Hydro was forecasting a tide of rising prices,[4] but those prices, in fact, were beginning to ebb. A 2016 forecast by the company put the average KWh export price for 2018 at C$0.64, the same year that Xcel Energy, Manitoba Hydro's single largest export customer, could acquire wind and solar energy with backed-up storage in the US at C$0.28 per KWh.[5] In 2025, just four years after Keeyask becomes operational in 2021, Xcel Energy's contract with Manitoba Hydro will expire with no guarantee and perhaps little likelihood of renewal.

On the cost side of the ledger, the blanks are difficult to fill in because the company guards the information for individual generating stations. However, the expected "levelized" generation costs per KWh from the Keeyask generating station can be reasonably approximated at C$0.12 including transmission.[6] The upshot for Manitoba Hydro is that the relationship between export market prices and costs has turned upside down. Should the utility choose to keep its export prices above total levelized unit costs[7] and thus above the market prices from alternative sources, export customers will be hard to find or retain.[8] Meanwhile, the company's ongoing debt obligations remain fixed.

Adding to the utility's debt load is the new Bipole III transmission line, which was completed in 2018 and purportedly needed for shoring up the reliability of the transmission system. This is the same line of 180-foot tall towers—thousands of them—that I had worried about during my canoe trip over a decade earlier. In the end, Manitoba chose a route that spared the First Nations communities and boreal wilderness on the east side of Lake Winnipeg and instead, at greater distance and cost, sliced the 216-foot-wide right-of-way through the west side of the province, including prime agricultural areas where it was opposed by local farmers. Over the next few years, the accumulating costs of the Keeyask and Wuskwatim dams, the Bipole III line, and other projects are likely to double Manitoba Hydro's debt. The province's bond rating, having been downgraded twice, although still good, is not stellar, and in a controversial restructuring to reduce operating costs, the utility shed 15 percent of its workforce, putting 900 employees out of work.

To help blot up some of the fiscal hemorrhaging—some export revenue in excess of incremental operating costs is better than none—Manitoba Hydro will have to subsidize export prices by continuing to mark them down below their total unit costs. And, unless the government is willing to let Manitoba's premier Crown corporation go into default, continuing to pay for these mark-downs will entail a procession of annual rate hikes, a direct government bailout, or a combination of both. Whether it's the ratepayers or the taxpayers, the citizens of Manitoba will bear the burden, and Manitoba's historically competitive advantage of low electrical rates in attracting and retaining investment will be crippled.

Meanwhile, despite Hydro's diligent and generous efforts to partner with the First Nations communities directly impacted by the two most recent generating projects—the Keeyask and Wuskwatim dams—the broader impacts of the utility's hydrological alterations of the landscape persist, both in terms of global atmospheric carbon as well as those felt more directly within Manitoba's northern watersheds. Indeed, Big Hydro's promotion of "clean, virtually carbon-free renewable energy" doesn't fully square with the down-to-earth reality. During construction, these and other mega dams in Canada, such as British Columbia's Site C and Labrador's Muskrat Falls, gag with greenhouse gases—from the burning of slash to the methane released from decaying, submerged vegetation to the carbon released from the manufacturing of biblical amounts of concrete. In addition to destroyed wildlife habitats, the carbon sinks or, at the very least, the carbon neutral areas of forested catchments are displaced with reservoirs, which are actually carbon sources.[9]

One reason for this less-than-intuitive outcome is that successions of shoreline plant growth and die-off, due to manipulated and heightened water levels, result in accumulations of decomposing rot, which, in turn, emit carbon-based gasses. Additionally, the soils exposed during dam construction and those that are eroded by fluctuating water levels and augmented flows, such as those from the Churchill River diversion, have the effect of increasing phosphorous loads in the water.[10] These nutrients plus the inflows of upstream organic matter settle into the impoundment basins whose waters, now enriched, foster cycles of plant and algae growth, die-off, decay, and ultimately the off-gassing of CO_2 and, more critically, methane. In terms of reducing greenhouse gas emissions, a forest left intact is always better than making a lake or making an existing lake bigger with a dam.

Within the Manitoba Hydro's impacted watersheds, additional human and ecological troubles follow from the ongoing manipulation of water levels and boosting of flow rates. These unnatural regimens foul potable water supplies, increase flood hazards and risks, decimate stands of wild rice—a traditional food source—expose ancient burial sites, litter the waters with boating hazards—logs and the like—and in the winter, create treacherous, slush-covered, and unsupported ice sheets.[11] They also erode and degrade riparian wildlife habitats and play havoc with fish populations, choking their gills with silt and destroying their spawning areas.

When Manitoba Hydro obtained regulatory permission to increase water level fluctuations beyond its original licensure, the whitefish fishery in South Indian Lake, which once employed more than 150 indigenous residents, never recovered. Leslie Dysart of the South Lake Community Association recently told me that, in his First Nations community, hope is hard to find. For many people of the Far North, the "green dream" of Big Hydro remains a nightmare.

If Manitoba Hydro is not entirely green or eco-friendly, neither, by an even larger measure, is its rival, the fracking industry, which is essentially in the business of altering the earth's geology. The combusted CO_2 emissions of fracked oil and natural gas rank second and third relative to coal's emissions per BTU of energy, but it's the process of fracking that often draws our attention. Whether due to deficient monitoring, poor oversight, well-casing failures, or inherent risks, fracking operations have proven their capacity to trigger earthquakes, contaminate ground and surface waters, and release methane, the Darth Vader of greenhouse gases, into both the air we breathe and our groundwater supplies below.[12, 13, 14] Some sites have sickened neighbors with odors and airborne drifts of benzene, hydrogen sulfide, and formaldehyde.[15] And wherever fracking's footprint has tread—the Appalachian Mountains or the Great Plains of North America—

thousands of noisy drill pads and dust-choking service roads have followed. They fragment the landscape, drive out wildlife, and obliterate rangeland, woods, ranches, and farms.[16, 17] At night, the darkened, star-studded skies are washed away with the eerie, orangish glow of methane flares.[18] It's all part of the price we pay for cheap oil and gas. At the pump, though, we are a happy people.

At the extreme end of the scale is Western Canada's oil sands, which were formerly known as the tar sands until the oilmen objected to "tar" as being pejoratively inaccurate. The truth about the oil sands sometimes gets obscured, yet certain key facts are clear. Despite the improving efficiencies and mitigation of impacts, of all of the world's oil sources, only a rare few are as thirsty, dirty, energy intensive, or literally stinking as the oil extracted from the sands of Alberta.[19, 20] Getting oil from these sands involves the Leventhian tasks of either surface mining or injecting steam into the ground to coax the sludgy sands to the surface after which, with the addition of more energy, they are heated and processed to separate out the water and sand and upgrade the retained oil to refinery standards. As of 2013, Canada's oil sands industry had converted 345 square miles of boreal forest, an area greater than all the boroughs of New York City, into a barren, blackish, moonscape overlaid with toxic tailings ponds.[21]

One such "pond," the Mildred Lake Settling Basin, covers 8.5 square miles and is contained by no less than the world's largest earthen dam. To deter migratory waterfowl from imminent sludgy death, oil companies intermittently fire off propane cannons, but the earsplitting noises, scarecrows, and the like are only partially effective. For the birds that don't get the message and, instead, land there, the tailings ponds are deathtraps. Nor will reclamation, when it occurs, ever fully restore these altered landscapes to anything resembling a boreal forest or recover the lost muskeg wetlands. Aside from a few tiny demonstrations, the required reclamations to "equivalent land capability" remain distant, underfunded future obligations. In some respects, the wealth of the oil sands reminds me of Steinbeck's *Pearl*, nothing but trouble. The difference is that the pearl was a thing of beauty, which fit into the palm of a hand.

In 2009 and 2010, scientists from the University of Alberta conducted peer-reviewed studies on the environmental impacts of the oil sands industry. Their findings, confirmed by a panel of experts convened by Environment Canada, proved that industrialization of the oil sands—whether from airborne compounds falling on melting snow or from leaking pipes and tailings ponds— was causing low but increasing accumulations of lead, mercury, arsenic, aromatic hydrocarbons, and other toxins in the region's formerly unpolluted lakes and downstream rivers.[22] Another study in 2014 showed high concentrations of these heavy metals in the livers and kidneys of the game animals harvested by local First

Nations people.[23] These groups, whose cancer rates exceed national averages, claim that the fish they catch now have tumors and deformities never seen before.[24] The earlier and subsequently disproven claims by industry and government officials that the Athabasca River's downstream pollution was from naturally occurring seepage have only served to undermine trust and complicate communications. Meanwhile, hazy plumes of sun-addled aerosols veil the skies above and, without preference, permeate the lungs of all the living creatures below, and the odors, sometimes lauded as the smell of money, prompt complaints from nearby communities.[25] Apparently, money stinks.

What Alberta's oil sands industry makes, its Pacific Coast neighbor to the west takes, and if Canada's Trans Mountain pipeline "twin" is constructed, British Columbia will soon see dramatically more oil sands crude pumped to its coastal terminals for export to Asia and other parts of the world. Faced with mounting economic, political, and legal complications, the pipeline's former owner, Kinder Morgan Energy, jumped at Canada's recent offer to generously buy them out. By nationalizing the Trans Mountain pipeline, Canada's political leadership has chosen to expose her taxpaying citizens to the project's financial risks and to implicate them in the oil sands' degradation of the planet. Whether through the purchase of rail cars or pipelines, production subsidies, or tax breaks, Canada has and continues to divert resources that instead could be used for investments in renewable energy and efficiency improvements in buildings or, through a free and undistorted marketplace, simply put to use in the more productive sectors of her economy. In picking a winner, has Canada's leadership chosen a loser? Ultimately, Canadian voters will have to decide whether their politicians have made a brilliant investment or blundered the national treasury on a monumental boondoggle.[26]

Not surprisingly, British Columbians' support for the Trans Mountain project in their province and the province's role as "oil taker" is hardly unanimous. Aside from those who live in an oil train blast zone and might see fewer 100-car oil trains rumbling through their neighborhoods, no one wants a pipeline in their backyard, nor if ocean fishing or tourism is their livelihood, do they want to see lines of oil tankers plying the waters of nearby channels and estuaries. The oil sands' heavy crude, which contains chemical thinners to reduce pumping resistance, is a vexing mix that makes spills nearly impossible to clean up, especially in water. In water, the thinners separate from the oil, leaving heavy "tar" balls—the stuff of roofing cement—to coat the bottom.

Although pipeline safety records are statistically impressive, proponents' assurances of total failsafe operation, while going beyond the pale of reasonable credibility, also seem to imply an expectation of total public trust. To reflect on why they might not be so trusting, British Columbians only have to think back to prior accidents in their province. One of these included the rupture of a high-pressure pipeline that sprayed a Burnaby neighborhood with a thick coat of glistening black crude and required the evacuation of 250 residents.[27] The Mount Polley copper mine in central British Columbia is another reason why residents might be wary about the rosy assurances of mega project boosters. In 2014, the earthen dam containing the copper mine's four-square-mile tailings "pond" ruptured and released a tidal wave of arsenic and lead-infused tailings' water. The turbid wall of water, moving like an avalanche, wiped out the riparian habitat of the downstream valley, polluted formerly pristine lakes and streams, and prompted the issuance of local water consumption advisories.[28, 29]

But I admit it. The foregoing evidence is limited, and none of it means that power projects, oil and gas fracking, or oil sands extraction should be summarily banned any more than I want to shut off the natural gas to my furnace this winter, unplug my refrigerator, or throw away the keys to my car. The point is that every source of energy, even solar and wind, leaves a footprint, some larger and harder than others, except for one, which is making do with less—conservation. For all of others, their external costs and impacts should be understood, mitigated, and then shouldered, not by society and the biosphere writ large, but directly by the producers and their customers. If the benefits are privatized, so should the costs. All the costs.

Of course, what we extract or take from the earth—oil, minerals, and the like—is only one side of the coin. The other is what we *do to* the earth with those extracted resources. A case in point, close to my home, is the twenty-two-mile-long widening of the Mississippi River known as Lake Pepin. Separating Minnesota and Wisconsin, this serpentine segment, the widest in the entire Mississippi, is once again becoming the Lake of Tears, but not for the sad death of the Indian Chief who long ago died there. Our beautiful, bluff-lined lake is shrinking. It is filling up with the chemically-laced sediments draining into it from the plowed fields of corn and soybeans that now blanket the former prairies of my home state. Renewable fuel mandates, ethanol subsidies, and crop price supports and "insurance" have induced farmers to tile and drain more fields, to draw down aquifers with more irrigation, to intensify fertilizer regimens, and to plow up fence rows and woodlots.[30] Interestingly, corn-based ethanol, which diverts food from the table to the gas tank, has an energy output-to-input ratio that barely exceeds 1:1. Ethanol, in other words, makes oil sands producers look like paragons of virtuous efficiency. Moreover, researchers at the University of Minnesota have found that corn production fouls the air and, in the US alone, causes 4,300 premature deaths, primarily from the fine particulates of ammonia emitted from nitrogen-based fertilizers.[31]

One of Lake Pepin's tributaries, the Minnesota River, drains the heartland of Minnesota's corn belt before merging its opaque waters with those of the clearer Mississippi just upstream from Lake Pepin. Muddied with eroded topsoil and spiked with farm fertilizers, herbicides, and pesticides, the Minnesota River is essentially an open, agricultural sewer—one that is prone to flooding from the added runoff sheeting across the open fields.

In the halls of the state capitol in St. Paul, where the legions of agribusiness lobbyists do their political sausage-making and who collectively have never seen a plowed acre of land they didn't like, a modest proposal recently came to life. It called for vegetated buffer strips along the state's waterways and ditches to help filter the farm chemicals and retain the runoff. Miraculously, the legislation became law, but not before the bill's opponents had gutted it. The untold miles of private ditches were exempted from the buffer requirement, and the ubiquitous drain-tile pipes already snaking under the buffer strips would still be allowed to flush their contents directly into public streams. It is from these outlets that the chemical and sediment-burdened waters from plowed fields begin their continental journey—into the Minnesota River, into the Mississippi, into Lake Pepin, and ultimately into the expanding dead zone of the Gulf of Mexico.

Alas, I could wander far and touch upon innumerable environmental issues, including the proposals for deep-rock mining of copper and nickel ore in northern Minnesota near the natural and untouched Boundary Waters Canoe Area, but the focus of this book is northern Canada, and it's not limited to just what we take from and do to our Mother Earth. It is also about what human beings take from and do to each other, although the two sets of issues are often intertwined.

In Canadian vernacular, the word "sorry" is reputedly said so often and in so many ways that its meaning has become muddled and the subject of some reflective amusement among Canadians.[32] True statements of contrition, of course, are more serious matters. In this vein, Canada has distinguished itself, even if belatedly, by issuing formal apologies for the tragedies of the residential schools, for the forced relocations of Inuit communities, and for the flooding of Cree homelands—all of them chronicled in the main text of this book.

With the issuance of several more recent apologies, Canada has continued this legacy. These include, in 2017, the extension of the 2008 apology and reparations for the abuses of the residential schools to include the indigenous populations of the Atlantic provinces of Labrador and Newfoundland, which were omitted from the earlier apology applicable to the rest of Canada. They also include two other apologies: one in 2011 for the sled dog slaughters in Nunavik (northern Quebec) and the other, in 2017, to First Nations' adults who were the children of the "Sixties Scoop."

In the case of the sled dog slaughters of the 1950s and 60s, the white man wanted all dogs chained, but the non-English-speaking Inuit had difficulty understanding English, and for that matter, they didn't have any chains, and the dogs themselves were accustomed to roaming freely. For the Inuit, dogs were their working companions and means of mobility, but the authorities considered them a "menace." Dogs, they said, competed for scarce food supplies, and they were "loose," so the Mounties shot and poisoned them, hundreds of them—often before their owners' eyes. And the real reason, according to Inuit, was not public safety but to get them, the Inuit, off the land and into the settlements and onto Federal programs.[33]

On August 8, 2011, the Premier of Quebec, Jean Charest spoke to the Inuit of northern Quebec and expressed his regret on behalf of the people of Quebec: "[W]e need to. . . close the chapter on these sad events. . . so that never again something like this should happen . . ."[34] The apology included C$3 million in reparations and a recommendation to use the money to organize sled dog races, promote Inuit art, and advance the teaching of Inuktitut.

The Sixties Scoop was named for the period of time spanning the 1960s through the early 1980s when welfare workers "scooped" up thousands of First Nations, Metis, and Inuit children from their families, often little notice and often without consent, and then adopted them out to primarily white families, some as far away as Louisiana, Europe, and New Zealand. For the scooped children, there was the shock of losing their family and then being raised by one they didn't know in places where they were often teased and bullied for being different, but there was also the loss of their language, their traditions, and their culture. Some children, when they were intercepted, were old enough to remember seeing the tears of their elders as they packed suitcases and embraced in farewells.[35]

The Sixties Scoop drew from the legacy of residential schools that began earlier in both Canada and the United States. My country's first residential boarding school, the Carlyle Indian Industrial School, opened in 1879 and was guided by its founder, Henry Pratt, who stated that the school's mission was to "save the man and kill the Indian."[36] Pratt is also quoted as saying, "I believe in immersing the Indians in our civilization and when we get them under, holding them there until they are thoroughly soaked."[37] Forced adoptions and residential schools, as such, were different, yet similar means to the same end: abrupt and total assimilation. In each case, well-intentioned beginnings left, at best, a mixed legacy, opportunity for some but abuse and conflicted identities for many.[38] By today's sensitivities, their underpinnings of intolerance and arrogance are hard to fathom.

The announcement by the Canadian Federal government in October of 2017 of a settlement to apologize and compensate the 20,000 survivors of the

Sixties Scoop was a watershed event. However, even though moratoriums on adoptions have curtailed their use, aboriginal children are still overrepresented in Canada's foster care system. They make up 7 percent of the country's children but nearly half of all the foster children. Yet, if adoptions and especially adoptions to non-aboriginal families are not the answer, then neither is trapping children in a succession of foster homes. This fostering of children has all the markings of "Scoop-II" written on it and the imminent requirement for yet another apology. However, given the likelihood of diminishing returns and even if eloquently written and accompanied by a candlelight vigil, an apology sequel may carry no more weight than the casual "Sorry, eh?" or the more condescending version, "Sorry you're feeling badly about this."

In January of 2016, the Canadian Human Rights Tribunal ruled that the government was guilty of providing lower levels of child welfare services on First Nations reserves than the rest of Canada despite the reserves' higher levels of need. Both the Tribunal's ruling and the Truth and Reconciliation Commission's *Calls to Action* report in 2015 pointed to the need for more resources "to keep Aboriginal families together . . . in culturally appropriate environments."[39] They also recommended shifting the control of child-welfare services to aboriginal governments.

In the hamlet of Arviat where our canoe trip ended, I can report that the population—growing at nearly 7 percent per year—is still booming, the jobs are still scarce, and, with the caribou herds in a period of decline, "food insecurity" is once again a concern.[40, 41] "Store bought" groceries for supplementing local "country foods," are still being shipped by seasonal ocean vessel or airfreight and are still priced 30-40 percent higher compared to southern Canada.[42] Given that nearly half of Arviat's population of 2,600 are under twenty years old,[43] there are a lot of hungry mouths to feed and expensive groceries to buy.

In 2010, the opening of Agnico Eagle's Meadowbank open pit goldmine northwest of Arviat, made it the only actively operating mine in all of Nunavut. Although workers from Arviat were able to land several dozen jobs at the mine, the reserves were expected to run out by late 2019. As operations at Meadowbank wind down, the company plans to shift excavation work to the new, nearby Whale Tail deposit and thereby extend operations, but only for an additional five years.[44] Such is the boom-and-bust nature of mining in the Far North.

The minutes of recent Hamlet Council meetings in Arviat suggest a leadership consensus in favor of making local education programs more rigorous, reducing social promotion at the schools, improving attendance, and providing more training in the trades. With a better educated and higher skilled workforce, the thinking is that Arviat could promote its workers for FIFO (fly-in-fly-out) jobs throughout Canada. Arviat workers could also gain a larger share of skilled trades jobs in their settlement that are now, by necessity, taken by itinerant southerners.

Among the leaders on Arviat's Hamlet Council and Nunavut's Legislative Assembly are the two members of the family that welcomed us into their home at the end of our 2004 canoe trip. When Joe Savikataaq and his son Jamie plucked us from Hudson Bay's choppy waters, Joe's regular weekday job was serving as Arviat's conservation officer, an important position in a community where hunting and fishing provide much of the local food supply. Joe was capable, reassuring, and bilingual, fluent in both English and Inuktitut. He introduced us to his whaler friends, he invited us into his house, he fed us, he let us sleep in his house's loft overnight, and then he valiantly tried to resist our offers to pay him. Really, there was something very special about this kind and gracious gentleman. And I swear this is true: I thought at the time that if this man ever ran for office and I became a Nunavut voter, without hesitation, I'd mark the "X" next to his name.

Apparently, I wasn't alone in these sentiments. Since we last saw him, the Honorable Joe Savikataaq became not only a Member of the Nunavut Legislative Assembly (MLA) at the territory's capital city, Iqaluit, on Baffin Island but also the Cabinet Minister for Community and Government Services. Education and consensus building are among Premier Savikataaq's top priorities. I say Premier because in 2018 Joe's fellow legislators elected him to be the Premier of Nunavut, Canada's most northern and largest territory, a place the size of all of Western Europe. Yes, it is true. I can now say that I was saved on the high seas of Hudson Bay by the Premier of Nunavut, that I ate caribou roast at his kitchen table, and that I slept in the Man's house!

It is also noteworthy that, among the various Savikataaq generations, political leadership is establishing itself as a family tradition. In 2015, the Premier's other son, Joe Savikataaq, Jr., in a multiple candidate race, decidedly won a seat on the Arviat Hamlet Council. Joe Jr., in a career move that again followed his father's footsteps, also became Arviat's newest conservation officer. Thus, the mission of sustainably managing the community's critical wildlife resources now rest in the hands of the next generation.

As Arviat's conservation officer, one of Joe Jr.'s challenges is the wandering of polar bears through the settlement during the bears' fall migrations. More specifically, the challenge is that of keeping humans and bears safely apart without either one killing the other. Instead of staying out on Hudson Bay, closer to the seals, the bears' preferred food source, the absence of sea ice has forced them to stay on shore. The ice on Hudson Bay continues to form later in the fall, stay thinner, and melt sooner. This means more bears on main street and particularly at the town's dump where the hungry animals scavenge for food scraps. In 2014, Halloween festivities in Arviat had to be moved into the community hall for fear of trick-or-treater run-ins with polar bears.[45]

Brother Jamie, meanwhile, is still a Mountie with the RCMP. In 2016, he was stationed in Iqaluit where his father worked as an MLA and cabinet minister. Jamie is among the small group of ground-breaking Inuit officers working not only to enforce the law but to diversify the Nunavut RCMP. Although they comprise nearly 90 percent of the territory's total population, only a little over 10 percent of the RCMP force is Inuit. According to RCMP commanding officers, reducing these imbalances and hiring more police and other civil servants from the Inuit population will require better educational outcomes and higher graduation rates.

The Margaret Aniksak Visitor Center and Museum is still open. This is the museum, where, in 2004, I asked the docent why the people moved into the coastal settlements. The museum welcomes visitors with displays about Inuit history and customs and collections of early photographs, recorded elders' stories, examples of beautifully beaded skin clothing, tools and games from the past, and other artifacts. The center also offers classes in inukshuk building, throat singing, and sewing. It's a long way to Arviat, but someday I'd like to return.

Owing to the book's timeline ending in 2006, there is a story about the Ahiarmiut relocations to Arviat that, except for a passing reference, I did not include in the main text of the book. It is the story about a woman named Kikkik and her infant daughter Elisapee (Nokahhak) Karetak that begins in the mid-twentieth century and then saw important developments in 2008 and also 2019. In 2019, Karetak was one of only a handful of Ahiarmiut relocates still alive and, owing to these recent developments, I've included the updates to her story below.[46]

It was the winter of 1958, when Karetak was just an infant, that she and her four older siblings lived under the care of their mother, Kikkik, and their father, Halo. They sheltered themselves in a snowhouse dug in along the shores of North Henik Lake, but the winter was bleak and hunger was constant. Meanwhile, Kikkik's half-brother, Ootek, and his family camped nearby, barely clinging to life. By February, blizzardy weather and caribou scarcities in their newly government-designated homeland had begun to take their toll.

One of Ootek's emaciated children slipped into the long sleep, and then Ootek, delusional with hunger and grief, took it upon himself to shatter the skull of his unsuspecting friend and neighbor, Halo, with a point-blank rifle shot to Halo's head. He then went after his half-sister, Kikkik, who still retained a measure of strength and thus was able to push the rifle away from Ootek's hunger-weakened hands. Desperately and instinctively, to save herself and her children, Kikkik wrestled Ootek to the ground, stabbed him, and killed him.

The next day and with little time to mourn for her murdered husband, Kikkik tucked Karetak into her amauti and put two of the younger children on a makeshift canvas toboggan. With the older children trailing behind her on foot and Karetak on her back, Kikkik began to pull the toboggan to the Padlei trading post in search of help and food, some forty-five miles away. After several days, she could no longer pull the child-laden toboggan, carry Karetak on her back, and lead the others across the wind-swept, snow-scoured tundra, so she wrapped two of the younger children in a caribou skin and placed them inside a small igloo, which she had built along the way.

Kikkik and the other three children—small trudging forms in the swirling whiteness—continued toward Padlei and were eventually rescued by a Royal Canadian Mounted Police aircraft. Of the two children left behind, the rescue team found only one still alive. Yes, Kikkik had lived and she had saved four of her five children, but she would soon face another hardship, this time at the hands of her rescuers. The RCMP arrested Kikkik and had her prosecuted for murder and child neglect. Mercifully, she was found innocent and properly acquitted.

And what of Karetak, the baby who rode to safety on her mother's back? She grew up to become a documentary filmmaker and a leader among the Ahiarmiuts who, in 2008, filed an official claim seeking an apology and compensation from the Canadian government. In 2014, the Nunatsiaq News reported that Karetak's third and final documentary about the Ahiarmiut relocations was not about the painful memories of her people's multiple trails of tears but about their strength and perseverance. Karetak said that her film is a celebration of "a great people, how strong we are and forgiving."[47]

As for the Ahiarmiut's long sought apology for the starvations and hardships endured in their forced relocations during the 1940s and 1950s, in 2019, a settlement was finally reached. I reflect with interest that the interval between the beginning of this chapter in Canadian history and its official resolution has mirrored the duration of my own lifetime of 70 years. On January 22, 2019, a standing-room-only crowd gathered in Arviat's community hall and heard Ottawa's Indigenous Relations Minister present the official statement. The emotional ceremony began with drum dancing and traditional singing and then the Minister read the statement: "We are sorry you suffered so immensely . . . We are sorry that you were not treated with the kindness, respect, and humanity you deserved." Of the original 67 surviving Ahiarmiut, at the time of the filing of their claim in 2008, Elisapee Karetak and twenty-two others remained. From these survivors, there were 167 direct descendants. Each of the twenty-three direct survivors received C$100,000 and each of the direct descendants, C$3,000. It was a time to forgive but not to forget.[48] As for our neighbors in Canada with whom we share this continent, *O Canada*, from my perspective, your anthem is true: *With glowing hearts we see thee rise*.

And so it is. The beat of the drum continues, the questions remain, and the words of the questions will echo into the future. Who are we? Are we the harbingers of a brighter dawn? More importantly, who will we become? Can we proudly claim that there are certain answers here, as certain as black or white? I don't think so. But as long as we can value the purity of the air we breathe and the waters that bring us life, there is hope. Yes, as long as we can recognize that we do not stand apart from the planet's web of living creatures, as long as we can see the beauty of the earth as clearly as her gifts of energy, and as long as we can look into the hearts of others and begin to see our own, there is hope. And that hope will be the dawn that grays the night.

Selected Bibliography

Articles and Proceedings of Conferences

Adamson, J. D., et al. Poliomyelitis in the Arctic. *Canadian Medical Association Journal 61,* no.4 (1949).

Bell, Jim (1996). Exiles Denied Apology. *Nunatsiaq News* (March 15, 1996) www.nunatsiaq.com/archives/back-issues/week/60315.html#1.

Bergman, Bria. Dark Days for the Inuit. MacLean's 109, no. 10 (1996).

CBC News. Flame Retardants in Inuit Breast Milk (2003) http://www.cbc.ca/gsa/?q=pollutants030917.

Coltrain, J. B., M. G. Hayes, and D. H. ORourke Sealing whaling and caribou: the skeletal isotope chemistry of Eastern Arctic foragers, Archaeological Science 31(2004).

Coulsen, Art. Our cheap energy floods Manitoba Cree with grief and hardship. *St. Paul Pioneer Press* (June 15, 2003).

Dallaire, Frédéric et al. Acute Infections and Environmental Exposure to Organochlorines in Inuit Infants from Nunavik. *Environmental Health Perspectives 112* (October 14, 2004).

Dewailly, Éric et al. Susceptibility to Infections and Immune Status in Inuit Infants Exposed to Organochlorines. *Environmental Health Perspectives103 n*o. 3 (2000).

Diubaldo, Richard J. The Absurd Little Mouse: When Eskimos Became Indians. *Journal of Canadian Studies, 16,* no. 2 (1981).

Eegeesiak, Okalik and Sheila Watt-Cloutier. The strange politics of the Marine Mammal Protection Act. *Toronto Mail and Globe* (July 26, 1999).

Fitzhugh, W. W. Environmental Factors in the Evolution of Dorset Culture: A Marginal Proposal for Hudson Bay. In M. S. Maxwell (Ed.), Eastern Arctic Prehistory: Paleoeskimo Problems, *Memoirs of the Society for American Archaeology, 31* (1976): 139-149.

Freeman, Milton M. R. Adaptive innovation among recent Eskimo immigrants in the eastern Canadian Arctic. *The Polar Record 14,* no. 93 (1969).

Goehring, Brian and John K. Stager, The intrusion of industrial time and space into the inuit lifeworld, *Environment and Behavior 23* (1991).

Grant, Shelagh D. A Case of Compounded Error: The Inuit Resettlement Project, 1953, and the Government Response. *Northern Perspectives, 19,* no. 1, Spring (1990).

Guyer, Ruth Levy (2006). The Power of Water. *Commentary, National Public Radio.*

Harrington, Richard. The Padleimiuts. *Canadian Geographic Journal, 44* (1952).

Irwin, Colin. Lords of the Arctic: wards of the state. *Northern Perspectives, Vol. 17,* no. 1, Canadian Arctic Resources Committee (1989).

Jull, Peter. A Personal Response to Frank J. Tester and Peter Kulchyski, Tammarniit (Mistakes): Inuit Relocation in the Eastern Arctic, 1939-63, *The Northern Review 12/13* (1994).

Kieth, Darren. Caribou, river and ocean: Harvaqtuurmiut landscape organization and orientation. *Inuit Studies 28,* no. 2 (2004).

Kuyek, Joan. After the Mine: Lynn Lake, Manitoba. *MiningWatch Canada* (2004) http://www.miningwatch.ca/en/after-mine-lynn-lake-manitoba.

Lacroix, Marc. Integration or Disintegration. *The Beaver, Spring 1959. The Beaver* was the quarterly publication of the Hudson's Bay Company. This entire issue has articles that are reflective of the tenor of the times.

Laugrand, F., Oosten, J., & Serkoak, D. Relocating the Ahiarmiut from Ennadai Lake to Arviat (1950-1958). In Collignon B. & Therrien M. (Ed.) *Orality in the 21st century: Inuit discourse and practices. Proceedings of the 15th Inuit Studies Conference.* Paris: Inalco (2009). Retrieved from http://www.inuitoralityconference.com.

Laugrand, F., Oosten, J, & Serkoak, D. The saddest time of my life': Relocating the Ahiarmiut from Ennadai Lake (1950–1958). *The Polar Record 46:02* (2010)Loney, Martin (1987). The construction of dependency: The case of the Grand Rapids Hydro Project. *The Canadian Journal of Native Studies 7*, no. 1 (1987).

McCartney, A.P. The nature of Thule Eskimo whale use. *Arctic Institute of North America 33*, no. 3 (1980).

McGhee, Robert. Disease and the development of Inuit culture, *Current Anthropology 35* (1994).

McKibbon, Sean and Michaela Rodrigue. Pelly Bay's marionettes are coming home. Kiviuq's oddysey is almost over. *Nunatsiaq News* (August 13, 1999).

McNicoll, Paule, Frank Tester, and Peter Kulchyski. Arctic abstersion: The Book of Wisdom for Eskimo, modernism and Inuit assimilation. *Inuit Studies 23*, no. 1-2 (1999).

Oosten, Jarich and Frédéric Laugrand. *Qaujimajatuqangit* and social problems in modern Inuit society. An elders workshop on *angakkuuniq*. *Inuit Studies 26,* no. 1 (2002).

Owen, James. Study: Siberian Bogs Big Player in Greenhouse Gas. *National Geographic News* (January 15, 2004) http://news.nationalgeographic.com/news/2004/01/0115_040115_siberianpeatbog.html.

Rasmussen, Derek. Cease to Do Evil, Then Learn to Do. *Cultural Survival Voices 1.1*(2001).

Nelson, Odile. Study tracks effects of contaminants in Nunavik infants. *Nunatsiaq News.* Iqaluit, Nunavut, (March 14, 2003).

Waldram, James B (1984). Hydro-electric development and the process of negotiation in Northern Manitoba, 1960-1977. *The Canadian Journal of Native Studies, 4*, no. 2 (1984).

Woodburn, James (1982). Egalitarian Societies. Man, New Series 17, no. 3 (September, 1982).

Government Documents and Reports

Allen, Rod J., et al. *Ecological Assessment of the Boreal Shield Ecozone.* Ottawa: Environment Canada, Minister of Public Works and Government Services 2000. www.ec.gc.ca/Publications/1F4C0C47-4E18-4988-8514-A842EED6F774%5CEcologicalAssessmentOfTheBorealShieldEcozone.pdf.

Anand-Wheeler, Ingrid *Terrestrial Mammals of Nunavut.* Iqaluit: Nunavut Department of Sustainable Development 2002.

Arctic Monitoring and Assessment Programme. *Arctic Pollution 2002: Persistent Organic Pollutants, Heavy Metals, Radioactivity, Human Health, Changing Pathways.* Oslo, Norway 2002.

Canada, Northern Contaminants Program. *Canadian Arctic Contaminants Assessment Report.* Minister of Indian Affairs and Northern Development, Ottawa 2003.

Dahl, Jens, Jack Hicks, and Peter Jull (Eds.). *Nunavut - Inuit Regain Control of their Lands and their Lives* Copenhagen, Denmark: International Work Group for Indigenous Affairs (IWGIA) 2000.

Lake Winnipeg Implementation Committee. Restoring the Health of Lake Winnipeg (2005) http://www.redriverbasincommission.org/lake_wpg_final.pdf.

Nunavut, Canada. *Keewatin Regional Land Use Plan 2000.* Nunavut Planning Commission 2000. This plan includes information about the climate, vegetation, geology, geography, people, population, economy, and resources of Keewatin (Kivalliq) region of the Barren Lands.

Nunavut, Canada. Report from the September Inuit Qaujimajatuqangit Workshop. Iqaluit, NU: Department of Culture, Language, Elders, & Youth, Government of Nunavut Printing Office 1999.

Royal Commission on Aboriginal Peoples. *The High Arctic Relocation: A Report on the 1953-55 Relocation.* Canada Communication Group 1994.

Royal Commission on Aboriginal Peoples. *Report of the Royal Commission on Aboriginal Peoples, Volume 1* 1996. See the following: Volume 1, PART TWO, Looking Forward Looking Back, False Assumptions and a Failed Relationship, sections 10 (Residential Schools) and 11(Relocation of Aboriginal Communities, including subsection 2.2, To Improve the Lives of Aboriginal People).

Spencer, Robert F. *The North Alaskan Eskimos: A Study in Ecology and Society.* Smithsonian Institution Burea of American Ethnology Bulletin 171. Washington, D. C.: U.S. Government Printing Office 1959.

Stocks, Brian J. Fire management in Canada. In *Global Fire Assessment, 1990-2000.* Forest Resources Assessment WP-55. Food and Agricultural Organization of the United Nations (FAO) 2001.

U.S. Energy Information Administration, Department of Energy. "Energy in Brief: What are greenhouse gases and how much are emitted by the United States?" http://www.eia.gov/energy_in_brief/article/greenhouse_gas.cfm.

Wakelyn, Leslie. *The Qamanirjuaq Caribou Herd — An Arctic Enigma.*

Beverly and Qamanirjuaq Caribou Management Board 1999, www.arctic-caribou.com/PDF/qcs.pdf.

Watt-Cloutier, Shelia. Testimony of Sheila Watt-Cloutier Chair, Inuit Circumpolar Conference, to the U.S. Senate Committee on Commerce, Science and Transportation.

Washington DC, September 15, 2004. http://inuitcircumpolar.com/index.php?auto_slide=&ID=261&Lang=En&Parent_ID=&current_slide_num.

Books, Manuscripts, and Theses

Alia, Valarie. *Names, numbers, and northern policy: Inuit, Project Surname, and the politics of identity.* Halifax, N.S.: Fernwood Publishing 1994.

Arima, Eugene Y. A contextual study of the Caribou Eskimo kayak. Toronto: Doctoral Thesis in Anthropology, University of Toronto 1972.

Barrow, John, ed. *The geography of Hudson's Bay; being the remarks of Captain W. Coats on his many voyages to that locality during the years of 1727 and 175.* London: Hakluyt Society 1852.

Birket-Smith, Kaj. *The Eskimos.* London: Methuen and Co. 1936.

Boas, Franz . *The Central Eskimo,* Lincoln, NE: University of Nebraska Press.1888, 1964.

Brody, Hugh. *The People's Land: Eskimos and Whites in the Eastern Arctic.* Harmondsworth, England: Penguin Books 1975.

Brody, Hugh. *Living Arctic: Hunters of the Canadian North.* Seattle: University of Washington Press 1987.

Brody, Hugh. *The Other Side of Eden: Hunters, Farmers, and the Shaping of the World.* New York: North Point Press 2001.

Brooks, et al. (2002). *Clearing the Forest, Cutting the Rules.* Toronto: Sierra Legal Defense Fund and Earthroots 2002. www.earthroots.org/clearing_the_forest_FINAL.pdf.

Bruemmer, Fred. *Seasons of the Eskimo: A Vanishing Way of Life.* Toronto: McClelland and Stewart, Limited 1971.

Burch Jr., Ernest S. The Caribou Inuit. In Morrison and C. Wilson (eds.), *Native Peoples, the Canadian Experience.* Oxford University Press 2004.

Crowe, Keith J. *A history of the Original Peoples of Northern Canada* (Rev. Ed.). Arctic Institute of North America, 1974, and McGill-Queen's University Press 1991.

Damas, David (Ed.). *Handbook of North American Indians, volume 5, Arctic.* Washington DC: National Museum of Natural History, Smithsonian Institution 1984.

Damas, David. *Arctic Migrants Arctic Villagers.* Montreal: McGill-Queen's University Press 2002.

Davids, Richard C. *Lords of the Arctic.* New York: Macmillan Publishing 1982.

Dorais, Louis-Jacques. Inuit. In Paul Robert Magocsi (ed.), *Aboriginal Peoples of Canada.* Toronto: Toronto University Press 2002.

Eber, Dorothy Harley. *When the Whalers were up North.* Boston: David R. Godine, Publisher 1989.

Fletcher, Christopher Continuity and Change in Inuit Society. In Morrison and C. Wilson (eds.), *Native Peoples, the Canadian Experience.* Don Mills, ON: Oxford University Press 2004.

Fossett, Renee (2001). *In Order to Live an Untroubled Life: Inuit of the Central Arctic, 1550-1940.* Winnipeg: University of Manitoba Press.

Grygier, Pat Sandiford. *A long way from home: the tuberculosis epidemic among the Inuit,* Montreal & Buffalo: McGill-Queen's University Press 1994.

Hearne, Samuel. *A Journey from Prince of Wales's Fort in Hudson Bay, to the Northern Ocean.* London: Printed for A. Strahan and T. Cadell 1795.

Hall, Charles F. *Arctic Researches and Life among the Esquimax.* New York: Harper 1865.

Harrington, Richard. *The Face of the Arctic.* New York: Abelard-Schuman 1952.

Hoebel, E. Adamson (1967). *The Law of Primitive Man.* Cambridge, MA: Harvard University Press.

James, Thomas. *The Strange and Dangerous Voyage of Captain Thomas James in his Intended Discovery of a North West Passage into the South Sea.* London: John Legatt 1633, reprinted in 1740 for O. Payne.

Jenness, Diamond. *The People of the Twilight.* New York: The MacMillan Company 1928.

Jenness, Diamond. *Eskimo Administration: II. Canada.* Arctic Institute of North America, Technical Paper No. 4. 1964.

Jenness, Diamond. *The Life off the Copper Eskimo, Part A of Voulme XII, A Report of the Canadian Arctic Expedition 1913-1918.* New York and London: Johnson Reprint Corporation 1970.

Kirmayer, Laurence J., Christopher Fletcher and Lucy Boothroyd. Suicide among the Inuit of Canada. In Antoon A. Leenaars, Susanne Wenckstern, Isaac Sakinofsky, Ronald J. Dyck, Michael J. Kral, and Roger C. Bland (Eds.), *Suicide in Canada.* Toronto: University of Toronto Press 1998.

Lopez, Barrry. *Arctic Dreams* (Rev. Ed.). New York: Vintage Books 1986.

Marcus, Alan R. *Out in the Cold: The Legacy of Canada's Inuit Relocation Experiment in the High Arctic.* Copenhagen: The International Work Group for Indigenous Affairs 1992.

Marcus, Alan R. *Relocating Eden: The Image and Politics of Inuit Exile in the Canadian Arctic.* Hanover, NH: University Press of New England 1995.

Marsh, Donald Ben. *Echoes into Tomorrow.* Three Hills, Alberta, Canada: Prairie Graphics and Printing 1973.

Maxwell, Moreau S. *Prehistory of the Eastern Arctic.* Orlando: Academic Press, Inc. 1985.

McGhee, Robert. Canadian Arctic Prehistory. Gastineau (Hull), Quebec: Canadian Museum of Civilization 1990.

McGhee, Robert. *Ancient People of the Arctic.* Vancouver: UBC Press 1996.

McGhee, Robert. The Prehistory and Prehistoric Art of the Canadian Inuit. In Alma Houston (ed.), *Inuit Art: An Anthology.* Winnipeg: Watson & Dwyer 1998.

McGhee, Robert. *The Arctic.* Gastineau (Hull), Quebec: Canadian Museum of Civilization Corporation 2001.

McGhee, Robert. *The Last Imaginary Place: A Human History of the Arctic World.* Don Mills, ON: Oxford University Press 2005.

Morrison, David and George Hébert Germain. *Inuit, Glimpses of the Arctic Past.* Gastineau (Hull), Quebec: Canadian Museum of Civilization 1995.

Mowat, Farley. *Walking the Land.* South Royalton, Vermont: Steerforth Press 2001.

Newman, Peter C. *Merchant Princes.* Toronto: Viking 1991.

Nuttall, Mark. *Protecting the Arctic: Indigenous Peoples and Cultural Survival.* Amsterdam: Harwood Academic 1998.

Oswalt, Wendell H. *This Land was Theirs*. California:Mayfield Publishing Company 1988. See Chapter Three: The Netsilik: Seal hunting and snowhouse Eskimos.

Petrone, Penny. *Northern Voices: Inuit Writing in English*. Toronto: University of Toronto Press 1998.

Rasmussen, Knud. Intellectual Culture of the Hudson Bay Eskimos. *Report of the Fifth Thule Expedition, 1921-1924, Vol. 8.* Copenhagen: Gyldendal 1930.

Rasmussen, Knud. Intellectual Culture of the Copper Eskimos. *Report of the Fifth Thule Expedition, 1921-1924, Vol. 9*. Copenhagen: Gyldendal 1932.

Rigby, Bruce, John MacDonald, and Leah Otak. The Inuit of Nunavut, Canada. In Milton M.R. Freeman (Ed.), *Endangered Peoples of the Arctic: Struggles to Survive and Thrive*. Westport, CT: Greenwood 2000.

Ross, W.G. *Whaling and Eskimos: Hudson Bay 1860-1915*. National Museums of Canada, National Museum of Man, Publications in Ethnology, No. 10, Ottawa 1975.

Ross, W. G. Whaling, Inuit, and the Arctic Islands. In Zaslow (Ed.), *A Century of Canada's Arctic Islands*. Ottawa: The Royal Society of Canada 1981.

Sahlins, Marshall. *Stone Age Economics*. New York: Aldine Publishing Company. See Chapter 1, "The Original Affluent Society."

Smith, Eric Alden. *Inujjuamiut Foraging Strategies: Evolutionary Ecology of an Arctic Hunting Economy*. New York: Walter de Gruyter, Inc. 1991.

Soubliee, Marion (Ed.). *Nunavut Handbook: Traveling in Canada's* Arctic. Iqaluit, Nunavut: Nortex Multimedia Inc. 1998.

Stefansson, Vilhjalmur. *My Life with the Eskimo*. New York: The MacMillan Company 1913.

Taylor, J. Garth. *Labrador Eskimo Settlement of the Early Contact Period*. National Museums of Canada, National Museum of Man, *Publications in Ethnology*, no. 19, Ottawa 1974.

Tester, Frank James and Peter Kulchyski (1994). *Tammarniit (Mistakes):Inuit Relocation in the Eastern Arctic 1939-63*. Vancouver: UBC Press 1994.

Thompson, Shirley. Sustainability and Vulnerability: Aboriginal Arctic Food Security in a Toxic World," Chapter Three, in Fikret Berkes, Alan Diduck, Helen Fast, Rob Huebert, and Micheline Manseau (eds.) *Breaking Ice: Integrated Ocean Management in the Canadian North*. Calgary: University of Calgary Press 2005.

Waldram, James *As Long as the Rivers Run: Hydroelectric Development and Native Communities in Western Canada*, Winnipeg: The University of Manitoba Press 1990.

Wilson, Roderick C. and Carl Urion. First Nations Prehistory and Canadian Hisotry. In Morrison and C. Wilson (eds.), *Native Peoples, the Canadian Experience*. Don Millss, ON: Oxford University Press 2004.

Walker, Brittenia (Ed.). *The tip of the iceberg: Chemical contamination in the Arctic*. Oslo: Norway: WWF International Arctic Programme 2005.

Waterman, Jonathan. *Arctic Crossing: A Journey Through the Northwest Passage and Inuit Culture*. Guilford, CT: Lyons Press 2001, 2002.

Wenzel, George. *Animal Rights, Human Rights: Ecology, Economy and Ideology in the Canadian Arctic*. Toronto: University of Toronto Press 1991.

Wright, J. V. *A history of the Native People of Canada*. Gatineau, Quebec: Canadian Museum of Civilization 1999.

Zaslow, Morris. *The Northward Expansion of Canada, 1914--1967*. Toronto: McClelland and Stewart. 1988.

Web Sites and Online Sources:

Archaeology in North America, University of Waterloo: http://anthropology.uwaterloo.ca/ArcticArchStuff/culturehistory.html.

Arctic Circle, History and Culture, Norman Chance: http://arcticcircle.uconn.edu/.

The Arctic Council. The Arctic Council is an intergovernmental forum for addressing many of the common concerns and challenges faced by the Arctic states; Canada, Denmark (including Greenland and the Faroe Islands), Finland, Iceland, Norway, the Russian Federation, Sweden and the United States: http://arctic-council.org/.

Arctic Institute of North America, Website of the Arctic Journal: http://www.arctic.ucalgary.ca/sections.php?sid=publications&cid=arctic_journal.

Arctic Monitoring and Assessment Programme. AMAP is an international organization established in 1991 to implement components of the Arctic Environmental Protection Strategy (AEPS). http://www.amap.no/.

Arviat Muncipal (Hamlet) Website: http://www.arviat.ca/.

Arctic Travel (where the Nunavut Handbook can be purchased): www.arctictravel.com.

Beverly and Qamanirjuaq Caribou Management Board: www.arctic-caribou.com.

Boreal Forest Network: www.borealnet.org.

Canada's Polar Life: www.arctic.uoguelph.ca.

Canadian Arctic Resources Committee (CARC) – dedicated to the environmental and social wellbeing of northern Canadians: www.carc.org.

Canadian Museum of Civilization: http://www.civilization.ca/cmc/exhibitions/hist/frobisher/fr57702e.shtml; http://www.civilization.ca/cmc/exhibitions/archeo/paleoesq/peexheng.shtml.

Canadian Council for Ministers of the Environment – climate change and other topics: http://www.ccme.ca/ourwork/air.html?category_id=33.

Chesterfield Inlet Website (History Section): www.chesterfieldinlet.net/chester_then.htm.

Cultural Survival Quarterly: www.culturalsurvival.org.

Culture and Public Action: http://www.cultureandpublicaction.org/conference/introduction.htm.

Inuit Circumpolar Conference, an international non-government organization representing approximately the 150,000 Inuit of Alaska, Canada, Greenland, and Chukotka (Russia): http://inuitcircumpolar.com/index.php?ID=1&Lang=En.

Inuit Tapiriit Kanatami. The ITK negotiated the Inuit land settlement claims with Canada and continues to promote the rights, interests, and living conditions of the four Canadian Inuit regions: Nunatsiavut (Labrador), Nunavik (northern Quebec), Nunavut, and the Inuvialuit Settlement Region in the Northwest Territories: http://www.itk.ca.

International Work Group for Indigenous Affairs: http://www.iwgia.org/sw153.asp.

Kitikmeot Region of Nunavut: http://www.polarnet.ca/.

Manitoba Wildlands, a good source for information about Manitoba Hydro: http://www.manitobawildlands.org/develop_hydro.htm#future.

MiningWatch Can: http://www.miningwatch.ca/.

National Library of Canada: http://www.nlc-bnc.ca/north/norint-e.htm.

Nunavut Territory Governement: http://www.gov.nu.ca/.

Nunavut Tunngavik Incorporated, the organization responsible for the implementation of the Nunavut Land Claims Agreement: http://www.tunngavik.com/.

Nunavut Wildlife Management Board: www.nwmb.com.

Nunavut '99, a Website sponsored by Nunavut Tunngavik Incorporated and devoted to the history, background, and celebration of the creation of Nunavut: http://www.nunavut.com/nunavut99/english.

Nunatsiaq News (Iqaluit, Nunavut): http://www.nunatsiaqonline.ca/.

Park, Robert W. (1999). *Archeology in Arctic North America*. University of Waterloo Department of Anthropology Web Site. See section entitled "The Sequence of Cultures in the Arctic." https://uwaterloo.ca/anthropology/about/people/people-profiles/archaeology-arctic-north-america.

Polar Bears International: http://www.polarbearsinternational.org.

Prince of Whales Northern Heritage Center – Arctic Harpoons: http://pwnhc.learnnet.nt.ca/exhibits/nv/harpoon.htm.

Radford University, Biogeography, Introduction to Biomes of the Earth: http://www.runet.edu/~swoodwar/CLASSES/GEOG235/biomes/intro.html.

Royal Canadian Corps of Signals History Web Site: http://www.nwtandy.rcsigs.ca/stations/ennadai.htm.

The Royal Commission on Aboriginal Peoples. See the *Report of the Royal Commission on Aboriginal Peoples* (1991) on the Indian and Northern Affairs Canada Website: http://www.collectionscanada.gc.ca/webarchives/20071115053257/http://www.ainc-inac.gc.ca/ch/rcap/sg/sgmm_e.html.

Smithsonian Museum of Natural History Arctic Studies Center: http://www.mnh.si.edu/arctic/index.html.

Statistics Canada (Tables by Province): http://www.statcan.gc.ca/tables-tableaux/sum-som/l01/pro01/pro113-eng.htm.

Taiga Rescue Network: http://www.taigarescue.org/.

End Notes

Chapter 1

1. Richard C. Davids, *Lords of the Arctic* (New York: Macmillan Publishing, 1982), chapters 15 and 16. Also see Polar Bears International website www.polarbearsinternational.org.
2. For details on this tragic encounter, see Richard C. Davids, Lords of the Arctic, 114.
3. The episode in this paragraph was reported in Usha Lee McFarling, "A Lot of Bad News for Bears," *Los Angeles Times* (November 28, 2002): 1.

Chapter 2

1. Thomas James, *The Strange and Dangerous Voyage of Captain Thomas James in his Intended Discovery of a North West Passage into the South Sea* (London: John Legatt, 1633).
2. Diamond Jenness, *The People of the Twilight* (New York: The MacMillan Company, 1928), 247.
3. Jonathan Waterman, *Arctic Crossing: A Journey Through the Northwest Passage and Inuit Culture* (Guilford, CT: Lyons Press, 2002).

Chapter 3

1. For a sobering analysis, see the Canadian Council of Ministers of the Environment website: www.ccme.ca/ourwork/air.html?category_id=33.
2. Canadian Council of Ministers of the Environment, *Climate, Nature, People: Indicators of Canada's Changing Climate* (Winnipeg, Manitoba: Canadian Council of Ministers of the Environment, 2003). The reference to barn owls was taken from the speech by Shelia Watt-Cloutier.
3. For further information, see Canadian Council of Ministers of the Environment, *Climate, Nature, People: Indicators of Canada's Changing Climate*, 27–28.
4. Lake Winnipeg Implementation Committee, *Restoring the Health of Lake Winnipeg* (2005), www.redriverbasincommission.org/lake_wpg_final.pdf.

Chapter 4

1. Flows in the Nelson River have been increased by 40% while those in the Churchill River have been reduced by 60%. Retrieved from www.hydro.mb.ca/corporate/water_regimes/churchill_river_diversion.shtml.
2. Bodaly, R. A., R. E. Hecky, and R. J. P. Fudge, "Increases in fish mercury levels in lakes flooded by the Churchill River diversion, northern Manitoba," *Canadian Journal of Fisheries and Aquatic Sciences* 41 (1984a): 682-691.
3. Bodaly, R. A., T. W. D. Johnson, R. J. P. Fudge, and J. W. Clayton, "Collapse of the lake whitefish (Coregonus clupeaformis) fishery in southern Indian Lake, Manitoba, following lake impoundment and river diversion," *Canadian Journal of Fisheries and Aquatic Sciences* 41 (1984b): 692-700.
4. *Mercury In Fish & Guidelines For The Consumption of Recreationally Angled Fish In Manitoba* (Winnipeg: Manitoba Water Stewardship Water Quality Management Section, undated, but more recent than 1994). "Scientific evidence," according to this provincial publication, "shows that long-term flooding of lands following construction of reservoirs accelerates the conversion of naturally occurring in organic mercury to methyl-mercury, an organic and more toxic form of mercury that is readily accumulated in fish." This effect lasts for 25-30 years after the construction of a reservoir. Also see the Summary Report and Technical Appendices of the Canada-Manitoba Agreement on the Study and Monitoring of Mercury in the Churchill River Diversion Submitted to The Minister of Environment and Workplace Safety and Health, Province of Manitoba and The Minister of Environment, Canada (Winnipeg, Manitoba, March 23, 1987).

5. Martin Loney, "The Construction of Dependency: The Case of the Grand Rapids Hydro Project," *The Canadian Journal of Native Studies* 7:1 (1987): 58.
6. James B. Waldram, "Hydro-Electric Development and the Process of Negotiation in Northern Manitoba, 1960–1977," *The Canadian Journal of Native Studies* 4:2 (1984): 218. The excerpts from the Van Ginkel report are cited in this article.
7. Van Ginkel Associates, *Transition in the North: The Churchill River Diversion and the People of South Indian Lake* (1967). Study prepared for the Manitoba Development Authority. This reference is cited in James B. Waldram (1984).
8. James B. Waldram, "Native People and Hydroelectric Development in Northern Manitoba, 1957–1987: The Promise and the Reality," *Manitoba History* 15 (Spring 1988).
9. Art Coulsen, "Our Cheap Energy Floods Manitoba Cree with Grief and Hardship," *St. Paul Pioneer Press* (June 15, 2003): A14.
10. Brian J. Stocks, "Fire Management in Canada," *Global Fire Assessment, 1990–2000* (Food and Agricultural Organization of the United Nations, 2001), www.fao.org/DOCREP/006/AD653E/ad653e86.htm.
11. Richard Brooks, et al., *Clearing the Forest, Cutting the Rules* (Toronto: Sierra Legal Defense Fund and Earthroots, 2002). This report provides an impressive appendix on clear cutting statistics in Ontario, the number, and the size of the cuts.
12. Joan Kuyek, "After the Mine: Lynn Lake, Manitoba. Ottawa: MiningWatch Can" (2004), http://www.miningwatch.ca/en/after-mine-lynn-lake-manitoba. Also discussions with the author.
13. Ibid.
14. Author's telephone conversation with Audie Dulewich, Lynn Lake's Mayor, in August 2006.
15. Rod J. Allen, et al., *Ecological Assessment of the Boreal Shield Ecozone* (Ottawa: Minister of Public Works and Government Services, 2000), 18.
16. The Town of Lynn Lake paid Santec Consulting to conduct a critique of the government's study. In January 2004, the town wrote to the government setting out their concerns.

Chapter 5

1. The concepts in this paragraph were drawn from those developed by Robert McGhee and Moreau Maxwell. See McGhee's handbook, *Canadian Arctic*

Prehistory (Ottawa: National Museums of Canada, National Museum of Man, 1978). See page 31 of Maxwell's *Prehistory of the Eastern Arctic* (Orlando: Academic Press, 1985). See also, Keith Crowe, *A History of the Original Peoples of Northern Canada* (Montreal, Quebec: Arctic Institute of North America Mcgill-Queen's University Press, 1974).

2. Robert McGhee, "The Prehistory and Prehistoric art of the Canadian Inuit," *The Beaver* 1981 (Summer): 22–30.
3. W. W. Fitzhugh, "Environmental Factors in the Evolution of Dorset Culture: A Marginal Proposal for Hudson Bay," *Eastern Arctic Prehistory: Paleoeskimo Problems: Memoirs of the Society for American Archaeology* 31 (1976): 139–49.
4. Roderick C. Wilson and Carl Urion, "First Nations Prehistory and Canadian History," *Native Peoples, the Canadian Experience* (Don Mills, Ontario: Oxford University Press, 2004): 26.
5. J. B. Coltrain, M. G. Hayes, and D. H. O'Rourke, "Sealing Whaling and Caribou: The Skeletal Isotope Chemistry of Eastern Arctic Foragers," *Archaeological Science* 31:1 (2004): 41.
6. Moreau S. Maxwell, *Prehistory of the Eastern Arctic* (Orlando: Academic Press, 1985), 240.
7. These two islands, Arviajuaq (shaped like a bowhead whale) and Qikiqtaarjuk (the little island), are now designated Canadian National Historic Sites.
8. The content in this paragraph reflects information provided to the author by David Morrison and Robert McGhee during telephone interviews with each them on May 18 and May 19, 2005, respectively. The explanation that disease may have been a significant factor in the demise of the Thule whaling culture is credited to McGhee. See McGhee's "Disease and the Development of Inuit culture," *Current Anthropology* 35:5 (1994): 565–94.

Chapter 7

1. Samuel Hearne. *A Journey from Prince of Wales's Fort in Hudson Bay, to the Northern Ocean.* London: Printed for A. Strahan and T. Cadell 1795.

Chapter 9

1. David Morrison and Georges-Herbert Germain, *Inuit, Glimpses of an Arctic Past* (Hull, Quebec, Canada: Canadian Museum of Civilization, 1955), 22.
2. J. J. Hatch, *Arctic Tern (Sterna paradisaea)* (Philadelphia: The Birds of North America, 2002), 707. Also see, Tara Ramroop and Kara West, "To the Ends

of the Earth," *National Geographic Education* (January 16, 2011), http://education.nationalgeographic.com/education/news/ends-earth/?ar_a=1
3. http://education.nationalgeographic.org/news/ends-earth/
4. K. M. Walter, et al., "Methane Bubbling from Siberian Thaw Lakes as a Positive Feedback to Climate Warming," *Nature* 4:43 (September 7, 2006): 71–75. Also see Robert T. Watson, Marufu C. Zinyowera, Richard H. Moss, and Bert Bolin, eds., *The Regional Impacts of Climate Change: An Assessment of Vulnerability* (Port Chester, NY: Cambridge University Press, 1997).
5. James Owen, "Study: Siberian Bogs Big Player in Greenhouse Gas," *National Geographic News* (January 15, 2004), http://news.nationalgeographic.com/news/2004/01/0115_040115_siberianpeatbog.html.
6. Chapter 12.
7. CircumArctic Rangifer Monitoring & Assessment (CARMA) Network, www.rangifer.net/rangifer/herds/herds.cfm?regid=na&mark=Beverly.
8. Anand-Wheeler, Ingrid, *Terrestrial Mammals of Nunavut* (Iqaluit: Nunavut Department of Sustainable Development, 2002).
9. Ernest S. Burch Jr., "The Caribou Inuit," ed., R. Bruce Morrison and C. Wilson, *Native Peoples, the Canadian Experience* (Toronto: Oxford University Press, 2004), 84.
10. H. V. Kuhnlein and N. J. Turner, *Traditional Plant Foods of Canadian Indigenous Peoples* (Amersterdam: Gordon and Breach Science Publishers, 1991), 38. Also see the Porcupine Caribou Herd Management Board, *Unit Two: The Value of Caribou*; check for online availability at www.taiga.net/pcmb/documents/teachers_manual_02.pdf.
11. Kersten Madsen, *Project Caribou: An Educator's Guide to Wild Caribou of North America*. Yukon Department of Environment. Check for availability online at http://taiga.net/projectcaribou. Also see the Inuit Tapiriit Kanatami website: http://www.itk.ca/sites/default/files/Arctic-Wildlife.pdf
12. U.S. Fish and Wildlife Service. *Caribou Biology*, http://arctic.fws.gov/carcon.htm#general.
13. Ibid.
14. See the Beverly and Qamanirjuaq Caribou Management Board website: www.arctic-caribou.com/value.html.

Chapter 13

1. John Barrow, ed., *The geography of Hudson's Bay; being the remarks of Captain*

W. Coats on his many voyages to that locality during the years of 1727 and 175 (London: Hakluyt Society, 1852), 29. Cited in Ross (1975), 37.
2. David Owingayak, "David Owingayak's Short History of Arviat," Unpublished.
3. Keith J. Crowe, *A history of the Original Peoples of Northern Canada.* (Montreal: McGill-Queen's University Press for the Arctic Institute of North America, 1974), 82.
4. Dorothy Harley Eber, *When the Whalers were up North* (Boston: David R. Godine, 1989), 16.
5. Hugh Brody, *Living Arctic: Hunters of the Canadian North* (Seattle: University of Washington Press, 1987), 191.
6. W. G. Ross, "Whaling and Eskimos: Hudson Bay 1860–1915," *National Museum of Man Publications in Ethnology* 10 (1975), 15.
7. W. G. Ross, "Whaling, Inuit, and the Arctic Islands," ed. Kenneth Coates and William R. Morrison, *Interpreting Canada's North* (Toronto: Copp Clark Pitman, 1989), 252–77.
8. Crowe (1991), 107. Also, see Damas (2002), 10–15.
9. Bruemmer (1971), 1. Also, see Jenness (1964), 11 and Ross (1975), 63–85.
10. Eber (1989), 43, 89, 119.
11. Crowe (1991), 171.
12. Bruemmer (1971), 14.
13. Ross (1975).
14. Franz Boas, *The Central Eskimo* (Lincoln, NE: University of Nebraska Press, 1964), 18.
15. Crowe (1991), 129.
16. Taylor, Richard R. (1976). Medical Department, United States Army Preventative Medicine in World War II, Volume III, edited by John Lada and Curtis Hoff, Office of the Surgeon General, Department of the Army, Washington, DC, 1976, p176. This 1944-45 diphtheria epidemic was followed outbreaks of tuberculosis and polio. See: Adamson, J. D., et al. (1949). Poliomyelitis in the Arctic, *Canadian Medical Association Journal*, Vol. 61, Number 4, p339-348.
17. Keith Hay, *Final Report of the Inuit Bowhead Knowledge Study* (Iqaluit, Nunavut: Nunavut Wildlife Management Board, 2000).
18. Brian Goehring and John K. Stager, "The intrusion of Industrial Time and Space into the Inuit Lifeworld," *Environment and Behavior* XX:23 (1991), 666.

19. Burch Jr. (2004), 82.
20. Eugene Y. Arima, "A contextual study of the Caribou Eskimo kayak," PhD thesis in anthropology, University of Toronto, 1972. Also see J. Garth Taylor, "Labrador Eskimo Settlement of the Early Contact Period," National Museum of Man Publications in Ethnology No. 9 (1974), 74–75. Although kinship relationships and camp memberships tended to follow the father's side, in the case of the Caribou Inuit, no particular preference was shown in this regard.
21. Burch Jr. (2004), 80.
22. Robert F. Spencer, *The North Alaskan Eskimoes: A Study in Ecology and Society* (Washington, D.C.: U.S. Government Printing Office, 1959), 153.
23. Morrison and Germain, (1995), 28.
24. Ibid, 28.
25. Renee Fossett, *In Order to Live an Untroubled Life: Inuit of the Central Arctic, 1550–1940* (Winnipeg: University of Manitoba Press, 2001), 207.
26. Colin Irwin, "Lords of the Arctic: wards of the state," *Northern Perspectives* 17:1 (1989). See the section titled "Inuit Education and Enculturation: Past."
27. Christopher Fletcher, "Continuity and Change in Inuit Society," ed. R. Bruce Morrison and C. Wilson *Native Peoples, the Canadian Experience* (Toronto: Oxford University Press, 2004), 80.
28. Kaj Birket-Smith, *The Eskimos* (London: Methuen and Co., 1936), 156.
29. Fossett (2001), 207–210. Also, see Knud Rasmussen, *Intellectual Culture of the Copper Eskimo* (Copenhagen: Gyldendal, 1932), 17; and Taylor (1974), 92–93.
30. T. E. Lawrence, in *The Seven Pillars of Wisdom*, wrote of the nomadic Bedouin at the beginning of the twentieth century: "The Beduin of the desert, born and grown up in it had embraced with all his soul this nakedness too harsh for volunteers, for the reason, felt but inarticulate, that there he found himself indubitably free. He lost material ties, comforts, all superfluities and other complications to achieve a personal liberty. . . . He saw no virtue in poverty herself: he enjoyed the little vices and luxuries—coffee, fresh water, women—which he could still preserve. In his life he had air and winds, sun and light, open spaces and a great emptiness. . . . There unconsciously he came near God . . . a comprehending Being, the egg of all activity, with nature and matter just a glass reflecting Him."
31. Vilhjalmur Stefansson, *My Life with the Eskimo* (New York: The MacMillan Company, 1913).

32. Samuel Hearne, "Arctic Dawn: The Journeys of Samuel Hearne," http://web.archive.org/web/20050219104536/web.idirect.com/~hland/sh/title2.html.
33. James Woodburn, "Egalitarian Societies," *Man* 17:3 (September 1982), 431–51.
34. Marshall Sahlins, *Stone Age Economics* (New York: Aldine Publishing Company, 1972). See Chapter 1, "The Original Affluent Society."
35. Ibid, 11.
36. Woodburn (1982), 442. According to Woodburn, the sanctions against the accumulation of personal possessions, among certain hunter-gatherer societies, goes beyond the limitations imposed by the requirement of portability. Deeply imbedded in the cultures of many of these groups are prohibitions against the excessive accumulation of the lightest of objects, even useful ones like arrowheads.
37. Jared Diamond, "The Worst Mistake in the History of the Human Race." *Discover Magazine* (May 1987), XX. Diamond argues that hunter-gatherers led healthier and less perilous lives while enjoying greater equity and leisure than the workers of the agricultural and industrial societies that succeeded them and eventually pushed the foragers to the marginal corners of the earth.
38. Sahlins (1972), 13–14 and Chapter 1, "The Original Affluent Society."
39. Diamond Jenness, *The People of the Twilight* (New York: The MacMillan Company, 1928), 197.
40. Franz Boas (1964), 174. Also, see Rasmussen (1924) and Taylor (1974).
41. The famine that occurred among the traditional Inuit was a reality that had many causes. More so than native people's prodigality, the capricious and deteriorating quality of the Arctic climate during this period accounted for most of these hardships. To keep matters in perspective, Marshall Sahlins, in *Stone Age Economics*, reminds us that in our current era of unrivaled industrial achievement, world starvation is still an enduring institution. At the time that he wrote his book (1972), Sahlins claimed that world hunger was growing both relatively and absolutely.
42. Crowe (1991), 24.
43. E. Adamson Hoebel, *The Law of Primitive Man* (Cambridge, MA: Harvard University Press, 1987), 9–10. Also, see Jennesss (1928), 209; Fossett (2001), 229; and Freuchen (1951).
44. Hoebel (1967), 9–10.

Chapter 14

1. For more information on the land claims settlement, see www.polarnet.ca/polarnet/nunavut.htm.
2. Morrison and Germain (1955), 22.
3. Jenness, *The Life off the Coper Eskimo, Part A of Voulme XII, A Report of the Canadian Arctic Expedition 1913–1918* (New York and London: Johnson Reprint Corporation, 1970), 189.
4. This paragraph paraphrased from Ernest S. Burch's "The Caribou Inuit," ed., R. Morrison and C. Wilson. *Native Peoples, the Canadian Experience* (Toronto: Oxford University Press, 2004), 87–8.
5. Brody (1987), 207.
6. Crowe (1991), 148. Also, see Valarie Alia. *Names, numbers, and northern policy: Inuit, Project Surname, and the politics of identity* (Halifax, N.S.: Fernwood Publishing, 1994), 26.
7. Brody (1987), 207–209.

Chapter 15

1. Pat Sandiford Grygier, A long way from home: the tuberculosis epidemic among the Inuit (Montreal; Buffalo: McGill-Queen's University Press, 1994), 30.
2. Mary Roach, "My Dinner with Nartok." Health 8:7 (1994). Also, see Shirley Thompson, "Sustainability and Vulnerability: Aboriginal Arctic Food Security in a Toxic World," ed., Fikret Berkes, Alan Diduck, Helen Fast, Rob Huebert, and Micheline Manseau Breaking Ice: Renewable Resource and Ocean Management in the Canadian North (Calgary, Alberta, Canada: University of Calgary Press, 2005).
3. Richard Harrington, The Face of the Arctic (New York: Abelard-Schuman, 1952). Also, see Hugh Brody, The People's Land: Eskimos and Whites in the Eastern Arctic (Harmondsworth, England: Penguin Books, 1975), 22–3, and others.
4. Richard Harrington, "The Padleimiuts," Canadian Geographic Journal (XLIV):1 (1952), 2–15.
5. Harrington, The Face of the Arctic, 30.
6. Diamond Jenness, Eskimo Administration: II. Canada (Montreal: Arctic Institute of North America, 1964), 30, 36.
7. David Damas, Arctic Migrants Arctic Villagers (Montreal: McGill-Queen's University Press, 2002), 31. Also, see Frank James Tester and Peter Kulchyski, Tammarniit (Mistakes):Inuit Relocation in the Eastern Arctic 1939–63

(Vancouver: UBC Press, 1994), 242–4. This paragraph reflects concepts developed in both of these sources.

8. Peter C. Newman, Merchant Princes (Toronto: Viking, 1991), 241.
9. The High Arctic Relocation: A Report on the 1953–55 Relocation (Ottawa: Canada Communication Group, 1994), 47–8.
10. Leslie Wakelyn, "The Qamanirjuaq Caribou Herd: An Arctic Enigma," www.arctic-caribou.com/PDF/qcs.pdf. The actual extent of the decline of the caribou populations during this era (mid-twentieth century) is debatable. Some earlier observers attributed poor hunting conditions among the Ahialmiut and other Caribou Inuit to shifting caribou migration patterns, not to actual declines in the caribou populations. While shifting caribou migration patterns may have exacerbated the Inuit hardships, current information suggests that the herds during the mid-twentieth century were less than half what they were in 2010. Caribou population declines, therefore, were a reality.
11. William D. Church "Chapter VI: The North Atlantic Area," ed. John Lada and Curtis Hoff, Preventive Medicine in World War II, Volume VIII (Washington, D.C.: Office of the Surgeon General, Department of the Army, 1976), 176. Also, see J. D. Adamson et al., "Poliomyelitis in the Arctic," Canadian Medical Association Journal 61:4 (1949), 339–48.
12. Canada and the United States erected the DEW Line in the 1950s to provide early warnings of possible sneak attacks by Soviet Russia. Only a single bomber flight over the top of the North Pole separated the Cold War combatants, and the only territory that stood between their population centers was the Canadian tundra. The DEW Line, like a gigantic electronic picket fence, marked the top of the continent and separated these antagonists.
13. Donald Ben Marsh, Echoes into Tomorrow (Three Hills, Alberta, Canada: Prairie Graphics and Printing, 1973), 147.
14. Peter Jull, "A Personal Response to Frank J. Tester and Peter Kulchyski, Tammarniit (Mistakes): Inuit Relocation in the Eastern Arctic, 1939–63," The Northern Review 12/13 (1994), 197–202.
15. Frank James Tester and Peter Kulchyski, Tammarniit (Mistakes): Inuit Relocation in the Eastern Arctic 1939–63 (Vancover: UBC Press, 1994), 74–6.
16. Frank Tester McNicoll and Peter Kulchyski, "Arctic Abstersion: The Book of Wisdom for Eskimo, modernism and Inuit assimilation," Etudes Inuit Studie 23:1/2 (1999), 199–220. Also, see "Build a New Igloo." Time Magazine (July 7, 1947).

17. Frank James Tester and Peter Kulchyski (1994), 70.
18. Today, visitors can reach this remote site by charter aircraft or by boat or canoe, the same way it was reached by traders and trappers for nearly three centuries.

Chapter 16

1. CBC News: "Nunavut grapples with housing crunch," May 31, 2004. Referenced in "$2B demanded from feds for Nunavut," September 30, 2004, housing http://www.cbc.ca/canada/story/2004/09/30/nunavuthousing_040930.html
2. See the *Nunavut Ten-Year Inuit Housing Action Plan* (Iqaluit, Nunavut, Canada: Nunavut Housing Corporation and Nunavut Tunngavik, September 2004).
3. Pat Sandiford Grygier, *A long way from home: the tuberculosis epidemic among the Inuit* (Montreal & Buffalo: McGill-Queen's University Press, 1994), 135.
4. Jenness (1964), 88.
5. Grygier (1994), 96–7.
6. Marsh (1973), 183.
7. Grygier (1994), 95–8.
8. Ibid.
9. Jenness (1964), 88.
10. Crowe (1991), 178.
11. Bria Bergman, "Dark Days for the Inuit," *MacLean's* 109:10 (1996), 66–9.
12. Jean Briggs, *Never in Anger: Portrait of an Eskimo Family* (Cambridge, MA: Harvard University Press, 1970).
13. Franz Boas, *The Central Eskimo* (Lincoln, NE: University of Nebraska Press, 1964), 172. Also, see Richard Harrington, *The Face of the Arctic* (New York: Abelard-Schuman, 1952), 11, and many others. Also, see Eric Anoee, quoted in Ulli Stelzer's *Inuit: The North in Transition* (Vancouver, British Columbia: Douglas and McIntyre Ltd., 1982), 131.
14. Crowe (1991), 198.
15. Royal Commission on Aboriginal Peoples (1996). *Report of the Royal Commission on Aboriginal Peoples, Volume 1*, 314. See Part TWO, Looking Forward, Looking Back, False Assumptions and a Failed Relationship, Section 10, Residential Schools,
16. Crowe (1991), 198

17. Ken Harper, "Hunters and high finance." www.nunavut.com/nunavut99/english.
18. Harper (1999). See last paragraph of "Governement Looks Northward" Section.
19. The regulated harvest of harp seals continued in Newfoundland. Newborn whitecoats could not be taken, only animals approximately twenty-five days old and older. Increased effort was being made to promote, process, and commercially market seal meat, but the biggest market was in China where the male seal's penis was sold as an aphrodisiac. The pelts also had commercial value. The harvest maintained political currency in Canada as a controversial means of reducing seal predation on cod fisheries.
20. Fletcher (2004), 62.
21. Federal Transfers to Provinces and Territories, http://www.fin.gc.ca/fedprov/mtp-eng.asp
22. Statistics Canada. "Crimes by offences, by province and territory," http://www.statcan.gc.ca/tables-tableaux/sum-som/l01/pro01/pro113-eng.htm
23. NWT Bureau of Statistics. 1996 NWT Alcohol & Drug Survey: Rates of Use for Alcohol, other Drugs and Tobacco. Yellowknife, Northwest Territories.
24. Sandy Isaacs, Susan Keogh, Cathy Menard, and Jamie Hockin, "Suicide in the Northwest Territories: A Descriptive Review," *Chronic Diseases in Canada* 19:4 (2000), 152–156.
25. Peter Freuchen, *Arctic Adventure: My Life in the Frozen North* (New York: Farrar & Reinhardt, 1935), 209.
26. Crowe (1991), 116.
27. Shelagh D. Grant, "A Case of Compounded Error: The Inuit Resettlement Project, 1953, and the Government Response, 1990," *Northern Perspective* 19:1 (Spring 1990). See "Promises and Expectation Section." www.carc.org/pubs/v19no1/2.htm.
28. Grant (1990). See "Unnecessary Hardships."
29. From a quote by John Amagolik cited in Alan R. Marcus, *Out in the Cold: the Legacy of Canada's Inuit Relocation Experiment in the High Arctic* (Copenhagen: International Work Group for Indigenous Affairs, 1992), 21.
30. Milton M. R. Freeman, "Adaptive innovation among recent Eskimo immigrants in the eastern Canadian Arctic," *The Polar Record* 14:93 (1969), 774.
31. Alan R. Marcus. *Relocating Eden: The Image and Politics of Inuit Exile in the Canadian Arctic.* Hanover, NH: University Press of New England 1995, 98-99.

32. Tester and Kulchyski (1994), 166-174; Marcus (1995), 202-206.
33. Grant (1990), "Financial Irregularities" section.
34. Royal Commission on Aboriginal Peoples, (1994), 159. Also see Marsh (1973), 156–7.
35. David Damas, *Arctic Migrants Arctic Villagers* (Montreal: McGill-Queen's University Press, 2002), 57.
36. Jim Bell, "Exiles Denied Apology," *Nunatsiaq News* (March 15, 1996). www.nunatsiaq.com/archives/back-issues/week/60315.html#1.
37. The hardships that befell the Ahiarmiut in the 1940s and 1950s started ominously with the departure of the traders. Unable to continue their losing venture, Revillon Freres abandoned its remote Ennadai Lake trading post in the early 1930s, and by 1940 the HBC ceased operations at Nueltin Lake, the next nearest post to the south. The handful of independent traders that had filtered into the area in pursuit of the white gold rush also left shortly after World War II.
38. Tester and Kulchyski (1994), 217.
39. Damas (2002), 89–90.
40. "History," http://nwtandy.rcsigs.ca/1940_49.htm#1949. Also, see Tester and Kulchyski (1994), 214–15.
41. This paragraph draws from FrédéricLaugrand, Jarich Oosten, & David Serkoak, "'The saddest time of my life': relocating the Ahiarmiut from Ennadai Lake (1950–1958)," The Polar Record 46:02 (2010), 116-118. The Ennadai Lake Inuit relocations to Nueltin and Henik lakes are described in various sources (Tester and Kulchyski, Marcus, and others). The account cited here by Laugrand et al. provides the best Inuit perspective.
42. Marcus (1995), 137.
43. Richard Harrington, *The Face of the Arctic* (New York: Abelard-Schuman, 1952). See chapter 15. Although the time period reported is 1950, the conditions, we can safely assume, probably were no different, and hardly better. Also, see Walter Rudnicki's "Report Field Trip to Eskimo Point" in Tester and Kulchyski, (1994), 230.
44. Farley Mowat, *Walking the Land* (South Royalton, VT: Steerforth Press, 2001), 53. Mowat directly quotes statements by an Ennadai Inuit survivor.
45. Tester and Kulchyski (1994), 220.
46. Royal Commission on Aboriginal Peoples. See Section 2.2, "To Improve the Lives of Aboriginal People," http://www.collectionscanada.gc.ca/webarchives/20071211055134/http://www.ainc-inac.gc.ca/ch/rcap/sg/sg38_e.html

47. Walter Rudnicki "Report: Field Trip to Eskimo Point," March 1958, findings p.1 (document supplied by author to and quoted by Tester and Kulchyski (1994), 234. Also quoted in Frédéric Laugrand, Jarich Oosten, David Serkoak.
48. Damas (2002), 102.
49. Frédéric Laugrand, Jarich Oosten, & David Serkoak, (2009). Relocating the Ahiarmiut from Ennadai Lake to Arviat (1950-1958). In Collignon B. & Therrien M. (Ed.) *Orality in the 21st century: Inuit discourse and practices. Proceedings of the 15th Inuit Studies Conference (2009)*, 26.
50. Crowe (1991), 173.

Chapter 17

1. Derek Rasmussen, "Cease to Do Evil, Then Learn to Do," *Cultural Survival Voices,* http://www.culturalsurvival.org/ourpublications/voices/article/cease-do-evil-then-learn-do
2. *Arctic Pollution 2002: Peresistent Organic Pollutants, Heavy Metals, Radioactivity, Human Helath, Changing Pathways* (Oslo, Norway: Arctic Monitoring and Assessment Programme, 2002), xi and "Human Health" section.
3. *Canadian Arctic Contaminants Assessment Report* (Ottawa: Minister of Indian Affairs and Northern Development, 2003). See "Highlights" and "Human Health" sections.
4. Frédéric Dallaire et al., "Acute Infections and Environmental Exposure to Organochlorines in Inuit Infants from Nunavik," *Environmental Health Perspectives* 112:14 (October 14, 2004). Also, see Éric Dewailly et al., "Susceptibility to Infections and Immune Status in Inuit Infants Exposed to Organochlorines," *Environmental Health Perspectives* 103:3 (2000), and Odile Nelson, "Study tracks effects of contaminants in Nunavik infants," *Nunatsiaq News* (March 14, 2003).
5. Arctic Monitoring and Assessment Programme, (2002), xi and "Human Health" section.
6. CBC News (2003). Flame Retardants in Inuit Breast Milk. http://www.cbc.ca/gsa/?q=pollutants030917
7. U.S. Energy Information Administration, Department of Energy. "Energy in Brief: What are greenhouse gases and how much are emitted by the United States?" http://www.eia.gov/energy_in_brief/article/greenhouse_gas.cfm

8. Sean McKibbon and Michaela Rodrigue, "Pelly Bay's marionettes are coming home. Kiviuq's oddysey is almost over," *Nunatsiaq News* (August 13, 1999).
9. Okalik Eegeesiak and Sheila Watt-Cloutier, "The strange politics of the Marine Mammal Protection Act," *Toronto Mail and Globe* (July 26, 1999).
10. Jarich Oosten and Frédéric Laugrand, "*Qaujimajatuqangit* and social problems in modern Inuit society. An elders workshop on *angakkuuniq*," *Inuit Studies* 26:1 (2002).

Afterword

1. Boden, T.A., Marland, G., and Andres, R.J. (2017). National CO2 Emissions from Fossil-Fuel Burning, Cement Manufacture, and Gas Flaring: 17512014, Carbon Dioxide Information Analysis Center, Oak Ridge National Laboratory, U.S. Department of Energy, di 10.3334/CDIAC/00001_V2017.
2. Ibid. The 2017 population information was taken from the "U.S. and World Population Clock." Retrieved from https://www.census.gov/popclock/.
3. Boston Consulting Group. (2016). Bipole III, Keeyask, and Tie-Line review.
4. Revised Attachment 16, Export and Domestic Revenue MFR 1, January 21, 2016. (Winnipeg, CA: Manitoba Hydro, 2016) Retrieved from https://www.hydro.mb.ca/docs/regulatory_affairs/pdf/electric/supplemental_filing_2015/18_attachment_16_export_and_domestic_revenue_mfr_1.pdf. In this revised, supplemental filing before the Public Utilities Board, Manitoba Hydro forecasted that unit revenues from the US would increase from C$0.037 per KWh in 2015 to C$0.064 in 2018 and then continue upward to over C$0.10 in 2034/35.
5. Walton, R., "Xcel solicitation returns 'incredible' renewable energy storage bids," Utility Dive (January 2018), retrieved from https://www.utilitydive.com/news/xcel-solicitation-returns-incredible-renewable-energy-storage-bids/514287/.
6. An Assessment of Hydroelectric Power Options to Satisfy Oil Sands Electricity Demand. Study 155.(Canadian Energy Research Institute, 2016). In this assessment of hydroelectric power options, the CERI estimated that the KWh cost of electricity from a new dam just upstream of the Keeyask, at the Conawapa rapids, if it were built, would be slightly over C$0.12 and C$0.085, with and without transmission. This finding

confirms the reasonableness of the C$0.12 KWh estimate for the Keeyask dam.
7. Levelized unit cost measures the present value of the total costs of building and operating a power plant divided by the energy produced per year.
8. It is noteworthy that Manitoba Hydro obtains about two-thirds of its export revenue from "opportunity" sales, meaning sales on the spot market for immediate delivery.
9. Deemer, et al., "Greenhouse Gas Emissions from Reservoir Water Surfaces: A New Global Synthesis," BioScience, Volume 66, Issue 11, 1 November 2016, Pages 949–964. Retrieved from https://doi.org/10.1093/biosci/biw117.
10. Mueller, David K. et al. Nutrients in the Nation's Waters—Too Much of a Good Thing? (Washington, DC: U.S. Geological Survey Circular 1136, U.S. Government Printing Office, 1996), pages 9-11. Many research studies have corroborated the fact that "soil erosion can carry a considerable amount of particulate phosphate to streams."
11. Thompson, S. (2015). "Flooding First Nations and Environmental Justice in Manitoba: Case Studies of the Impacts of 2011 Flood and Hydrodevelopment in Manitoba," Manitoba Law Journal: 38(2), 220-259. Retrieved from http://themanitobalawjournal.com/wp-content/uploads/articles/MLJ_38.2/Flooding%20of%20First%20Nations%20and%20Environmental%20Justice%20in%20Manitoba%20Case%20Studies%20of%20the%20Impacts%20of%20the%202011%20Flood%20and%20Hydro%20Development%20in%20Manitoba.pdf.
12. Magnani, et al., "Discriminating between natural versus induced seismicity from long-term deformation history of intraplate faults," Science Advances 3:11(November 24, 2017). In "Drilling Reawakens Sleeping Faults in Texas, leads to Earthquakes," Scientific American, November 24, 2017 (https:// Anna Kuchment reports that "(s)ince 2008, Texas, Oklahoma, Kansas and a handful of other states have experienced unprecedented surges of earthquakes. Oklahoma's rate increased from one or two per year to more than 800. Texas has seen a six-fold spike." The explanation of this increased seismic activity is attributed to the injection of fracking wastewater and, to a lesser extent, injected fracking fluids near dormant fault lines. The pressure from the injected water nudges the potential energy held in check by formerly "dead" faults and, like the pin that pops the balloon, it triggers them into movement. They become kinetically energized earthquakes that may continue to shake and rumble for years to come.

In Oklahoma, earthquake insurance coverage, once an extreme rarity, has now become a booming business even as insurers resist providing coverage and, after policies are issued, often attempt to deny earthquake claims on the grounds that they are man-made, "fracked" events. See Cary Jones' article, "'Extraordinary denial rate' of 9 in 10 earthquake claims rattles Oklahoma Insurance Commissioner John Doak," Tulsa World (March 5, 2015).

13. For a good overview of the sources and some of the incidents of surface and groundwater contamination associated with hydraulic fracturing processes, see Dave Levitan's post, "Inhofe on Fracking, Water Contamination," http://www.factcheck.org/2015/03/inhofe-on-fracking-water-contamination/; also Nicholas Kusnetz's "North Dakota's Oil Boom Brings Damage Along with Prosperity," ProPublica (June 7, 2012). Retrieved from https://www.propublica.org/article/the-other-fracking-north-dakotas-oil-boom-brings-damage-along-withprosperi. Land areas and surface waters are contaminated by spills of oil, briny wastewater, or fracking fluids (water, sand, and chemicals). Kusnetz reports that in 2011, 1,000 reported releases of oil and wastewater occurred in the NorthDakota's Bakken oil fields, the largest one sterilizing 24 acres of land with 2 million gallons of brine. Kusnetzcited sources claiming that many more spills went unreported. The sources of groundwater contamination stem from underground seepage of liquids and gases, primarily through cracked or corroded well pipes. These deep, underground cement-encased steel pipes must contain fluid pressures as high 15,000 pounds per square inch and, through fracking and refracking, are repeatedly tested to their performance limits. Pressurized methane gas, drawn up through the pipes, pushes through any cracks that might be present whence it can eventually move into groundwater supplies.

14. While it is unfair to imply that the fugitive emissions of methane from fracked oil wells are significantly higher than conventional wells, methane flare-off (combustion), venting, and leakage remain serious environmental and economic concerns. Many of the wells that target oil reserves also tap into natural gas. Lacking infrastructure and storage systems to contain the less valuable methane, these facilities, rather than capturing it, simply waste it by onsite venting or flaring.

15. Gregg P. Macey et. al., "Air concentrations of volatile compounds near oil and gas production: a community-based exploratory study," Environmental Health 13:82 (July 16, 2004). This study found, at multiple wells in three different states, that the levels of eight volatile chemicals exceeded federal guidelines and that benzene, formaldehyde, and hydrogen sulfide were the

most common compounds to exceed acute and other health-based risk levels.

16. Caldwell, Jennifer A., A Policy and Impact Analysis of Hydraulic Fracturing in the Marcellus Shale Region: A Wildlife Perspective, Master's Thesis, University of Delaware. 2015.

17. Green, A. W., Aldridge, C. L. and O'donnell, M. S. (2017), "Investigating impacts of oil and gas development on greater sage-grouse," *Journal of Wildlife Management*, 81: 46–57. doi:10.1002/jwmg.21179. The second paragraph of this article is excerpted here: "Development associated with oil and natural gas extraction is an increasing threat to sagebrush habitats as the number of wells associated with oil and natural gas extraction increase across the landscape. Construction of oil and gas wells results in the direct loss of sagebrush, but impacts have negative consequences at larger scales than the well pad and after drilling is complete, including alteration due to road and pipeline construction and changes in wildlife behavior (Northrup and Wittemyer 2012). Sawyer et al. (2006) reported that mule deer (Odocoileus hemionus) avoided well pads out to approximately 4 km and shifted their habitat use to less suitable areas in response to increased development. Other large mammals have changed home ranges, movement, and behavior in response to human activity (Dyer et al. 2002, Sawyer et al. 2009, Wasser et al. 2011, Northrup 2015). Disturbance from oil and gas development may also cause local declines in avian populations (Bayne et al. 2008, Gilbert and Chalfoun 2011, Jarnevich and Laubhan 2011), shifts in community structure (Bayne et al. 2008, Francis et al. 2012), and behavior modifications in response to increased noise pollution or other disturbance (Pitman et al. 2005, Francis et al. 2011). The cumulative effects of these impacts are not well studied but have potential negative consequences for ecosystem function (Francis et al. 2012)."

18. In the two small islands of remote land comprising the Theodore Roosevelt National Park Grasslands, the famous night skies, once illuminated by the Milky Way and Northern Lights, are now aglow with the eerie orange of the thousands of gas flares surrounding it in the Bakken oil fields of North Dakota. In the United States, proposed federal rules to require reductions in venting and flaring and to require more inspections for curtailing gas leakage have been postponed by the Trump administration.

19. According to Natural Resources Canada, one barrel of oil requires 2 to 4.5 barrels of fresh water for processing, water that is typically drawn, without payment, from the Athabasca River, one of North America's last and longest free-flowing rivers.

20. The energy input per barrel of tar sands oil produced is about 1.3 million BTUs, meaning that the ratio of energy output to input, known as "energy returned on energy invested," varies somewhere between 3:1 and 7:1, compared to roughly 15:1 to 20:1 for conventional oil. It should be noted that much of this energy input is or can be produced internally from the byproducts of processing oil sands. See Adam R. Brandt, Jacob Englander, Sharad Bharadwaj, "Energy Efficiency of Oil Sands Extraction: Energy Return Ratios from 1970 to 2010," Energy, Volume 55, Issue null, Pages 693-702.
21. According to Alberta Energy, http://www.energy.alberta.ca/oilsands/791, the total surface and open-pit mined oil sands areas comprise 895 square kilometers. According to Sam Roberts, "It's Still a Big City, Just Not Quite So Big," (2008, May 22), New York Times, the total land area of New York City is 305 square miles (790 square kilometers).
22. Prajulee, A. & Wania, F., "Evaluating officially reported polycyclic aromatic hydrocarbon emissions in the Athabasca oil sands region with a multimedia fate model," Proceedings of the National Academy of Sciences, 111:9 (January 2, 2014).
23. McLachlan, S. M., Environmental and Human Health Implications of the Athabasca Oil Sands—Phase Two Report (Winnipeg: University of Manitoba in collaboration with Mikisew Cree First Nation Athabasca Chipewyan First Nation, 2014). See "Results" section, pages 138-150 and Executive Summary. Access to full report obtained through http://onerivernews.ca/health-studypress-release-2014/.
24. McLachlan (2014).
25. Liggio, J. et al, "Oil sands operations as a large source of secondary organic aerosols," Nature 534, (June, 2016), 91–94.
26. The controversial Keystone-XL (Phase 3) Pipeline across the Great Plains of the USA is another oil sands transport export route. Although recently approved by the Nebraska Public Service Commission and cleared by the Trump administration, obstacles remain. The multi-billion-dollar price tag, the hundreds of easements on private land that still need to be negotiated, and legal obstacles, including a recent injunction order by a U.S. District judge in Montana all combine to encumber this pipeline with a less than certain future.
27. Uechi, J., "Survivors of Kinder Morgan's Burnaby pipeline spill fear company's plan to twin the line," Vancouver Observer (October, 24, 2013).
28. Hadden, J., "Natural disasters make 2014 a year to forget for many,"

Global News (December 30, 2014). Retrieved from https://globalnews.ca/news/1746702/watch-natural-disasters-make-2014-a-year-to-forget-formany/. The video in this website posting is worth more than any words of description that I might offer.
29. Mount Polley Mine Tailings Storage Facility Breach (Victoria, BC: British Columbia Ministry of Energy, Mines & Petroleum Resources, November 30, 2015), 12-14.
30. Spawn, S., Lark, T. & Gibb, H., "US Cropland Expansion Released 115 Million Tons of Carbon (2008-2012)." Presented at America's Grasslands Conference 11/15/2017, Fort Worth, TX, Seth A. Spawn.
31. Hill, Jason et. al., "Air-quality-related health damages of maize," Nature Sustainability (April 1, 2019).
32. Some examples of the use of the word "sorry": In place of "excuse me," there is, "Sorry (I bumped into you)." Alternatively, to transfer blame to the victim or to assert superiority, one might say "I'm sorry you're feeling badly about this," or "Sorry (somebody has to be the winner here)." To avoid a more direct insult, such as "You are a feckless ingrate," there is the matchless passive-aggressiveness and cool efficiency of this singular word when delivered emphatically: "Sorry?!" Finally, to charitably unburden the perpetrator of guilt while still reinforcing a sense of awkwardness fitting for the occasion, one might say "Sorry (I must have stepped in your way)."
33. Woodward, S. "Sled dog slaughter: Nunavik Inuit demand inquiry," retrieved from https://stephaniewoodard.blogspot.com/2011/09/sled-dog-slaughtercanadian-opposition.html. This paragraph draws from content in this article.
34. Makivik and the Quebec Government Achieve Historic Resolution! The Fan Hitch, Journal of the Inuit Sled Dog International 13:4 (September 2011).
35. For a video of one adoptee's story, see https://www.cbc.ca/news/canada/manitoba/marlene-orgeron-on-being-taken-during-60s-scoop-1.2584742).
36. "History and Culture—Boarding Schools," American Indian Relief Council. Retrieved from http://www.nativepartnership.org/site/PageServer?pagename=airc_hist_boardingschools.
37. Carlisle Indian Industrial School Historical Marker. Retrieved from http://explorepahistory.com/hmarker.php?markerId=1-A-228.
38. Ibid.
39. Calls to Action (Winnipeg, Manitoba: Truth and Reconcilliation Commission of Canada, 2015).

40. Zerehi, Sima Sahar, "Nunavut Inuit back caribou calving grounds protection," CBC News (March 17, 2016). Retrieved from http://www.cbc.ca/news/canada/north/nunavut-inuit-caribou-calving-groundsprotection-1.3494752.
41. Tarasuk, V, et al. Household Food Insecurity in Canada (Toronto: PROOF Food Insecurity Policy Research, University of Toronto, 2017).
42. 2016 Nunavut Food Price Survey (Iqaluit: Nunavut Bureau of Statistics, June 2016).
43. Census Profile, 2016 Census—Arviat, Nunavut (Statistics Canada, 2016).
44. For more information about these mines, see Agnico's website: https://www.agnicoeagle.com/English/operations-and-development-projects/operations/meadowbank/default.aspx.
45. "Polar bears push Halloween activities indoors in Arviat, Nunavut," *CBC News* (October 16, 2014) https://ca.news.yahoo.com/polar-bears-pushhalloween-activities-115045250.html.
46. Mowat (Walking the Land), Tester and Kulchyski (Tammarniit), and others have chronicled the story of Halo's murder and Kikkik's rescue in more detail. I have drawn from these accounts to present a more condensed version.
47. Sarah Rogers, "Ahiarmiut hope to close third and final chapter of their story," Nunatsiaq News (May 20, 2014).
48. Sarah Rogers, "Ennadai Lake Inuit get long-awaited apology for forced relocations," *Nunatsiaq News* (January 23, 2019). Much of the content of this paragraph is summarized from Rogers' article.

www.ingramcontent.com/pod-product-compliance
Lightning Source LLC
Chambersburg PA
CBHW051543010526
44118CB00022B/2560